Postliterary America

p 111. Testimonial imaginative,
p. 139 'strategies of innocence'.
p. 146 re. poetry & poetics?

CONTEMPORARY NORTH AMERICAN POETRY SERIES

Series Editors Alan Golding, Lynn Keller, and Adalaide Morris

MARIA DAMON

Postliterary America

From Bagel Shop Jazz to Micropoetries

UNIVERSITY OF IOWA PRESS
Iowa City

University of Iowa Press, Iowa City 52242
Copyright © 2011 by the University of Iowa Press
www.uiowapress.org
Printed in the United States of America

Design by Teresa W. Wingfield

The University of Iowa Press is a member of Green Press Initiative and is
committed to preserving natural resources.

Printed on acid-free paper

Library of Congress Cataloging-in-Publication Data

Damon, Maria.
    Postliterary America : from bagel shop jazz to micropoetries / Maria Damon.
        p.   cm.—(Contemporary North American poetry series)
    Includes bibliographical references and index.
    ISBN-13: 978-1-58729-957-5 (pbk.)
    ISBN-10: 1-58729-957-7 (pbk.)
    1. American poetry—20th century—History and criticism.   2. American
poetry—21st century—History and criticism.   3. American poetry—
Minority authors—History and criticism.   4. Poetry—Social aspects—
United States.   5. Experimental poetry, American—History and criticism.
6. Identity (Psychology) in literature.   I. Title.
    PS323.5.D26 2011
    813'.54093529—dc22

                                                          2010041462

Contents

Acknowledgments

GRATEFUL ACKNOWLEDGMENT is due to the following books and journals in which versions of these essays first appeared: "The Jewish Entertainer as Cultural Lightning Rod: The Case of Lenny Bruce," *Postmodern Culture* 7:2 (January 1997) n.p.; "Jazz-Jews, Jive, and Gender: The Ethnic Politics of Jazz Argot," in *Jews and Other Differences: The New Jewish Cultural Studies*, ed. Daniel Boyarin and Jonathan Boyarin (Minneapolis: University of Minnesota Press, 1996) 150–75; "Triangulated Desire and Tactical Silences in the Beat Hipscape: Bob Kaufman and Others," *College Literature* 27 (Winter 2000) 86–105; "Displaysias: Writing Social Science and Ethnicity in Gertrude Stein and Certain Others," in *Modernism, Inc.: Body, Memory, Capital*, ed. Jani Scandura and Michael Thurston (New York: New York University Press, 2001) 133–50; "Imp/penetrable Archive: Adeena Karasick's Wall of Sound," in *Radical Poetics and Secular Jewish Culture*, ed. Stephen Paul Miller and Daniel Morris (Tuscaloosa: University of Alabama Press, 2009) 379–96; "Kinetic Exultations: Postliterary Poetry, Counterperformance, and Micropoetries," in *Class Issues: Pedagogy, Cultural Studies, and the Public Sphere*, ed. Amitava Kumar (New York: New York University Press, 1997) 33–47 and in *Poetry and Pedagogy: The Challenge of the Contemporary*, ed. Joan Retallack and Juliana Spahr (New York: Palgrave Macmillan, 2006) 129–47; "When the Nuyoricans Came to Town: (Ex)Changing Poetics," *XCP: Cross Cultural Poetics* 1.1 (1997) 18–42; "Avant-garde or Border Guard: (Latino) Identity in Poetry," *American Literary History* 10.3 (Fall 1998) 478–96; "Loneliness, Lyric, Ethnography: Some Discourses on/of the Divided Self," *XCP: Cross Cultural Poetics* 3 (1998) 137–47 and *XCP: Cross Cultural Poetics* 11 (Spring 2003) 31–60; "Poetries, Micropoetries, Micropoetics: Elegy on the Outskirts," *Iowa Journal of Cultural Studies* special issue on Poetries (Winter 2006) 86–105; "Electronic Poetics Assay: Diaspora, Silliness, and—?Gender?," is an altered version of two essays, one in *Cybertext Yearbook 2002–2003*, ed. Markku Eskelinen et al. (Saarijärvi: University of Jyväskyla, 2003) 141–62, and the other in *Diasporic Avant Gardes: Experimental Poetics and Cultural Displacement*, ed. Barrett Watten and Carrie Noland (New York: Palgrave Macmillan, 2009) 51–76.

Thank you to the University of Minnesota for numerous forms of support, including single-semester leaves, Faculty Summer Research Grants, sabbaticals, and grants-in-aid for the completion of this project; to department chairs Shirley Garner, Michael Hancher, and Paula Rabinowitz; to Sara Cohen, Michael Eldridge, Laura Czarnecki, Anca Parvulescu, Jason Peck, and Scott Hreha for their assistance with research and editing. Thanks to Joseph Parsons, Adalaide Morris, Alan Golding, and Lynn Keller at the University of Iowa Press for their generous assessment of and work on the volume. Thanks to the many friends, colleagues, students, and family members who read, commented on, or endured the different forms of labor embodied in this book. In particular, I want to acknowledge the research help of Steve Waksman, Carolyn Krasnow, Rachel Buff, and Frieda Knobloch, especially the latter's editorial skills, in preparing "The Jewish Entertainer as Cultural Lightning Rod." I also learned much from Albert Bendich, Rebecca Mark, Riv-Ellen Prell, Robert Danberg, Judith Halberstam, and David Antin. Thanks are equally owed to the following people for the formation of "When the Nuyoricans Came to Town": Ed Cohen, Solomon Deressa, Laurie Dickinson, Bob Gale, Carolyn Holbrook, Bob Holman, Mark Nowak, Joanna O'Connell, and Deirdre Pope, who made the Loft's videotapes of events available to me. All faults herein are, obviously, my own.

Introduction

IN HIS LIVE ACT, Dizzy Gillespie famously developed the following routine: at the appropriate moment, he would announce that he would introduce the band. Turning his back to the audience and abandoning the microphone, he would walk about the stage, earnestly urging the band members to shake hands with each other, presumably proffering each one's name to the others, inviting them to focus closely on each other, while the audience watched the intimate, convivial ritual from an excluded position of either knowing or surprised amusement and appreciation for Diz's wit. By introducing his band members to each other rather than to the audience, Gillespie was not just exercising his prodigious sense of humor. Though what makes the joke funny is the redundancy of the gesture—this band of skilled musicians clearly knew each other already—its nonredundancy is less immediately apparent. The process of creative performance in time, and the ever-changing same of the principles of the music these artists play, remakes each of its elements, redynamizes the intricacies of improvisation, and thus remakes the world in each performance: it is a *poiesis*. They, and we, may think they already know each other, but in the Heraclitean flow of the ensemble process, there is always more to be revealed and learned, new combinations to be experimented with, new changes to ring, unanticipated sounds to trip over or trip out on. While jazz improvisation is a familiar trope for life, social organization, and creativity itself in modernist and postmodern discourse and analyses thereof, it is still a powerful way to understand internal organization that is fluid and teetering along the intelligent edge of structural anarchy. It also occasions a meditation on the nature of an introduction in which the terms for intelligibility are established.

Intelligibility? When Gillespie revolutionized jazz in the 1940s, bebop, the style he helped initiate, was barely intelligible to its first audiences, although its practice was quite rigorous: a steady rhythm overshot with melodic lines improvised and defamiliar-ized from the individual pitches making up the chord progressions of Tin Pan Alley pop tunes, which were wittily renamed to draw attention to the speed and inventiveness of the new versions. Now these noteflights are themselves canonized and referred to as jazz standards. The gesture's theatricality and communality resonate with the ambivalent hermeticism of another closely related art form, poetry, the subject of this collection of essays, which, though they are intimately related to each other, are for-mally collected here for the first time. As with jazz, accessibility and in-accessibility are not fixed characteristics, and poetry's status as both vox populi and the rarified distillation of literary art makes it a cultural terrain full of endless and often contentious analytic possibilities. By "accessibil-ity" and "inaccessibility" I do not mean primarily understandability, as we tend to think in the poetics world: How easy is this poem to grasp? To teach? How transparent or opaque is its meaning to a readership—and which readership? Usually this is approached as an issue of "difficulty," both in jazz and in poetics. However, if we reunderstand the question of intelligibility and accessibility, other questions become more relevant. What traces of history, culture, and consciousness can be grasped through conscientious attention to the poetic fragment? What remains hidden beyond reach, and what does this distance do to our reception, our po-etic experience? How is this in/accessibility itself interesting? What is it? And how does our own situatedness—in the United States, in early twenty-first century—refract poetries of the recent past and muffled pres-ent? Thinking of poetry or jazz as a social practice, of Diz's playful re-minder of the specificity, the particularities of knowing (we are allowed to watch these musicians get to know each other, but we're safe on the side-lines) that make expressive culture a social enterprise, we can move into a poetic space where shtick, side effects, ephemera, the paratextual and paraliterary—the postliterary, in these times—are as charged with signifi-cance as the main event, the standards, the readings, the displays of skill that people have come to consume.

A concern with social locations at differing removes from a power center—that is, with dissidence and its expressive cultures—and an inter-est in "diaspora poiesis," another trope for uprootedness and swirl rather than fixedness, for the process of making rather than the made object, led me to publish a series of essays on verbal art made by people with non-normative identities vis-à-vis the U.S. mainstream. Approaching overlap-ping material from different angles, the pieces revisit a consistent set of themes, concerns, and ambitions in the poetics. They bounce off each other tangentially or directly like planets derailed from their wobbly orbits, like people or poems wandering over time and space in search of community, exhibiting the "art of being off-center":[1] "[Poems] cannot live alone any more than we can."[2] The same could be said about these essays. Strictly speaking, they are siblings, and they configure and reconfigure themselves in relation to each other in shifting proximity, alliance, distance, and tension as family members, colleagues, or the members of Diz's highly trained but always slightly anarchic ensembles do. They are worn and raggedy, naive and stubborn: I could say, with Barrett Watten, rewriting Pound in a different context, "My errors and wrecks surround me . . . error was part of my aesthetic."[3] The essays, in other words, aspire to participate in rather than to domesticate the creative demimonde they describe.

Referring to the suggestion of the muffled present, the in/accessibility of the past in the present, the fragments of alien history embedded in our current poetics, we can move from the lightheartedness of Diz's performances to harsher forms of public-private artistic address, more recent and more fraught. In a March 2007 discussion of outsider art on the Buffalo Poetics List, an institution devoted to the discussion of experimental poetries, Milwaukee visual poet and outsider artist David-Baptiste Chirot wrote a long, impassioned manifesto about the ways in which even the seemingly most compromising forms of institutionalization (museumification, in this case, rather than confinement to prisons or mental hospitals, an experience so common for outsider artists that the category "art brut" originated in Jean Dubuffet's attempt to describe the work he collected from mental patients) cannot really extinguish the spark of subversive, vibrant oddness and vitality of the art or artist. Chirot's work consists primarily of the rubBEings he collects and collages from street forms such as telephone poles, manholes, and street signs. In response to Chirot's extended post, San Francisco poet and publisher Stephen Vincent, one of the stalwarts of the Bay Area alternative publishing scene (his Momo's Press was the first to publish Jessica Hagedorn and other members of the countercultural, multiracial arts scene of the 1970s and 1980s) made a haunting and astute observation:

> Funny, how it . . . makes me think of 14th century German . . . iconic
> Christian paintings in devotion to and in celebration of various Biblical
> allegories. I remember a CAA [College Art Association] annual conference
> in Boston in which the lecturer showed infra-red (?) slides of the under-
> painting (preliminary sketches) for various works. Instead of stiff depic-
> tions of iconic allegorical figures, we were given a very naturalistic view of
> the models—men, women and children—drawn from the village around
> the school where the works were painted, definitely made to conform to

and please the strictures of the Church. Following the argument here, the "outsider" art was actually secreted into the interior life of the "inside" of the Church. I guess we might call these "under paintings" a case of "insider" art. Ironically it's taken 6 centuries to bring the work into view. . . . it's definitely of the material world, and not of allegory made. Somehow brings up the recollection of the story of prisoners in Quantanamo [sic] making poems on thin strips of the paper pealed back from paper cups—and passing those strips among each other. Definitely "insider" art by "outsiders."[4]

There's much to be digested and reworked here, but the notion of an outsider art at the foundation of the canonical, palimpsestically concealed, and yet central to the shape, energy, and spirit of culturally central, even iconic, work, suggests a useful model for thinking about the current poetryscape in the now globalized United States. Just as in every piece of clothing a story of labor and exchange is embedded, a book, poem, or word reifies a set of relationships that can be rendered fluid and mobile again by the hermeneut, the attentive and curious critic, the co-poetic conspirator, the archaeological and attitudinal snoop. In particular, the syncretic cultural emanations that crystallize into poems and other verbal quirks, especially those that emerge from a matrix of unseen and fraught power relations, hold special interest for the scholar investigating poetry as social formation.

The essays presented here explore this outsider-within phenomenon in the aesthetically pressured language we call poetry, addressing the ways in which power relations and social positioning play themselves out in and are shaped by and through non-normatively creative language artifacts. The pieces explore a wide range of such artifacts known to their multitude of producers and consumers as poems, engaging the broad, unanswerable, but provocative question, what is poetry? "Historically situated, aesthetically pressured language" starts to answer, but only just, because what constitutes poetry varies widely across cultures, classes, and myriad other contexts. The book attends to both demotic, vernacular poetries and avant-garde, high literary poetry with similar tools, bringing together traditional close readings and the materialist analysis known as cultural studies to bear on a genre often cordoned off by virtue of its special aesthetic status. While such studies are no longer anomalies, historically, poetry scholarship has been a latecomer to this particular incarnation of materialist criticism; the seminal works on the sociology of literature in a cultural studies vein concerned romance or historical novels and other forms of popular or mass-genre fiction. Indeed, although sociohistorical contextualizing is now de rigueur in most literary scholarship, including poetry scholarship, attention to poetry deemed aesthetically lacking or poetry that embraces a messy or unfinished aesthetic is still relatively rare. However, precisely because the term poetry has such strong resonance in people's affective and expressive lives, and because it proves significant in community formation, popular investment in the genre, especially in new populist forms such as poetry slams and spoken word performances, begs for engaged literary as well as sociological attention. These selected essays attend to this phenomenon, as well as to other unusual or extreme poetries. Because the extant analytic lexicon of literary theory inadequately describes the ragtag, generative edges of poetic production that compose this field of inquiry, these investigations into the nature of the poetic have led to new coinages such as "micropoetries" (glossed at some length below), "*écriture brute*" (outsider writing), and "postliterary poetics" (by which is meant not digital or postliterate poetics but rather an aesthetic that embraces the entire range of poetry, including what lies beyond literary or fine-art poetry). A 2006 issue of the *Iowa Journal of Cultural Studies* devoted to what one might call subaltern poetics used the simple but effective term "poetries" to suggest the multiple varieties of verse (and transverse) that can usefully name a disciplinary and generic category that once happily restrained itself to art poetry—that is, high literary endeavor.

Because the category of micropoetries is both explicitly invoked and implicitly attended to throughout these essays for a postliterary America (it is the primary focus of two of the essays, and informs the whole collection), a brief dilation on the term follows here. *Micropoetries* refers positively to the rawness of fragmentary, ephemeral, nonliterary, unintentional, or otherwise considered unviable poetry: doggerel, occasional verse by amateurs, and other paraliterary detritus that, because of its high degree of defamiliarization, achieves the poetic in its effect on reader, audience, or recipient. In a sense, micropoetries are the cultural studies equivalent of the Aeolian harp, open to/dependent on the sensitivities of the hearer and the vagaries of the surrounding habitus, the social weather that creates tone and content. Because audiences and poetic discourses vary widely, micropoetries are intensely context-specific and often arise out of the cultural practices of subcultures or informal communities with little public acknowledgment or power. For example, graffiti, prison poetry by nonliterary inmates (as distinct from figures such as Oscar Wilde or Osip Mandelstam), slogans, private (scrapbook or diaristic) or semiprivate (correspondence, blogs, or social network) writing, poetry written by children or their strange and charming utterances, *écriture brute*, thieves' cants, and other argots or vernaculars may be considered micropoetries, as might newspaper poetry, greeting-card verse, prayers, and idiolects.

Intended as a capacious term, micropoetries widens the field of the poetic by valorizing artifacts that may be considered clumsy, awkward, and inadmissible among professional poetry circles.

The poetic nature of micropoetries inheres as much in the critical intervention as in the artifact itself, thus requiring a level of engagement beyond acceptance of received wisdom about what constitutes poetic value. Micropoetries scholarship draws on the Russian formalist principle of *ostranenie*, or estrangement, as an index of poetic language, but, in accordance with the insights of the Russian sociolinguists of the 1920s and British cultural studies scholars of the 1970s and 1980s, it aims to broaden the nature of this defamiliarization. That is, not only is the micropoetic fragment estranged from its quotidian environment, it may also, in a double displacement, be estranged from normative notions of the poetic; in other words, it may be considered "bad poetry" in any given era or context (the increasing acceptance and even success of Flarf, a contemporary poetry movement that seeks out "not okay" material as its poetic medium, indicates the provisional, contingent nature of aesthetic standards). Methodologically, these studies are also indebted to Walter Benjamin's combination of observation of linguistic, haptic, or other phenomenological effects with social analysis and to ethnographer Clifford Geertz's celebrated "thick description" as a way of making the micropoetic or subcultural artifact meaningful to non-insiders. Genealogically, the term derives from ethnomusicologist Mark Slobin's term "micromusics," or musical subcultures that fall outside mainstream (classical, popular, folk, and other commercial) networks of production and distribution but enjoy a relationship of productive adjacency to these mainstreams, challenging and combining with them to create new styles and otherwise refresh popular musical culture. While Slobin's study of expressive culture in out-of-the-way places lacks the political bite of Dick Hebdige's powerful exposition of "subcultural style," his systematic discussion of the interactions between different registers of musical cultures addresses the slipperiness and contingent nature of any divisions in the largely fluid relationships of commercial, academic, fringe, and outsider cultures to and with each other.

Close attention to sensory minutiae, the micronics of attentive hearing, is one of the virtues implied in the title of Charles Bernstein's anthology of poetry performance, *Close Listening: Poetry and the Performed Word*, and plays a key role in the scholar's training for work in micropoetries. Both Slobin's emphasis on subcultural, minoritarian, or highly eccentric but context-dependent expressive practices and Bernstein's heightened awareness of minutiae (subtextural as well as subtextual), with an eye (or ear) to enhanced aesthetic experience as well as social and linguistic (and for Bernstein, delightfully incongruous or dissonant) information, indicate the micropoetic object's contingency, ephemerality, and dependence on the contexts of its production and reception. As a diffuse phenomenon, micropoetries compose a subterranean but ubiquitous presence, a verbal force field from which emerges "fine-art" poetry generally referred to as such, although the critical apparatus that has congealed around the latter is often at pains to disavow this connection, seeking instead an absolute difference under the rubrics of "quality" and "craft." In fact, there is by necessity a fluidity between the spheres of practicing poets who are recognized as such by their institutions and the many sites of micropoetic uprupture that don't make it past the gatekeepers; as in the worlds of music Slobin outlines, there is constant and dynamic traffic between them. Diz's joke, though it became part of his standard performance behavior, could usefully be considered a jazz improvisation in itself, part of the musical performance that is as ripe for analysis as the notes and their sequence, the culture from which bebop arose, or the still radical gesture of estrangement the play on "introduction" enacts.

It may appear that we have left politics far behind in our celebration of the minutiae of phenomenological appreciation and Slobin's measured relativism and disinterested tracking of musical commerce at the edges of the mainstream. But the prefix *micro*, of course, in addition to suggesting the preciosity of, say, microgreens in your baby red oak leaf salad, is also intended to connote the minoritarian status of disenfranchised, dispossessed language and those who produce it, as Gilles Deleuze and Félix Guattari have famously elaborated in introducing the term "deterritorialization" into "minor" literary studies.[5] The fluidity with which these sounds and artifacts, micropoetic bits of poetic detritus, these po-emes, circulate does not, of course, obliterate differences in material privilege and access to power that operate in such interactions, as again exemplified by Benjamin's attention to specific haptic experiences in the swirling confusion of nineteenth-century industrial Paris. Constituted of the actual linguistic materials that flare up from the social environment before they've been codified into or participate in the economics of poetic institutions or discourses, micropoetries mediate between discourses of poetry as a genre and cultural studies as an analytic orientation, one that combines attention to the popular and ephemeral with an emancipationist vision. Attempting to democratize American poetry still further, we listen to and for ever-deeper layers of micropoetries, and participate with those poetries in their subjection to the pressures of whatever analytic or creative making they undergo or are taken through. Within every normative poet there is a ragingly abject survivor, and acknowledgment of this continuum can illuminate a "politics of transgressive subjectivity" (to quote Joseph Lease[6]) that subtends whatever emancipatory potential attached to poetry as a cultural practice.

Meanderment: A Walk in Milwaukee

This would be a suitable moment to devote a bit of attention to the work of Chirot, the street poet and visual artist who lives in unstable conditions (with a succession of landlords, one of whom was so moved by one of Chirot's haunting images that he planned to have it tattooed on his body) in Milwaukee, a Midwestern industrial/postindustrial city that, like Detroit, has a lively vernacular art scene: close-to-the-ground, anarcho-punk, experimental, and other furtive but fertile subcultures thrive there. Chirot, unemployed and living on SSI, and thus an endangered person, embarks daily on collecting expeditions in streets and alleys, to gather, using the cheapest of materials, what he calls rubBEings: the living but submerged life forms that manifest themselves when he puts paper to rough street surface—manhole covers, telephone poles, street signs—and applies charcoal (reminiscent of the gravestone rubbings of the 1970s). He is committed to summoning the spirits trapped in these forms, whom he considers members of the sentient world, and to awaken more conventionally embodied humans to the multidimensionality of the block, the street, the city, the world they and he move through, waking and sleeping. One might say that these rubBEings embody a sort of memory of another plane of understanding, another medium of knowing. Hollow-eyed, not quite recognizably formed, rough drafts of people, places, and things, or leftover residue, ash of Pompeii or Hiroshima lives, they are blurry-edged and vulnerably open to our interpretive projections. Pre- or posthuman, intimations of distorted and wobbly immortality, they also eerily imply mortality of the most disturbing and pathetic kind. They are like the Guantánamo prisoners, wrapped in eloquent but muffled half-existence, expressive but so highly mediated by distance and material obstacle that their lives, like Daphne's in the laurel, are barely perceptible even to those who try hard to project empathically, and at the same time are magnified in intensity by multiple layers of thwarting circumstances. His own artist's statement for *RubBEings*, a volume published by Xexoxial Editions, a cultural anarchist press housed at Dreamtime Village, an intentional community in rural Wisconsin, says it best:

The One whose Oracle is at Delphi neither speaks nor conceals but gives signs   —HERACLITUS

Visual poetry is a hieroglyph of site/sight/cite. . . .

    I have a deep belief in the uncanny existence and experience of the found. Found materials are all around us—"it is not the elements which are new but the order of their arrangement" (Pascal). Since I spend a great deal of time walking about in the world, there is no end to the materials for use. Each day, no matter how many times one may have walked the same streets & alleys, there is every something new—or something that one had not noticed before—to work with, to learn from, dream on. . . .

    I began making rubBEings in Spring 1999. Walking a great deal, finding materials to bring home to use—I realized I was already in an immense work room—surrounded by letterings, words, signs—that I could copy on site and make arrangements from directly. Immediately I purchased a lumber crayon and cheap note pad and the rubBEings became not only part of daily life but of my dreams and memories as well. . . .

. . .

    I feel an uncanny affinity with these rubBEings—others of my I. . . .

    I have met both these rubBEings and a great many people along the way. As well as the friends uncannily encountered among wood grains, sidewalk cracks, battered metals and walls, I have gotten to know many new friends. . . . To me this is the greatest gift—community/communication among rubBEings and Human Beings. . . . my works are a form of Thanks for this.

Chirot cites the modernist heroes Picasso, Rimbaud, and Henry Miller (as well as premodern Heraclitus and early modern Pascal, who could be said to occupy extremely different places on the continuum, or perhaps to represent dissonant lineages of rational/intuitive traditions), and observes that he sees himself in direct communication with a European tradition of Old Masters both representational and avant-garde, a tradition sharply called into question by other aspects of his practice. Chirot is an outsider artist not in the sense of being untaught but rather in his highly marginal social location, indeterminantly multiethnic heritage, thoroughly noncareerist orientation toward what's often referred to as the "po biz," and close connection with a host of nondominant artistic and verbal traditions, such as the devotional element of his practice and his credo that, though he conducts these spiritual disinterments solo, this is a communitarian and community-building ritual, a street spiritualism. Walter Benjamin's sympathetic description of the ritual value of premodern art (pre-art, as it were) resonates here, though it is inevitably complicated by the multiplicity of influences and idioms that converge in Chirot's and many other contemporary poets' practices. For example, another influence Chirot cites is Bob Cobbing, the folksy, rough-hewn London avant-gardist whose grainy, photocopied work is palpably present as a direct antecedent. So clearly, while the poetics world Chirot inhabits is not "naive" or unmediated by a self-conscious vanguardism, it is nonetheless highly unstable and tenuous. The works are powerful but also powerless, articulating a position that abdicates social and existential certainty and the material benefits that accrue to those who act with certainty. Compelling in their abjection, their simultaneous resonance and indecipherability index the dynamic interzone between animate and inanimate that haunts the poetic from Orpheus's enchantment of rocks and trees to the digital yoking of cybertechnology and human aspiration.

Emerging from our dream sequence in urban Wisconsin with our alleyway Virgil, we acknowledge that the abject gives us a signal perspective. It signifies emphatically in the following essays. Perhaps the work that appeals to me most is that which inhabits the charged, disturbing overlap between the avant-garde and the world of outsider poetries: the work of brilliant word artists under the strain of mental illness, trauma, addiction, or other conditions that destabilize a coherent sense of self, or the work of communities that, despite their vibrance and creativity, are continually relegated to the edges of access, and thus perforce all the more ingenious. These writers and their work wear out the standard concept that poetry expresses a self that, though under pressure, basically coheres, except for the splitting that necessarily attends any moment of Enlightenment-authorized self-reflection. These poets produce work that supercedes reliance on understood notions of the self (namely, that it is self-questioning but guided by a basic faith in its own integrity) and of literary language (it is mildly defamiliarized, but along recognizably literary lines) by inhabiting such received wisdom beyond its comfort levels: in these artifacts of extremity, the self is radically disturbed rather than quizzically self-reflective, as if Descartes never came back from his thought experiment to write the words that have become a triumphalist slogan for the West, "I think therefore—," without finishing the sentence. The language of these poets is fragmented and distressed rather than in flirtation with a sort of accessorized alterity. The collision of defamiliarized language (a benchmark of the literary taken to extremes) and incoherent subject makes for a disorienting aesthetic experience that stretches one's ethical and imaginative capacities, and it is this space that the current project seeks to tease out, interact with, and bring to the chiaroscuro of academic discussion.

Out of Wisconsin and into the Bagel Shop

A short explication of the first term in this book's subtitle and its organization is in order. "Bagel Shop Jazz," a poem by Bob Kaufman, an African American (and apocryphally Jewish) street poet usually identified with the Beat movement but also active during, if peripheral to, the black arts movement, is a text I return to because it captures my concerns: charged and performative relationships between and among the unstable categories of race, ethnicity, gender, and sexuality in a chess game in which the foregrounding or elision of one element reconfigures everything else: cold war bohemia and its legatees, (auto)ethnographic description, poetic subjectivity, memory, trauma, play. There's a risk to repeatedly mining one poem for new perspectives that is perfectly captured by Groucho Marx's shady real estate auctioneer in *Coconuts*: it's only one square foot, but it's yours as deep as you want to go. The risks are greater still when that territory is not static but porous and ever-shifting, a constant flux of self-disestablishment and reconception that is no sooner fixed than it becomes once again indeterminate. Though throughout the volume I address Kaufman's poem from a number of different perspectives, the felicitous phrase "Bagel Shop Jazz," which within the poem's logic names the Co-Existence Bagel Shop, a Beat hangout in San Francisco's North Beach during the 1950s, is metonymic for explorations across a wider range of inquiries into identity (indicated by what was in the 1950s a markedly ethnic food), community (the cluster of nocturnal and diurnal activity around a coffeeshop), and countercultural, dissident, and dissonant poetry (jazz), which both improvises and repeats, and which offers a perennial trope for the "changing same," and also for the virtuosic balance of competition, individualism, and *esprit de corps* achieved by the most powerful ensembles.

Permeably organized into two sets of case studies that overlap and resonate despite some historical distance, the book addresses both subterranean or hipster/bohemian poetries from the 1950s and 1960s—the outrageous standup comedy of Lenny Bruce, as well as the street verse of Bob Kaufman—and more contemporary instances of sonic, orthographic, and multimedia experimentation with language: spoken word poetry, micropoetries, and Internet, digital, or e-poetry coming from out-of-the-way places: rural Wisconsin, the infonet world of Google and MySpace, or art figures who struggle for legitimacy even within the movements they helped to create. Both sections of the book aim to adumbrate and lend increased resiliency to the literary countermemory of their respective eras: in the first instance, the disenfranchised in an otherwise booming post–cold war U.S. economy; in the second instance, as a counterweight to contemporary triumphalist narratives of ideological certainty that run top-down unchecked, hostile to nuance, expressive culture, and alterity ("inaccessibility") of any stripe. Attending to U.S. poetries that have been underrecognized because of their social locations, processes, idiosyncrasies, or idiolects, the book argues for and performs eccentric investments as foundational to the literary and political health of multiple communities, not least the scholarly communities in which poetry is simultaneously cherished and subject to analytic scrutiny.

The first section of the book, "Identity K/not/e/s," comprises some of the specific readings of the Kaufman poem as well as other discussions of apocryphal or self-eroding Jewish American identity, language use, and black–Jewish relations in bohemian circles, including attention to Gertrude Stein's circle and cold war USA. An essay on the contemporary feminist Kabbalah scholar and performance poet Adeena Karasick propels the book forward in time to the present moment. As I prefer to stay local, close to the artifact, these essays are immersions in clouds of diasporic detritus, notes, nodes, and fragments; their language cleaves to its subjects, hanging on for dear life in orbiting swirls of estrangement, notting and knotting—troubling, unraveling, contradicting—anything to stay in touch with these wounded words.

The second grouping of essays continues to explore the ragged edges of identity, community, and poetics in mutually reflecting, prismatic "takes" on a range of closely related materials: micropoetries, the spoken-word phenomenon, the strange nature of the "lyric I" and its postmodern descendants. Part II's title, "Poetics for a Postliterary America," announces the wider ambitions of the project, moving back panoramically to indicate the larger concerns embedded in the relatively focused close readings that make up part I. This section explores other, more contemporary ethnic (and postethnic?) readings of poetry and poetics, introduces new terms into the discourse of poetic scholarship (micropoetries, counterperformance), and branches out into electronic poetics as a diaspora aesthetics of the twenty-first century. In approaching the topics of poetry and poetics, I intend both terms in both their narrow and wide senses. Here, *poetry* is both conventionally understood as highly aestheticized language with particular attention to rhythm, tonality, imagery, and the repertoire of figurative language and figures of speech characterizing "the poetic" and, more broadly, as literary or defamiliarized language that does not particularly cleave to the protocols of Western lyric. Thus the language of a quasi-anarchist chopper bicycle club or a *LiveJournal* entry is considered under the sign of the poetic as much as Gertrude Stein's, Bob

Kaufman's, or John Wieners's literary efforts. Likewise, *poetics* means both the mechanics of poetry making and the broader sense of poiesis, making-ness itself, the processual unfolding of creative activity broadly construed, regardless of its degree of literary intentionality, recognition, or reception as such. The "post" in postliterary expresses a relationship generally but not exclusively characterized by both chronology and genealogy, implying some degree of supercession and transformation or mutation, but not a complete disavowal. Rather than reject the term "literary," it widens the scope of the literary and plays at its borders, taking under consideration online diaries and elegies, student writing, comedic improvisation, van-guard experimentation, spoken word, stammers, cries and whispers, and community (de)formation(s) as postliterary activities worthy of analysis. And "America" is certainly a contested term as well, though the publisher's house style prohibited my use of quotation marks around it.

As a whole, the book attempts a balance between conventional poetic reading strategies applied to eccentric though identifiably poetic materials and more probing inquiries that move poetic scholarship into conversa-tion with other disciplines such as ethnography, into the minutiae of the poetics of the everyday, into realms in which verbal art is taken seriously as poetic without recourse to aesthetically evaluative categories of bad or good. It may seem out of step to address the question of aesthetic value now that we have absorbed some of the wisdom of cultural studies, but poetry scholarship, even when it takes a historicist approach, still demon-strates tacit or explicit assumptions about what is worthy of study and what is peripheral or epiphenomenal. Arguments about taste abound, and taste still claims primacy in the realm of close reading and attention to systems of figurative language. Many chapters are characterized by a fair dose of autobiographical or poetic material—neologisms, anecdotes, alternative orthography, rhyme—so that one could fairly argue that the collection implicitly proposes an open style of critical writing that acknowledges the centrality of the idiosyncratic—the peculiar particular—to the whole. Each part contributes to a rough, imperfectly assimilated whole, which it-self continues to mutate. That whole in its turn, I hope, contributes—with the valuable off-kilterness of the bricoleur's improvisations—to the emer-gent and exciting discourse emanating from a renewed public interest in poetry and poetics, a gloriously motley whole of which this is a scrappy scrap, a shreddy thread, aspiring to enter into an asymptotic continuum reaching toward those muffled in/accessibilities, the outsider within.

Part 1

Identity K/not/e/s

1 The Jewish Entertainer as Cultural Lightning Rod

The Case of Lenny Bruce

To is a preposition, come is a verb.
To is a preposition, come is a verb.
To is a preposition, come is a verb, the verb intransitive.
To come. To come.
I've heard these two words my whole adult life, and as a child when
I thought I was sleeping. To come. . . . Now if anyone in this room or
the world finds those two words decadent, obscene, immoral, amoral,
asexual, the words "to come" really make you feel uncomfortable, if
you think I'm rank for saying it to you, and you the beholder gets
rank for listening to it, you probably can't come.

—LENNY BRUCE, ACCOMPANYING HIMSELF ON DRUMS,
"TO IS A PREPOSITION, COME IS A VERB"

IN THE SUMMER OF 1989 I got a copy of Lenny Bruce's 1962 obscenity trial transcript from Albert Bendich, the defense attorney for the case. As I drove home with the 352-page document, the radio told me of Jesse Helms's proposed muzzling of the NEA. Heretofore, my interest in Jewishness as a de facto and traditionally "traveling culture" with its own makeshift language(s) had been primarily a process of self-exploration. That moment of being trapped in a small, moving space with Jesse Helms and Lenny Bruce, and later reading the transcript itself, redirected my efforts toward exploring the ways competing masculinities overlap and intersect, and how these differences can be read through the hierarchies of culture represented in the trial, which was in effect a showdown between high-, low-, and middlebrow cultures as represented respectively by the academy, the entertainment world with its blurred sexual boundaries, and the discourse of the courtroom and the police force. The trial foregrounded and foreshadowed social change even as its protagonist was offered up for public consumption.

Bruce, the stranger who rode into town and said the right thing at the right time in front of the wrong people, suffered the consequences of a wayward hyperverbalism deployed in the interest of social criticism. Though the scholarship on Jewish diasporic language use suggests certain strategies—for example, the primacy of anecdotes and minutiae, the valuation of dialogue, commentary, and argument as pleasures and ends in themselves, the blending of the sublime and the earthy or its rhetorical analogue, the blending of the language of high abstraction and colloquialisms—as characteristic of Jewish written and oral culture, I want to stress that in identifying Bruce's strategies as "Jewish," I do not posit these strategies as inherently or only Jewish.[1] Indeed, Bruce's manic polyglot eclecticism and makeshift, survivalist logic share much with a more generalized, multiethnic urban sensibility, especially the African American jive idiom; his conversation mingled "the jargon of the hipster, the argot of the underworld, and Yiddish."[2] Nonetheless, I focus on the latter because it is, arguably, the primary constitutive element of Bruce's self-presentation, and because in the context of his San Francisco trial his Jewishness played a mediating role—the lightning-rod role—between San Francisco's civic structure, the intellectual and sexual countercultures, and the entertainment substratum of the city.

In addition, specific focus on the trial as a cultural and rhetorical event raises issues of censorship in terms that are all too relevantly urgent in light of attempts to regulate the languages of the Internet and to dismantle the NEH and NEA in the name of policing language, and even more recently the Patriot Act's raising of the stakes. It's easy to recognize in high-profile policings of social critique a reenactment of the anti-intellectualism and antipluralism so transparent in the transcript of Bruce's trial; the charge of obscenity is used to legitimate increased government surveillance of the art world, dissident cultures, and the academy. I do not argue that Bruce was under attack as a Jew in the same way that 2 Live Crew or Andres Serrano were under attack as men of color in the 1990s.[3] Rather, I argue that Bruce's outsiderhood and ethnic language use set him up to mediate cultural and political tensions in San Francisco—specifically, he was arrested for public references to male genitalia because the emerging gay men's community in that city posed a threat to mainstream civic discourse. His irreverence and outspokenness about sexuality and race, his willingness (compulsion, in fact) to question all norms of behavior implicated him in the local struggle over cultural expression.

Much lively work on ethnicity, gender, and language in American culture has provided the methodological and theoretical base for an investigation of Jewish performance texts and their reception: the approaches to ethnicity and culture provided by James Clifford's or Michael Fischer's "new ethnographies," the blend of close literary analysis with intuitive musings on the meaning of "vernacular" offered by Houston A. Baker's work on African American writers, Renato Rosaldo's discussion of subaltern wit as a weapon and tool for social analysis, Riv-Ellen Prell's attention to the specific ways in which gender and power relations are coded in Jewish and anti-Jewish humor. By contrast, with a few notable exceptions, what little scholarship there is on Bruce focuses on the personality-cultish aspects of his dramatic life story or on a simplistic reading of his "martyrdom," without close theoretical attention to how he generated texts through which we can read the conflicts of his times.[4] I hope to bring the questions generated by the first body of scholarship to bear on a moment in Bruce's and the nation's life: the moment in which his language use was labeled obscene, and he—not only his words—was censored.

Lenny Bruce stands on the slash between the words "inside/outside," balancing on that caesura like a carnival artist (his wife, Honey, grew up, in fact, in the extended-family carnie world). He teeters on that vertiginous edge, that "ethereal peak," as he phrased it, right before his plunge.[5] Lenny Bruce as Jewish entertainer is the caesura—the cultural lightning rod—that mediates the inside out from the outside in.

That caesura marking difference, the person of Lenny Bruce on stage, is furthermore positioned as an index of male sexuality, the erect penis— not the hegemonic, capital-P Phallus of the symbolic order but rather, in this case, Jewish male sexuality, which is as unstable and evanescent in its cultural significance as that liminal space between inside and outside, and encompassing both inside and outside, that characterizes modern Jewish life. If the veiled gentile Phallus is the elusive figure that, like the Wizard of Oz, governs the discursive institutions of American social life from behind the scenes, the exposed penis of the other is the vulnerable carrier of the subversive disease of "obscenity," which threatens the stability of those social institutions and calls down on itself the harshest recriminations.

Furthermore, using Renato Rosaldo's analysis of subaltern humor to posit Jewish humor as a weapon of self-defense, one can analyze Bruce's seduction/attack on his audience as a prototypical Jewish American male performance strategy for survival. His use of Yiddish to mark a boundary of inclusion/exclusion, his savaging of Jews in front of a Gentile audience as an oblique critique of that audience as well as a direct critique of Jewish hypocrisy and assimilation, the speed of his rap, and his preoccupation with sex and sexuality work together to destabilize normative social relations on all levels.[6] These tactics serve as much to confuse the opposition and get away—a tactic of survival—as to articulate an ethical and aesthetic position. Together, they constitute a general critique of stability, an assumption and affirmation of the role of Jew as floating signifier, and a rhetorical representation of the historical and often dire contingencies of Jewish life.

JEW as Diasporic Icon

It's painful to review the obvious. That Jews occupy the primary (non) space in the Western imagination as interlopers, counterfeits, transients, unknown quantities with chameleon-like qualities is such a truism that to attempt to document it would plunge the writer into an exercise bordering on the tautological. I use the singular to underscore ironically the monolithic power of this Western trope: "the Jew" (both genderless and hyperbolic in his invisible masculinity, like "his" "G-d") as icon of diaspora par excellence. The singularity and capitalization erase the history and materiality of diaspora. The false solidity of the phrase "the Jew," on the one hand, and the ethereal diffusion of rotten-sweet crematoria vapor on the other, mask the physical travails and psycho-emotional trauma of displacement. "The Jew" is in fact a floating signifier: the Anglo Christian imagination represents the Jew as embodying both the elitism of high culture and the bestiality of low culture, as both the threat of capitalism and that of communism, as both steeped in quaintly Old World ways and committed to dangerously modern and subversive philosophies that hold nothing dear. To some extent this is simply the classic double bind of an oppressed group. Feminists, for example, have for many years pointed to the virgin/whore/mother tropes constricting the possibilities of women's sexual expression and experience. And Henry Louis Gates, Jr., among others, has discussed the phenomenon of African slaves in the post-Enlightenment New World having to establish their humanity by writing—but not too well: cultivating the persona of the earnest counterfeit was the only way to succeed without being too threatening.[7] Unique to the Jewish trope is that Jews as a group represent nonrepresentability. To be Jewish, according to this master trope, is to be unpin-downable, without location, liminal.

The performance poet David Antin has pointed out that Jews served as "translators . . . of language and culture in Southern Spain and the strange fact that they as 'boundary-dwellers' in Spain so frequently had the name Marques, that is 'march-dweller,' 'border'- or 'boundary-man' or 'woman'—and furthermore that the names Marx, Marcuse, Marcus all come from an original Marques."[8] English-language speakers are most familiar with this name as the title Marquis, which in early examples provided by the *OED* refer to the owner of land of poor quality and low profit, or the prefect of a frontier town—a kind of consolation prize of title. That a name representing liminality itself—boundary-person—evolved into a title of (almost) nobility just prior to the Jews' forced exodus from Spain speaks to the longevity and profundity of Western ambivalence toward Jews as objects of desire (that is, of both hatred and intense desire for appropriation). It is commonly observed that one common form of anti-Semitism is the claim (by the non-Jewish majority) that Jews are the oppressor: that Jews "control the media" and have a secret plot to take over the world, that Jews are all rich and pull strings behind the scenes to get their way. The ambiguity of the title "marquis" instantiates this weird reversal; as in the word "snob" (*sine nobilitate*), the title granted the liminal character, the entertainer/trickster, evolves into ersatz, arriviste pseudorespectability, which can then be re(pre)sented as privilege.[9] Indeed, the theater marquee, that modern announcer of entertainers (inbetweeners/Jews), has its origins in the same word: a marquee was the open-air tent inhabited by marquises (inbetweeners/Jews). The multiple puns in Bruce's visual gag in *How to Talk Dirty and Influence People* comes to mind here: a photograph of the Strand Theatre's marquee announcing Bruce's engagement while the caption reads: "At last! My name in lights: S-T-R-A-N-D."[10] A strand is a border (beach), a marker of transition or inbetween-ness. Lenny Bruce was stranded on his own terrain as the standup (erect) comic; he had marked out the trickster's border realm for himself and was abandoned to die in that vanguard twilight zone after being encouraged and commended for occupying it. The other aspect of this joke, of course, treats the theme of naming, denaming, renaming so painfully prominent in diasporic histories. "Bruce," the name that appears on the marquee, is no more Lenny's real name than Strand is—nor was Schneider, the one before Bruce.

That one can both disavow and affirm an identity with perfect sincerity indicates the elusive power of Du Bois's double consciousness, and of the "ethnic id" aptly named by Michael Fischer.[11] The ability to maintain and tolerate seemingly contradictory positions, to live in multiple realities, is currently considered a characteristic of postmodernism,[12] alternately affirmed as a liberation of consciousness from the constraints of linearity and sequential time/space and bewailed as a loss of authenticity and stability, a numb sensibility lending itself perfectly to a dangerously high tolerance for and acquiescence to social trauma. This ability, however, is also profoundly and traditionally "Jewish."

Mr. Bruce Was Not Permitted to Represent Himself: Jews and the Crisis of Representation

Kimberle Crenshaw has outlined the inadequacy of current public systems of representation to acknowledge identity and subjectivity.[13] She tells of a group of black women who experienced harassment in the workplace and wanted to sue their employer for discrimination. They were told that they could not sue as black women, though that was the identity under fire in these instances of harassment; they had to sue either as black, in which case they had to demonstrate that black men were similarly harassed, or as women, in which case they had to demonstrate that nonblack women were similarly harassed. The legal system had no way of recognizing their subjectivity as they themselves experienced it; there was no means for them to represent themselves within the strictures of a categorical worldview that could not make room for them to grant themselves meaning.

As it is for many "minority" groups, the condition celebrated by postmodernists as the "crisis in representation" has long been a lived reality for Jews. The aesthetic and intellectual excitement of challenging those Western epistemologies that posit a simple one-to-one correspondence between empirical phenomena and "meaning" intersects pointedly with a struggle for the right to self-representation. Self-representation, according to Bruce, cannot involve a loyalty to a fixed identity; therein, to the extent that nationalism affords a spurious self-certainty, lies the devastating cynicism of his anti-Israel jibes in "Religions, Inc." ("We gotta . . . great man . . . to . . . tell us what to do with the Heavenly Land—Rabbi Steven H. Wise!" Rabbi Wise: "I tink vee should subdivide" . . .)[14] and "Christ and Moses Return" ("We're not [in temple] to talk of God—we're here to sell bonds for Israel!").[15] On the other hand, this refusal of a fixed geopolitical body champions a Jewishness with almost sentimentally universalist overtones, especially his famous anti-essentialist dicta:

> I neologize Jewish and goyish. Dig: I'm Jewish. Count Basie's Jewish. Ray Charles is Jewish. Eddie Cantor's goyish. B'nai Brith is goyish; Haddassah, Jewish. Marine Corps–heavy goyim, dangerous. . . . Koolaid is goyish. All Drake's Cakes are goyish. Pumpernickel is Jewish, and, as you know, white bread is very goyish. Instant potatoes—goyish. Black cherry soda's very Jewish. . . . Trailer parks are so goyish that Jews won't go near them. Balls are goyish. Titties are Jewish. Mouths are Jewish. All Italians are Jewish.[16]

Here, Bruce loads Jewishness with connotations of (ethnic) soulfulness, femininity, earthiness, and hipness. Refusing genetic, religious, or even cultural essentialism, he nonetheless incurs a different danger. He self-allegorizes a "Jewishness" so grandiose and omnipresent that it pervades all categories rather than being itself a category. Like carbon or chi (life energy), Jewishness is, as it were, *pre*-essentialistic (or pretaxonomic) in its transcendence, an inchoate *prima materia* that is nonetheless localized in the minutiae of daily life: music, food, consumer products, living arrangements, body parts. The delicate process of locating any human(e) universality in this kind of particularity (in, for example, anecdote, field observation, text, or incident) describes the dialectic between the local and the theoretically generalizable that is at the heart of much current academic debate in anthropology (pro/con ethnography), feminism (identity politics), and cultural studies.[17]

Self-representation, as distinct from representation by hostile or well-meaning others, is one attempt to avoid laboring under restrictive definitions superimposed on a necessarily fluid subjectivity. To return to the Crenshaw example, the right to self-representation means the right to represent multiple subjectivities, especially those not mandated as legal, racial, or institutional categories. Self-representation implies taking the proceedings into the realm of trans- or antidiscursivity, a move threatening enough to warrant censorship either by explicit silencing or by forcing a flamboyant rap (such as Bruce's performance) into the highly circumscribed courtroom format, limiting wide-ranging verbal potential to legal jargon. Although in the history of his courtroom dramas Bruce was granted the right to representation by others (and hired and fired an amazing number of lawyers, none of whom satisfied his need for total control), he was heavily discouraged—as defendants routinely are—from representing himself as his own counsel. Bruce was expected to stay silent while prosecuting and defense attorneys read his decontextualized routines from transcripts; his bodily presence was necessary to the trials, but his hyperverbality—arguably his "real" presence—was forcibly and repeatedly banished. The courts' ambiguous need for his presence put him in absurd legal quandaries sometimes. By scheduling his trials in two different states concurrently, the law prevented him from fulfilling even the basic requirement of physical presence since he could only be in one place at a time; thus he was de facto guilty in the court at which he could not appear.

Lenny Bruce, né Leonard Alfred Schneider, born in Brooklyn in 1926, came from a background of vaudeville (according to one etymology, *voix de ville*, voice of the city), the low culture of Lower East Side Jews, into public fame as a hip, autodidactically intellectual, socially relevant, and utterly irreverent standup comic whose routines ranged from "Psychopathia Sexualis" to "How to Relax Your Colored Friends at Parties." In this sense, his biographical data instantiate the (pace Muhammad Ali) float-like-a-butterfly, sting-like-a-gadfly signifier that is the Jew in the modern Western imagination. He was tried for obscenity and acquitted in March 1962, following the first of many arrests for obscenity. This initial obscenity arrest took place on October 4, 1961, at the Jazz Workshop on San Francisco's nightclub strip, conformity to the "community standards" of which might have qualified otherwise censorable "obscene speech" for protection. He was arrested for violating the Penal Code, the phallic order represented by the conservative elements in San Francisco's political makeup, its traditionally Irish-Italian-American police force and political machinery. His violation consisted of three instances of obscenity: use of the word "cocksucker," use of the term "kiss it" with implicit reference to an exposed penis, and the famous semantics lecture cum religious chant, "To Is a Preposition, Come Is a Verb." All of these transgressions target male sexuality as both subject and object of demystification, unveiling, uncovering, a verbal circumcisive display experienced by representatives of the normative order as an assaultive castration. It is important to see this cultural text, the obscenity trial, as a moment in which gender, sexuality, and language were on trial/in process, according to *Tel Quel*'s famous pun, capturing in an instance of dramatic confrontation San Francisco's postwar emergence as the front line for such transgressions.

Entertaining Anxiety

Lenny Bruce's 1962 obscenity trial marked a temporal instant in the cultural history of a city that is itself remarkable in American culture. The late 1950s and early 1960s witnessed a renaissance in the Gold Rush City; it established itself as the center of several different but overlapping countercultures noted for their flamboyant foregrounding of the aesthetic and their emphasis on alternative social organizing units (the gay relationship, the hippie "tribe," the Third World arts coalition). These new formations threatened assumptions about the interrelatedness of sexuality, reproduction, and traditional family life. Developing as a capital of anarcho-socialist activity (and, shortly, the free speech movement), and of avant-garde literature and life, the Bay Area fostered a literary community whose oxymoronic epithet was "Beat" (beatific, wasted, jazz-inspired) and a burgeoning gay community that for the first time in American history would have civic and political as well as cultural visibility as a cohesive unit. By the end of the sixties, the region had become a center for the culture of altered consciousness and experimental spiritual practice.

Language, ethnicity, gender, sexuality, consciousness—identity itself—all became contested terms in a celebratory and experimental atmosphere.

Traces of all the destabilizing elements of the countercultural discourses surfacing in the particularly volatile years of the shift from the McCarthy era to the civil rights era can be found in embryonic form in Bruce's controversial Jazz Workshop routine and in the trial that ensued. The trial's subtext concerned, among other things, mainstream discomfort with the emerging gay men's community (Bruce used the word "cocksucker" in a routine about being asked by his agent to do his gig in a newly gay bar). The trial displayed the town-gown politics of the Bay Area's own cold war between the police force and the "long beards" at Berkeley, who in Bruce's defense invoked figures like Rabelais and Swift to legitimize his satirical and ribald shpritzes. The trial embodied the tension between the protocol of juridical process and the carnivalesque nature of Bruce's deterritorialized language, dramatized by the constant disruptive laughter from the courtroom audience. Although he was neither San Franciscan, gay, literary, Beat, nor politically active in any conventional sense, the notoriety of Bruce's arrest and trial enabled, almost by accident, the emergence of these cultures' national visibility. Specifically, several of the dramatis personae of the trial indicated Bruce's affiliations with these circles. Lawrence Ferlinghetti, who published and distributed Bruce's pamphlet *Stamp Help Out*, was the contact person who supplied the defense attorney, Al Bendich, known among Beat circles as Ginsberg's successful ACLU defense counsel in the "Howl" obscenity case six years earlier. The presiding judge, Horn, had also presided over the "Howl" case. Bendich hypothesizes that Bruce owed his acquittal to Horn's having been "educated" about obscenity and the Constitution by the defense in the "Howl" case.[18] (The "Howl'" obscenity trial, also held in San Francisco, was likewise a bellwether instance of Jewish male verbal and sexual identity on trial.) Bruce's own status as an ethnic person, an outsider whose weapon was language—in short, as a Jewish entertainer—marked him for repercussion. He became a lightning rod mediating civic wrath and countercultural flamboyance.

I have discussed elsewhere the survivalist compulsion in Bruce's Jewish hyperverbalism: if I stop talking they'll kill me.[19] The hairpin turns in logic and association in Bruce's tragicomic spiel hold out against the closure that means death. Bruce told Bendich, "I can see around corners," evoking images of adrenaline-powered feats of psychic and physical strength.[20] The vision is always of disaster; the words are always chasing after the vision, trying to articulate it and to obscure it (you can't let them know you know), and racing to head it off at the pass. Hence the decentered, brilliantly precise imprecision of Bruce's rap, the mumbling, desultory delivery that never quite ends. The verb "to entertain" derives from *entretenir*, to hold in an in-between state. Entertainment means hanging on to a liminal stage where all manner of things are possible because everything is both in suspension and in transition, deterritorialized and resistant, holding disparate elements together, maintaining a state of unsettledness and nomadic consciousness. Entertainment, Bruce's philosophical rambling, enacts verbally a history not of aimless wandering but rather of a purposive, at times frantic, self-displacement. Thus, Judge Horn erred when he insisted to the packed and unruly courtroom crowd, "You are not here to be entertained."[21] As an attempt to salvage a career, the trial was a negotiation for survival, an *entretien*. Given the performance imperative of the Jewish American male, Bruce's "semantics" lectures become "semen-tics" and finally "see-my-antics" routines as the fight for survival becomes, poignantly, the struggle to please, to be entertaining.[22] The scene is shot through with tremendous vulnerability.

Positing Jewish male sexuality as a subversive element in this scenario does not mean celebrating it unambiguously. Male sexuality is, to say the least, a contested terrain, and different ideologies of masculine prowess—here, the Anglo Christian and the Jewish (the rhetoric of the trial recasts this opposition as straight and decent versus gay and obscene)—conflict with such seismographic force that the collision throws off sparks illuminating a historical and cultural transition. Consciously problematizing these masculinities and their interactions can be an emancipatory move toward dismantling a discourse that posits any construction of sexuality as normative or monolithic. The logistics of Bruce's trial do indeed lend themselves to the quasi-structuralist school of neat differences (viz. the dichotomized name of the case: *The Plaintiff, aka The People of San Francisco vs. the Defendant, aka Lenny Bruce*), appearing to be a showdown between the forces of the phallus and those of the vulnerable penis, between the symbolic and the imaginary, between the factual and the fanciful, between the straight and the hip, between several different masculine sexualities. However, in following such an analytic pattern, I feel torn between wanting to see the neat dichotomies I've just outlined as definitively separate, so that I can put myself safely on the side of vulnerable penile imaginary fanciful hipness, and wanting to portray the putative opposition as in fact indicating ambiguity: outside is always already inside, the potential disruptions in the hegemony of the Phallus are ultimately recouped anyway. (They're all men, the terms of their discourse exclusionary and closed to me.)

And in fact, both the heroes and the villains of this free speech debate are all men, all ostensibly straight, all white. Both the defense attorney, Albert Bendich, and the prosecuting attorney, Albert Wollenberg, were Jewish, so there goes any untroubled claim for Jewishness as subversive. (However, Bendich, from New York, was a Yiddish speaker who grew up, like Bruce, in an oppositional culture; Wollenberg's family consisted of multigenerational San Francisco Jews who had not, by and large, experienced the same kind of prejudice as their East Coast counterparts and who, having arrived at a more central civic position, had, arguably more at stake in upholding the status quo). Mary Brown, an audience member of the Jazz Workshop routine and the only woman called to testify on the comedian's behalf, is not permitted to answer the question, otherwise routine in an obscenity case, whether or not her prurient interest was stimulated by the show (the constitutional protection of obscene speech stipulates that the utterance "not arouse the prurient interest" of the listener or reader); that is, she may not define her own sexuality, even to deny it. Despite her status as an eyewitness rather than an expert witness, Wollenberg challenges her competence to answer such a question because her "expertise" on this matter has not been established.[23] Nonetheless, though it is staged and reads smoothly as a showdown of diametrically opposing sensibilities and values, permeated with anxiety over gender and sexuality as it is, the trial is exclusively dominated by male voices and male interests. Though the men read long passages from *Lysistrata*, "The Wife of Bath's Tale," and Molly Bloom's soliloquy, no female academics or authors are given the floor; Mary Brown, as we have seen, was thwarted in her efforts to speak on behalf of Bruce and her own subject position. This male entretien revolves around the dual discourses of male homophobia and homosociality, in which Jewishness plays a transitional though implicit role.

Entertaining Homophobia

I was working a burlesque gig with Paul Moer, in the Valley. That's the cat on the piano here, which is really strange, seeing him after all these years, and working together. And the guy says, "There's a place in San Francisco but they've changed the policy."

"Well, what's the policy?"

"Well, they're not there any more, that's the main thing."

"Well, what kind of a show is it, man?"

"It's not a show. It's a bunch of cocksuckers, that's all. A damned fag show."

"Oh. Well, that is a pretty bizarre show I don't know what I can do in that kind of a show."

"Well, no. It's—we want you to change all that."

"Well—I—don't that's a big gig. I can[t?] just tell them to stop doing it."[24]

John D'Emilio has documented the emergence of the gay men's community in postwar America and devotes considerable energy to detailing the historical dynamics by which San Francisco became a Mecca for gay men. The confluence of a number of progressive literary, political, and spiritual countercultures with the Bay Area's military centrality enabled a richly unorthodox milieu of marginalized men: creative artists, beatniks, anarchists, academics, and military men discharged after the war.[25] Some men, such as Allen Ginsberg (a gay man and a Beat poet), Peter Orlovsky (a naval dischargee and Bohemian demimondain), Gary Snyder (a poet and a Berkeley student), Kenneth Rexroth (a poet and an anarchist), and other "outcats" whose names will never be known, formed bonds that crossed over from one subculture to the others. The nightclub-entertainment scene contributed to and reflected this culturally potent mix: gay bars operated next to straight strip joints, jazz clubs that featured a new "intellectual" breed of comedy, and coffeehouses that specialized in poetry readings. The Bruce skit that introduces this section addresses this emerging network of countercultural communities and the resulting ambivalence on the part of the traditional entertainment business (which already had only a tenuous relationship to mainstream respectability). The rough narrative outline here is that Bruce was in hypothetical conversation with an agent who wanted to book him at Ann's 440, a club he used to work at (across the street from the Jazz Workshop, so he could expect that his audience would be somewhat familiar with it). In the meantime, since the time he worked there, Ann's 440 had become a gay bar. His agent's intention was to "change all that"—to restore it to straightness. Bruce's routine documents the increasing visibility of the gay men's community, even as his arrest for mentioning it attests to its ongoing, perhaps proportionally increasing, vulnerability. He asserts his own straightness even as he questions the impossible task of altering, ignoring, or denying the historical development of a solid alternative sexual community. "Well—I don't—that's a big gig."

At the moment of Bruce's arrest, the arresting officer Solden asked him, "Why do you feel that you have to use the word 'cocksuckers' to entertain people in a public night spot?" Bruce replies, "Well, there's a lot of cocksuckers around, aren't there? What's wrong with talking about them?" This moment is fraught. It is possible that Bruce is using the term here simply as an insult, implying that the policeman is a cocksucker in the generalized sense of "jerk." But given the saturated moment—Bruce has just come off the stage from his routine—it is more likely that he is engaging the more specific sense of the term as "gay men." The case is still complicated, however. On the one hand, Bruce, repeating uncritically and for "authentic" effect the homophobic term he attributed to the show-biz manager in his performance, complies with a larger social homophobia. On the other hand, the flippant answer foreshadows, if not the pro-active sentiment, the logic of the slogan so crucial to contemporary cultural survival in San Francisco and elsewhere: Silence = Death. (It bears reminding that Bruce's subsequent silence *was* materially related to his death.[26]) While his commitment to free speech and to unmasking hypocrisy necessitated his occasional attacks on homophobia, nowhere more than in his routines on gay men does he conform to the ineptly self-revealing liberal who is the usual butt of his vitriolic humor. In this particular routine, though, it is not liberal homophobia that is the target of his humor but gay men themselves, used as "bizarre" objects. The meaning of the routine is further complicated by its respective transcriptions as "I *can* just tell them to stop doing it" and "I *can't* just tell them," in response to his agent's desire that he intervene in the bar's gayness. The first instance implies that the bizarre show is itself comprised of men performing fellatio; by telling them to stop, he would put an end to their objectionability. "They" are "cocksuckers" only when they are sucking cock. In the second instance, "I can't just tell them to stop doing it," Bruce suggests that simply telling people not to be gay (in public) will not work; sexuality is an inclination rather than a set of actions. He calls attention to the disparity between the literal/descriptive and figurative/derogatory meanings of the term "cocksucker" even as he gets mileage out of his presumed straight audience by suggesting an inherent funniness in fellatio (though in "The Bust," he also proclaims its pleasures).

The police officers testifying against Bruce were witnesses for the People of the State of California, with a relationship of illusory grandiosity to people analogous to the Phallus's relationship to physical penises. Who are the people? Who gets to decide who is human? The right to talk about them/us because there are a lot of them/us implicates talk itself as a deciding factor in the constitution of personhood. Al Bendich said that language is what makes us human, it's a medium for getting our basic human needs met; the pragmatist would have it that the word be spoken beforehand, in the absence of the thing, to indicate lack, desire, need.[27] But it's also a medium for celebrating: the wild boy of Aveyron delightedly repeats "lait, lait," after the milk has been served, acknowledging its wonder.[28] Is Bruce calling "cocksuckers" into existence by naming them, or is he acknowledging their emerging visibility in San Francisco's public life? Clearly, the People were not happy with the possibility of alternative sexuality or the articulation of that sexuality. Truth is what is, Bruce insisted in his moments on the witness stand. If there are gay people, why not talk about them? The People's fear is that talking about "it" will create "it"; conversely, the hope is that not talking about it will keep it invisible.

Another twist to simple homophobia comes into play in this scenario to exacerbate the issue of what specifically constitutes "obscenity"— legally construed as a "morbid interest in nudity, sex, or excretion." During cross-examination the defense witnesses were asked, "Why did he have to use the word 'cocksucker'? Wouldn't 'faggot' or 'fairy' have done as well?"[29] The state objects not to derogatory epithets for gay men but to the explicit penile reference, which evinces morbid interest. The term "cocksucker" refers to an act; the terms "fairy" and "faggot" indicate a type of person that might engage in such an act. As Foucault has taught us, this is an important historical distinction. The discomfort engendered by the term "cocksucker" indicates that the People's true fear is of the homoerotic possibilities embedded in conventional homosociality—a fear implicitly suggested by Bendich when he elicited testimony about the frequency with which the word is in fact used in the police station, a public place.[30] The Jewish male is implicated in this mainstream fear by embodying for them that middle space, neither fully "homosexual" (or demonstrably homoerotic) nor conforming to the laws of Gentile male bonding through physical activity; as Daniel Boyarin has observed, the "Jewish sissy" occupies a place that conforms to neither mainstream heteromasculinity nor unambiguous homosexuality. Bruce understood this mainstream fear that the line between homosexuality and homosociality collapse: his subsequent skit "Blah Blah Blah" insisted on the People's proclivity for using the word covertly, and exposed their secret love of excess and celebration in language, which love implicated them as phatic fags, spewing Jews, redundant, secreting, and feminized—his semblables:

What I got arrested for in San Francisco . . . I got arrested for . . . uh . . . I'm not going to repeat the word because I want to finish the gig here tonight. It's . . . uh . . . all right. They said it was vernacular for a favorite homosexual practice. A ten-letter word. Uh. . . . It's really chic. That's two four-letter words and a preposition. I can't . . . uh . . . I wish I could tell you the word. It starts with a "c". . . . Well, you know what the word is. Now it's weird how they manifested that word as homosexual, 'cause I don't. That relates to any contemporary chick I know, or would know, or would love or marry.

You know. When I took the bust, I finished the show. And I said that word, you know, the ten-letter word and the heat comes over and says, "Uh, Lenny, my name is Sgt. B. . . . You know the word you said?"

"I said a lot of words out there, man."

"Well, that—that that word."

"Oh, yeah."

"Well Lenny, that's against the law. I'm gonna have to take you down."

. . . Now we really got into it, into it. Now we get into court. The chambers. The judge—Aram Avermitz, a red-headed junkyard Jew, a real ferbissiner with thick fingers and a homemade glass eye. Tough-o, right? He comes in. Swear the heat in, honk, honk.

"What'd he say?"

"Ya Hona. He said blah-blah-blah."

"He said blah-blah-blah?!?"

Then the guy really yenta-ed it up: "That's right, I didn't believe it. There's a guy up on the stage, in front of women and a mixed audience, saying blah-blah blah."

"This I never heard, blah-blah-blah. He said blah-blah-blah?"

"He said blah-blah-blah. I'm not gonna lie to ya." It's in the minutes: "I'm not gonna lie to ya. . . ."

The DA: "The guy said blah blah blah. Look at him. He's smug. He's not going to repent."

Then I dug something. They sorta liked saying blah blah blah. 'Cause they said it a few extra times . . . it really got so involved, the bailiff is yelling, "What'd he say?"

"Shut up, you blah-blah-blah."

They were yelling it in all the courts: "What'd he say?" "He said blah blah blah."

Goddam, it's good to say blah blah blah.

That blah blah blah.

That blah blah blah.

That blah blah blah.[31]

Entertaining Homer-phobia

A schematic take on the trial also reveals a glaring opposition between the strategies of the prosecution, the People, and the defense, Lenny Bruce and his counsel, which speaks to epistemological differences: what constitutes knowing, and what is the status of interpretation? The prosecuting attorney called only two eyewitnesses, the two arresting officers. They testified to the facts: they had indeed heard Mr. Bruce use the words "cocksucker," "kiss it," "I'm coming," and "Don't come in me." The defense, by contrast, was concerned not with facts but with the Constitution's protection clause for obscene speech: all but one (Mary Brown) were expert witnesses. Albert Bendich had called in a constellation of cultural critics, university professors, poets, musicians, and teachers, including Ralph Gleason, Grover Sales, Lou Gottlieb, and Don Geiger, then chair of the Rhetoric Department at Berkeley. Rather than disputing the facts, this stellar lineup of cultural interpreters mediated Bruce to the jury by dwelling on his semantic brilliance, as witnessed by his lecture on grammar in "To Is a Preposition, Come Is a Verb," on his redeeming social significance through his pedagogical discussions of "human problems," on his artistic merit through associating his name with those of the Western greats, and on his conformity to "community standards" in that he performed on the same street as drag shows and strip joints. According to this strategy, Bruce's legitimacy rested on his being translated by expert interpreters who compared him to the heavy hitters in the most conservative Western Civ major league. In one of the more astounding sequences of the trial, Kenneth Brown and Albert Bendich offer their respective plot summaries of *Lysistrata* (invoked for its overt references to penises) to Judge Horn, who rejects the former ("I know that is not the theme of *Lysistrata*") and approves the latter ("what you just stated is the correct answer") as if he were administering an oral exam for a Great Books course.[32] However, even though the judge gets caught up in this all-male intellectual revue, cultural capital is both a requisite and a liability in this trial. It is a requisite and a liability for the defense witnesses, whose professional credentials protect them (they routinely assign passages from Swift, Joyce, and Rabelais with no fear of reprisal) even while the prosecution attempts to discredit expertise as effete. Wollenberg, appealing to the jury rather than the judge, deploys a predictable anti-intellectualism: what does the "average citizen" know or care about Aristophanes, Rabelais, and Swift? The acquittal reflected the division of labor; when interviewed afterward, the jury avowed that it had desperately wanted to find Bruce guilty but couldn't, given the judge's carefully constitutional instructions.

And cultural capital was a liability for Bruce, the high school dropout court jester to the intelligentsia who, though well read and self-taught, lacked the insider's knowledge—a function of class and training—to understand the complicity between juridical and high cultural discourses (throughout the trial, he kibbitzed so disruptively that the judge threatened to have him removed).

Regardless of his defense's courtroom attempts to present him as a Great Master, Al Bendich stressed twenty-seven years later that Lenny

Bruce was a human being speaking to other human beings.[33] Therein lay the "disturbing" and "esthetically painful" quality of his performance.[34] Bruce's humanness underscores the absurdity of summoning expert witnesses—experts in literature and language, in comedy, in cultural critique, in "semantics"—to qualify him as someone entitled to use the words "cocksucker," "don't come in me," and "kiss it." Disciplinarity falls aside in conversation; in entertainment, it becomes ridiculous. I suggested to Al Bendich that Lenny had pushed language to its limits. He demurred. "Lenny was no Homer, no Whitman. He wasn't a poet. He was no Kant or Hegel, he wasn't a philosopher."[35] But a human being in conversation can push language to its limits as well or better than anyone—that's what a rapper, a raconteur, a comedian does. Because the organic intellectual can transgress the arbitrary boundaries of disciplinarity and of expertise, she or he gives the lie to the concept of a bounded field of knowledge. Bruce is not particularly avant-garde in the literal sense; the integrated thinking and talking person in performance predates the Western educational system of disciplinarity and expertise. Just as the Bacchanalian poetry readings in North Beach, greeted as cutting-edge, rowdy, revolutionary poetic praxis, reenacted a much earlier tradition of poetry as ritual, Bruce's performances enacted philosophical and moral inquiry in the vein of street raps such as Socrates' before they were domesticated and transcribed by his students. Bendich's strategy, establishing the expertise of his various witnesses to prove Bruce's right to First Amendment protection, worked. But the acquittal (the only one in Bruce's long trial career) was a Pyrrhic victory.

The question of expertise suspect to those of us whose expertise lies in the area of cultural critique becomes an embattled one for very different reasons when the subject comes under attack from the prosecution, particularly with regard to "community standards." For the district attorney representing the People, "expertise," a necessary qualification for "expert witnesses," is suspect, as de facto elitism experts by definition are outside the community to whose standards Bruce must conform. However, he appeals to the concept in order to disqualify Mary Brown from commenting on the putative prurience of her interest in Bruce's performance; she is not part of the People's community either. Furthermore, the elitism of high culture and the academy and the low culture of vaudeville vulgarity are played as both ends against what is represented as the mainstream populist interest; no denizens of the "strip strip" are called to the stand by the prosecution or by the defense except Bruce himself, stymied by the discourse of both his allies and his foes. In the closing argument, the People— via Wollenberg—appeal to the jury's sense of civic self-representation:

When you describe San Francisco to somebody, ladies and gentlemen . . . do you talk about our sewers? That's what we heard a performance of, the sewer; and that's comedy? . . . Now, the question isn't what the University of California professors or the high school teachers from Daly City feel is literature or comedy; the question is what the community feels—not the top of the community educationally, those people over in the ivory towers that say this is a literary work; it is what the people on the street, the conglomerate average, feel—not just the high and mighty or the self-appointed high and mighty.[36]

On the one hand, Bruce's language belongs to the realm of the "high and mighty" (academic literati, sexually suspect men) rather than the "conglomerate average" (middle-class family men); on the other hand, his language is low and vulgar, that of "stevedores down on the wharf loading a ship, . . . and the stevedores aren't saying ['cocksucker'] in a place crowded with people in an auditorium."[37] On the one hand, Wollenberg questions and impugns Bruce's "origins" (Jew as paradigmatic "white Negro")'s bastard rap: "What scurvy hole did it come from?"[38] On the other:

We would have a long beard up on the stage explaining the act of love and explaining the shortcomings. . . . We're . . . not called on to judge other than the community standard itself; not the standard of the University of California in a cultural environment under direction and control of a professor teaching in the school . . . . none of us are dealing with [either the top at the professors' level, or the bottom at the sewer]; we're dealing at the common level. . . . [Lenny Bruce] is a man who believes that he can go out amongst us in society, not just at the academic level in a class of speech or literature at the University of California, not down at the other end of the rainbow—out with the boys, maybe, let's say, doing a laborer's job, using vile and profane language; no, this is a man that is going out into the public and believes he has a license to use this language.[39]

Bruce's crime is spelled out, albeit redundantly and incoherently: he mixed up high, low, and center; he decentered culture by bringing to hypothetically mass audiences content that should be tightly constrained within academic contexts or all-male worksites. Wollenberg's closing speech implicitly associates high and low cultures with counterculture, and he casts the retrogressive populism represented by the People—the "authentic" American people's culture—as the beleaguered victim of attack from the effete above and vulgar below. The representative of this attack is the Jewish chameleon, inauthenticity personified, who infiltrates the high and the low (whose corrupting influence blurs the boundaries between high and low) but can never quite achieve the respectable invisibility of the middle. In the name of the People of the State of California, Wollenberg seizes public culture as the domain of a mythical middle America, which sometimes is "the man on the street" and sometimes is decidedly not the man on the street (especially if that man is a laborer or "out with the boys"); sometimes is "women and children" and sometimes it is decidedly not (especially if the women volunteer to testify for Bruce). In contrapuntal relation to contemporaneous black-Jewish relations (in which Jewish lawyers often defended black victims framed by racist courts, and Jews in general were a visible albeit sometimes ambiguous force in the civil rights movement), here the figure of the silenced Jewish entertainer stands in for the figure of the gay man, who has as yet no public discourse for self-legitimation, no political voice to silence.

Coda: Inside'r Out

Lenny Bruce once said, "People call me a sick comic, but it's society that's sick, and I'm the doctor."

Like the origins of the title Marquis, European Jews are only sort of white. Being a Jew of any gender is like being a middle-class white woman: oppression is privilege, and vice versa. It's not a quantitative issue—it's not that you're "in between" the most privileged and the most oppressed on some scale of comparative outsiderhood; rather, your insiderhood is simultaneously your outsiderhood; you occupy a particular subject position that has its own logic and exacts its own dues. The white middle-class housewife is oppressed in that her privilege is conditional on her man's status. Though European Jews share the privileges of whiteness in the sense of skin color, they are nonetheless by definition excluded from central participation in the groups that guarantee white privilege. They are oppressed in that (among other things) their safety still depends on the beneficent goodwill of non-Jewish power centers. But "inside/out" strikes in another way as well, as a pun: insight out. It points to the ostracism of the person with heightened social insight, who brings out of the closet the secret shame of the social body; and the converse and corollary position of insight afforded those who have traditionally been termed outsiders. In the words of Bob Kaufman, "Way out people know the way out."[40] If we think of the hyperverbal stranger who tells stories, the one who mediates heaven and earth, who mediates Beatitude and stolid populism, who enables a cultural and historical shift, the Jewish entertainer who may not represent himself but who must represent what is projected onto him by the various constituencies in this historical drama, we would have to consider the possibility that Christianity is the paradigmatic scene for this pageant. And lest anyone find obscene the suggestion of Jesus as Jewish phallus whose frictive movement engenders history, here are some alternative obscenities: infant mortality, starvation in a land of dollars. Child abuse, sexual violence, and the death penalty. Cross burnings, castrations, lynchings, queer-bashing. The routine plundering of Native American burial grounds and the episodic defacement of Jewish cemeteries. The inability to respond to pain or to honor beauty. The institutional ravaging of our bodies. Attempts to silence our creative and erotic powers, our powers to change the conditions of our lives, our powers to represent ourselves however we want.

2 Jazz-Jews, Jive, and Gender

The Ethnic Politics of Jazz Argot

BAGEL SHOP JAZZ

Shadow people, projected on coffee-shop walls
Memory formed echoes of a generation past
Beating into now.

Nightfall creatures, eating each other
Over a noisy cup of coffee.

Mulberry-eyed girls in black stockings
Smelling vaguely of mint jelly and last night's bongo drummer,
Making profound remarks on the shapes of navels,
Wondering how the short Sunset week
Became the long Grant Avenue night,
Love tinted, beat angels,
Doomed to see their coffee dreams
Crushed on the floors of time,
As they fling their arrow legs
To the heavens,
Losing their doubts in the beat.

Turtleneck angel guys, black-haired dungaree guys,
Caesar-jawed, with synagogue eyes,
World travelers on the forty-one bus,
Mixing jazz with paint talk,
High rent, Bartok, classical murders,
The pot shortage and last night's bust.

Lost in a dream world,
Where time is told with a beat.

Coffee-faced Ivy Leaguers, in Cambridge jackets,
Whose personal Harvard was a Fillmore district step,
Weighted down with conga drums,
The ancestral cross, the Othello-laden curse,
Talking of Diz and Bird and Miles,
The secret terrible hurts,
Wrapped in cool hipster smiles,
Telling themselves, under the talk,
This shot must be the end,
Hoping the beat is really the truth.

The guilty police arrive.
Brief, beautiful shadows, burned on walls of night.

In Bob Kaufman's poem "Bagel Shop Jazz," which serves as a demography of the shadowland of hip, the nameless women, Jewish men, and black men he eulogizes (*lacrimae rerum sunt* in the culture wars) may appear to constitute a unified, triangular front in opposition to the "guilty police." Their outsiderhood and marginal, always already to-be-memorialized existence ("brief, beautiful shadows, burned on walls of night") puts them in a conspiratorial league (breathing together, unified by the beat) with each other against the stultifying forces of convention. Jazz culture in the tellingly named Co-Existence Bagel Shop of San Francisco's North Beach area offered a liminal shelter made of dreams and shadows where these shadow people could mediate the straight world for each other. Yet these alliances were love-hate triangles, fraught with unease, ambiguous identifications and repudiations, affiliations and disaffiliations, instrumentalism and mutual objectifications ("smelling vaguely of mint jelly and last night's bongo player"), as well as friendship, productive and reproductive collaboration, and genuine bonds based on shared (counter)cultural and social concerns, similar worldviews, and mutual respect. Though structurally each grouping is given a stanza apiece of approximately equal length, the tensions underlying Kaufman's brief profiles in coolness contrast the (nonethnicized) women's and Jewish men's "dreams" with the African American men's "secret terrible hurts" and fatalistic addictions ("this shot must be the end"). In Kaufman's vision, the women's lives are organized around sex, the Jews' around high modernism, high rent, and the relatively innocuous marijuana high, and the African Americans' around historical pain, bebop heroes (Diz, Miles, and Bird rather than Bartok or last night's anonymous bongo drummer), and the high stakes involved in believing in jazz. Moreover, the African American men are endowed with a serious interiority not accorded the other two: though all three groups have misgivings about their lives on the edge, the women dispel their doubts in the rhythm of sex, and the Jews are "lost in a dream world." For black men the creative possibilities offered by the jazz world can provide a respite from the trauma of social pain (of which they are fully conscious), while for the women and the Jews, jazz life is the risk they take rather than a balm. The vague anxiety of the first two points of the triangle becomes a tragic self-consciousness in the third.

And all of them talk talk talk, about navels, classical music, or bebop. The names they drop and, especially, the language they use place them in relation to each other. Those relations are indeterminate, shifting as shadows do, rising, drifting, and receding as smoke does, as talk does, as the steam from a coffee on a cold San Francisco night does. Their talk mediates those relations, creates the texture, the noisy cups of coffee, the "idiomatic fog that veils the user" that provides the text for my inquiry.[1]

Kaufman drew his greatest inspiration for his verbal creations from jazz. The vibrant and dynamic language of the African American music world, this linguistic realm of belonging, functioned as an object of desire for nonblack counterculturals. I focus here on the phenomenon of the Jewish hipster, Norman Mailer's "white Negro," in order to generate a thick description of Jewish men entering communities composed primarily of non-Jews of color—sometimes to the extent of wanting to or actually adopting another ethnic designation. I examine how they negotiate race, class, and gender; how they use the women and the black culture available to them in their negotiations; and how they use language in turn to negotiate their relations to those black men and black, white, and Jewish women: how and why they talk. Attention to this paradigm of cross-cultural mimetic desire can further an analysis of the ethnic, class, and gender anxieties that seem to characterize American ethnic groups, particularly those undergoing a dramatic shift in social status. The subjects here will be, on the one hand, Mezz Mezzrow and Lenny Bruce as counterculturals, and on the other, Phil Spector and to a lesser extent Benny Goodman as examples of what Michael Rogin describes as the strange and theatrical mimesis of black Americans by wannabe white Americans in the service of the latters' upward (whiteward) social mobility.[2]

Among Kaufman's most memorable lines is "Way out people know the way out." This essay is dedicated to people who find their way out, and to people who don't.

(Some) Jews and Their Fathers: No Way Out?

My father, who died in 1973, made his living measuring the body parts of living, primarily dark-skinned people around the world. Mostly other men. As a second-generation Jewish American man-child growing up in Boston, he was searching for his place in the social continuum of races as it was played and fought out in the streets of his childhood, where Irish, Jews, and blacks battled each other with unequal resources for the living spaces left over by the Mayflower contingent. As an adult physical anthropologist at a prestigious research university, he channeled this obsessive self-searching into a discipline established by the nineteenth-century scientizing of the metaphysics of the great chain of being—a discipline (in all senses) that took him far from himself, desensitizing him to the felt pain of social difference (his own and others') as it legitimated his inquiry through words as dubious as they are Greco-Roman: epidemiology, somatotyping, anthropometry, medical anthropology. The use of these words placed him in the position of overseer, managing and interpreting the physical continuum of races imagined by this science. His attempt to master his ethnic and gender anxiety through intellectual discipline reinscribed him in that very intersection he found so problematic: a Jewish man—at least a Bostonian Jew from Eastern Europe growing up and living in the period spanning World War I through the Israeli nationalist experiment—was supposed both by Jews and by others to win battles not through physical prowess of the street but through verbal, scholarly performance.[3] What was he as a man? What was he as a Jew? He attempted to resolve some of these perceived contradictions through marriage with a Scandinavian Gentile woman. Together, they gave their three daughters unequivocally Christian names, sent us to aristocratic private day schools, and joined the Unitarian Church, which in Boston has the cachet of history, social register prestige, and old money. Although I resist the nakedly judgmental connotation that the term has come to carry in contemporary cultural politics, I have been urged by friendly critics to use the blunt language of ethnic commentary: his goal, they point out, was assimilation. I am uneasy with the word. It collapses complicated motives and means into a word that appears to mean something—one thing, one currently-tinged-with-negativity thing.

But what? (Whom did my father ever really fool, other than one of my girls' school classmates, who, on learning after his death that he had been Jewish, remarked in astonishment, "Dr. Damon? Jewish? But—he wasn't vulgar!") And is that what assimilation—whatever it is—is about anyway? Fooling people? My dictionary offers a definition of "assimilate" tailored to the occasion. "*vi.* 1. to become like or alike. 2. to be absorbed and incorporated: as, minority groups often assimilate by intermarriage." The two are distinctly different: to be like, or to be devoured by. The intransitivity of the verb in the second instance renders power invisible: Absorbed by what? Incorporated into what? To be absorbed, intransitive, means to be engrossed, fascinated, preoccupied (example: my father was completely absorbed in his studies).[4] That is not what is meant in the "minority group" example. To be incorporated, intransitive, means to adopt a legal status as a corporation, or to be united. Again, this is not what is meant by the example given for "assimilate." Obviously, we know the present absence signified here: to be absorbed or incorporated into the dominant, majority group. (My father wanted to be incorporated, devoured and digested, by the dominant Gentile mainstream.)[5] If this parenthetical example is so, he picked an unwitting mediator, a stranger in a strange land: my mother, who emigrated from postwar Denmark at age thirty, was the "foreigner" in our family, the one who spoke with an amusing accent, the one whose peasant roots (her family are pig farmers, no less) resonate with the nostalgia I hear from other Jews (never my own Jewish relatives) for shtetl cooking and customs. She is much more Tevye-like than my urbane father, who taught us how to eat artichokes, read us Greek myths from Bulfinch at bedtime, and celebrated Mozart's birthday. He was the polished cosmopolitan who had read everything, she the bumpkin with the love of nature and earthy humor who joked that she too had read a book once: Shakespeare in the original Danish. He couldn't change a lightbulb; she was the omnipotent earth mother (or her 1950s incarnation, Supermom) who did all the cooking, yard work, childcare, and housework and held a skilled professional position low prestige enough to not threaten my father's job. But Tevye-ality notwithstanding, she wasn't Jewish, and he was.

At certain jokes in Marx Brothers movies, however, at certain puns or Yiddishisms unexpectedly uttered by his less crypto-Jewish friends, my father's personality changed dramatically. He shed the cool and unassuming sophistication modeled after what he had seen of British manners in his year at Cambridge. Tears of laughter (or were they tears of pain and longing?) rolled down his cheeks as he jiggled with helpless mirth. The meek and decorous Anglophile scientist became for a moment a rowdy little boy—he was responding to real language. Sometimes, afterward, with a mixture of glee and shame, he would explain the jokes to us, sometimes not. These linguistically saturated moments have clued me in to the power of vernacular. Because of my removal from living traditions in Judaism and Jewishness and because, nonetheless, their cultural forms ruled unacknowledged from the depths of my family's psyche, I sometimes fear that I inhabit the unconscious of an earlier generation of American Jews and am still working out their complexes.

The alliances I examine here are not the ones my father made, but ones he could have made—ones I would like to make. Unlike him, many Jewish men of his generation resolved their anxieties about ethnicity and community by bonding with non-Jews of color. It was not shame about their outcast status as Jews that prompted these alliances but rather the sense that Jewish American culture, by assimilating upward, was abdicating the special role of critique available to social outsiders.

But first, another contextual digression: a word from our noncorporate (unincorporable, unassimilable) but corporeal sponsors-in-outrageousness about what words mean to them.[6]

Words, Words as if All Worlds Were There: A Way Out?

Most bebop language came about because some guy said something and it stuck. . . . Before you knew it, we had a whole language. . . . We didn't have to try; as Black people we just naturally spoke that way. People who wished to communicate with us had to consider our manner of speech, and sometimes they adopted it.[7]

Down to the Jewish ghetto on Maxwell Street I went, to look around in the second-hand stores. I came to one store where an old Jewish man with a long beard and a little yomelkeh stood in the doorway, and I heard something that knocked me out. An old-fashioned victrola setting out on the curb was playing a record, Blind Lemon Jefferson's "Black Snake Moan," and the old Jewish man kept shaking his head sadly, like he knew that evil black snake personally:
> Oh–oh, some black snake's been
> suckin' my rider's tongue.[8]

Quincy Troupe and Miles Davis's collaborative autobiography of Miles concludes with a brief statement by Troupe about Miles's language. It anticipates critics who may be offended by the vulgarity of the text, and functions not so much as an apology as it does as a manifesto:

Had we sanitized the language in the book, the voice of Miles wouldn't sound authentic. . . . Miles speaks in a tonal language . . . the same word can take on different meanings according to the pitch and tone, the way the word is spoken. For example, Miles can use motherfucker to compliment someone or simply as punctuation. . . . Besides, when I hear Miles speak, I hear my father and many other African-American men of his generation. I grew up listening to him on street corners, in barbershops, ballparks and gymnasiums, and bucket-of-blood bars. It's a speaking style that I'm proud and grateful to have documented.[9]

The language in which the story of Miles is told (the improvisational, tonal, and rhythmic quality) is at least as much the story as what we might call "narrative content" (melody). Language and music are coextensive, and verbal fluency in the jazz idiom is as crucial a talent as musical ability. As Ben Sidran has pointed out, "the musician *is* the document,"[10] and this text includes not only musicianship but also clothing, physical style, and verbal virtuosity. For example, when Duke Ellington invited Sonny Greer into his orchestra, there was much scrutiny of the flashy drummer, even after his successful audition: "He used a lot of tricks. . . . Maybe, we thought, he wasn't all that he was cracked up to be." The litmus test was verbal: "We stood on the street corner and waited for him. . . . 'Watcha say?' we ask him. . . . Sonny comes back with a line of jive that lays us low. We decide he's okay."[11] Similarly, even after his playing had been accepted by the other band members, Louis Armstrong was put off by what he perceived as the uptightness of Fletcher Henderson's band, for which he had left Chicago and come to New York, until the trombonist and the tuba player got into a fight and cussed each other out with imaginative and outraged invective. At that point, Armstrong says, "I commenced to relax—you know—feeling at home."[12]

While Michael Rogin has persuasively argued that Al Jolson used blackface in order to negotiate his assimilation away from Jewishness into the American mainstream, I argue that, in different ways for each of the men I write about, blackness becomes a way to be "more Jewish" by providing a New World context for social critique, community, and an understanding of suffering and the "human condition" both social and metaphysical.[13] Many European-descended Jews as well as non-Jewish performers used blackface as part of their acts, along with a host of other ethnic stereotypes: the "wop number" and the "sheeny number" had their moments in the spotlight, along with the "coon number." But observing the ubiquity of blackface, and indicating its function as enabling Americanization, cannot be elided into a generalization about Jewish European American[14]/African American relations, or about Jewish desires to assimilate—that is, to shed or camouflage their "Jewishness" in favor of a less socially opprobrious, nebulous "whiteness" purchased at the expense of the caricatured black man or woman. While Rogin points out the mechanisms whereby Jolson's blackface performance enabled his move toward American power centers—marriage with an Anglo woman, mainstream success with regard to public recognition and the acquisition of wealth—a number of Jews found in African American culture the resources for resisting absorption into a dominant culture they found stultifying, hierarchic, unjust, unaesthetic, and un-Jewish.

In each case, attention to the particulars of individuals' rapports with their own and others' cultures reveals a rich texture of motive, response, and artistic/cultural production that merits specific regard. I have chosen examples of Jews whose attraction to African American culture is motivated not by the impulse to assimilate but by the impulse to resist. The impulse is not unproblematic, and this essay is neither an apologia for these Jews' means of identification nor a condemnation, but an investigation of that move. Each of the three people I discuss here sought to associate himself with African American music culture differently: Mezz Mezzrow by realizing his childhood conviction that he would grow up to become a "colored musician," Lenny Bruce by adopting the language of the jazz milieu and by his outspokenness about civil rights issues and racism, and Phil Spector by producing black music and by trying on occasion to "act black" in ways that inadvertently come close to the caricatures of an earlier generation of white performers.

As for the role of music in this phenomenon, musicianship was one of the few pursuits in this country and in the Eastern European cultures these men descended from that provided both social and geographic mobility for members of traditional underclasses. Though *klezmorim* (Jewish male professional folk musicians) were of a special, not quite respectable class with their own argot, they were allowed to wander from town to town with minimal difficulty and were credited with the ability to represent and draw forth the human soul as no other artist could. On immigrating, many of these musicians became participants in New World forms of popular music.[15] In the past several decades' revival of interest in klezmer, which blends elements of Eastern and Western European folk music, Middle Eastern and North African music, and now American jazz, it is often referred to as "Jewish jazz."

But while the musical forms of jazz and the visual forms of performance are fully worthy of investigation, I focus on language as an index of cultural kinship and mimesis. Why language, and why these two ethnic groups? The first point is simply the obvious: language is culture. Language use is a primary element in self-constitution and self-representation for any group, ethnic as well as nonethnic. The second is that, though the foregoing is virtually a truism, it is also something of a truism (and here

IDENTITY K/NOT/E/S

all standard caveats about stereotypy apply) that African American and Jewish traditions share a love of verbal display and value language performance far beyond its strictly utilitarian, signifier-equals-signified status as a "tool" for communication. Jews and African Americans also share, as historic underclasses of Europe and the United States, respectively, a need for strategies of exclusion through language: codes, double entendres, and alternative languages protected emotional and political meanings from a series of overlords. Though he cautions against reading his work as an essentialistic demonstration of certain tropes as "black," Henry Louis Gates, Jr., has amply documented the dynamics of wordplay, the importance of mastering circumlocution, and the centrality of "signifyin(g)" practices in African American culture.[16] The Armstrong and Ellington examples, as well as the enormous body of scholarship on the practice of signifying, demonstrate a cultural appreciation for the well-turned phrase, the spontaneous and devastating repartee, the one-upmanship involved in games of utterance. There are Jewish works analogous to Gates's: Freud's, Benjamin Harshav's, and Max Weinreich's loving analyses of Yiddish styles of communication walk, like Gates's *The Signifying Monkey*, the shaky, challenging line of argument between cultural essentialism and historico-cultural investigation of "language skills" characteristic of Jewish practice.[17] But though these studies are far less well known to the general academic audience than Gates's endearingly subversive semiotic simian, the clichés about Jewish culture that signal a perception of Jews (by Jews) as loving smart talk are myriad at the colloquial level: "Three Jews, four opinions"; "A Jew always answers a question with another question"; the joke about the Jew stranded on a desert island who built two synagogues (when he was rescued and questioned about this he responded, waving his hand in the direction of one of them, "That's the shul I *don't* go to!")[18] —these clichés nevertheless indicate a high valuing of debate, expression, and difference of opinion and open-ended critique. ("Expressing opinions is one of the greatest human pleasures," a friend's father insisted when his wife asked him why he had to do it all the time.)

Texts: Finally

The following three examples offer windows onto different permutations of a Jewish desire for verbal participation in African Americanness, and particularly the ways in which African American language comes to have (for these Jewish men) a physical dimension, a *body*—specifically, a woman's body—that is likewise an object of desire. The first two are from Mezz Mezzrow's *Really the Blues*, a jazz autobiography, and Ronnie Spector's *Be My Baby*. In both cases the woman figures become emblematic occasions for their ethnic transitions, embodying their desire and discomfort; they are vehicles, in terms of the mimetic triangle, for these Jews' desire for black masculinity. The third text is supplied by Lenny Bruce, the man who made Jewishness hip, and who occupies a special place on this continuum of mimesis and appropriation.

First, here's Mezz:

> I was put in a trance by Bessie's moanful stories and the patterns of true harmony in the piano background, full of little runs that crawled up and down my spine like mice. Every note that woman wailed vibrated on the tight strings of my nervous system; every word she sang answered a question I was asking. You couldn't drag me away from that victrola, not even to eat.
>
> What knocked me out most on those records was the slurring and division of words to fit the musical pattern, the way the words were put to work for the music. I tried to write them down because I figured the only way to dig Bessie's unique phrasing was to get the words down exactly as she sang them. It was something I had to do; there was a great secret buried in that woman's genius that I had to get. After every few words I'd stop the record to write the lyrics down, so my dad made a suggestion. Why didn't I ask my sister Helen to take down the words in shorthand? She was doing secretarial work and he figured it would be a cinch for her.
>
> If my sister had made a table-pad out of my best record or used my old horn for a garbage can she couldn't have made me madder than she did that day. I've never been so steamed up, before or since. She was in a very proper and dicty mood, so she kept "correcting" Bessie's grammar, straightening out her words and putting them in "good" English until they sounded like some stuck-up jive from *McGuffy's Reader* instead of the real down-to-earth language of the blues. That girl was schooled so good, she wouldn't admit there was such a word as "ain't" in the English language, even if a hundred million Americans yelled it in her face every hour of the day. I've never felt friendly towards her to this day, on account of how she laid her fancy high-school airs on the immortal Bessie Smith.[19]

Here Mezz (advertised on the cover of his autobiography as "the first white negro") relates the final straw that sent him irrevocably into African American culture. The incident revolves around language use: in particular, the contrast between the way two women use language. To Mezz, his sister's "ethnic cleansing" of Bessie's soulful and sensual language, rendering it prissy and inauthentic, constitutes a cardinal violation against the profundity of the blues. Both his sister's preferred idiom and the fur coat he steals epitomize the upward mobility he scorns (the narrative, dictated to a more sympathetic male amanuensis more than twenty years later, still quivers with vital righteous wrath). In what he sees as a punishment fitting the crime of Helen's privilege, he uses the theft to buy his first alto sax and move out of the family home forever. That is, he uses his sister's accessory to the crime of upward assimilation to facilitate his own downward assimilation, prostituting his sister's coat to a prostitute in a gleeful act of what he considers Helen's degradation, not realizing that she may have as much in common with Bessie Smith as he does—and that his anecdote implicates him in her familial oppression.

Another early turning point for Mezz in his romance with African American culture is when he overhears the male partner of a dancing black couple cry out to the woman, "Perculate, you filthy bitch!" which inspires the name of his first band, the Perculatin' Fools. What Mezz perceives (rightly) as verbal inventiveness and uninhibited, "picturesque" language is also a misogynistic display; along with the participants in the forum on the "white Negro" (Norman Mailer, Ned Polsky, and Jean Malaquais), Mezz shares a distorted understanding that the freedom of expression he envies in black culture also, implicitly, confers permission to be overtly misogynistic. Although his language is respectful and reverent when he speaks of Bessie Smith, the women in his immediate life—his sister and the mother he mentions only once, early in the memoir—were domesticating and hence negative forces in his psychic life. Many Jewish men and women of the period found that pressure to assimilate and resistance to assimilation led to conflict between the genders.[20] Far from Rogin's description of Jolson's Oedipal scene, Mezz offers an anti-Oedipal desire to undermine the goodness—the purity—of his family of origin in favor of the earth goddess Bessie Smith and the social milieu her songs inhabit. This meeting of ethnic, class, and gender anxiety, represented by the two women Mezz constructs as opposites, plays out the conflict between the standard English to which his social group of origin aspired and the jazz argot Mezz loved and prided himself on mastering to the point of being able to pass as African American.

At one point much later in Mezz's career, during a prison sentence he is serving for selling drugs, he arranges to have himself put in the black section of the segregated prison by insisting that, appearances notwithstanding, he is actually black. At Christmastime, the Christian whites organize a carol choir, and the Jews, not to be outdone, counterorganize a Chanukah choir. Mezz remarks with amusement that "they ask me, a colored guy, wouldn't I care to lead it. I find out once more how music of different oppressed peoples blends together. . . . I don't know the Hebrew chants, but I give it a weepy blues inflection and the guys are all happy about it. They can't understand how a colored guy digs the spirit of their music so good."[21] Mezz has so deeply identified with African American culture that he greets the Jewish music as exotic but appealingly resonant with blues feeling, something he can identify with because of a common understanding of suffering. It is not clear to me whether he is being tongue-in-cheek or straight here; it doesn't appear to cross his mind that the Jewish prisoners have divined his ethnicity of origin.

My second example is drawn from Ronnie Spector's *Be My Baby*, an account of her abusive marriage to Phil Spector, boy genius of rock-'n'-roll musical production. Throughout the book, Ronnie identifies herself usually as a "half-breed" (of black and white parentage), and occasionally as black, as in the following passage, in which, after sending Ronnie and her unambiguously black mother to Watts to buy him some Afro wigs (Spector was sensitive about his thinning hair), he takes them to a gospel sermon at a church in Watts. Bearing in mind that this is not Spector in his own words but a portrait drawn by his abused ex-wife, there is much to be learned from the woman who has been the object of mediation between this Jew and the African American culture he loves:

> Phil loved his Afro wig. I guess it made him feel like he had soul or something, because after he got it, he wanted us all to go back down to Watts to hear some real gospel music at the Reverend James Cleveland's church. I wanted no part of it. I never liked straight gospel music because I could never understand what they were singing.
>
> Of course, Phil had his heart set on it. So we all piled into the back of his limousine—me, my mother and Phil. He also brought along a pair of bodyguards. Afro wig or no Afro wig, Phil wasn't taking any chances going down to Watts. He even brought one of his pistols, which he tucked into his jacket pocket.
>
> . . . We found seats in the back just as Reverend James Cleveland's choir started singing. They were wailing and moaning and singing out in that way that gospel people do, and Phil was moaning and wailing right along with them. He was rolling his shoulders and shaking his arms, and pretty soon he was sweating and shouting out "Amen" like he was at a Baptist revival meeting. It was funny, really. Here I was, this black girl, bored out of her mind at a gospel concert, sitting with a Jewish man in an Afro who looked like he was about to speak in tongues.
>
> After the singing, Phil kept on shouting "Amen" all through Reverend Cleveland's sermon. When the Reverend held out the collection plate, Phil

jumped to his feet with a hundred-dollar bill in his hand. "Oh, no!" my mom gasped under her breath. But it was already too late to stop him. . . .

After the service people were still staring at Phil. . . . My mother and I were embarrassed for him, but Phil actually looked proud as he smiled and wiped the sweat from his forehead."I guess I showed them I'm not just any white guy," he bragged.

"That you did, Phil," my mother agreed. "That you surely did."[22]

In this uncomplimentary scene, Spector tries to pass as an insider in an environment in which he feels he must carefully juggle his concern for personal safety (and the simultaneous perceived need to hide this concern), his display of wealth, which sets him apart from the majority of the congregation, and his performance of at-homeness and appreciation, which he hopes will affirm his presence and make him welcome. Yet Spector's gaucheries appear to have their origins in a desire to reconnect with a soulful quality of faith that has gone out of the respectability of secular, assimilated Jewish American life. And this involves a move down the scale of social prestige.

Ronnie Spector, née Bennett, wears her own ethnicity lightly; her autobiography introduces her as the daughter of a black mother and a white, failed-musician father who deserts the family (another ethnic stereotype challenged), who learned makeup tricks ("big hair" and exaggeratedly elongated eyeliner) from the Hispanic and Asian kids in the neighborhood in which she and her co-Ronettes—her sister and cousin—grew up. At one point she recounts witnessing from her dressing room a fight between black and Hispanic youths over whether the Ronettes were a black or a Hispanic girl group; she comments with amusement that they were both, since she and her sister are black and their cousin is Hispanic. ("Do you think we can pass for black?" she asks her sister, who responds, "We *are* black. *And* Spanish. And probably a whole lot of other things too that we don't know about. . . . We've got enough kinds of blood to keep everybody happy.")[23] Similarly, in the wig episode, she is amusedly embarrassed but not offended by her husband's behavior. Unlike her husband, Ronnie Spector is not fixated on ethnic identity as a social marker; her sense of identity is more nuanced, less insistent (less threatened) than his. Like Kaufman's "Caesar-jawed" Jews with "synagogue eyes," Spector, "lost in a dream," arouses her tolerant, if exasperated, compassion.

As a Jew, Phil Spector is indeed not just any white guy. He has specific historical reasons for identifying with African American history. At the same time, his controlling and abusive treatment of his wife, his role as producer of black talent, and his class status in comparison to many of the singers he helped midwife into stardom all implicate him in the parasitism of which black Americans have often accused Jewish and non-Jewish whites.

Mezz's distaste for his sister and passion for Bessie's soulful earthiness, as well as Spector's need to dominate his black wife and his welcoming of Ronnie's mother into his own family life (and his extreme disgust with his own mother—"a tiny woman. A real Jewish mother type," says Ronnie, who made unannounced appearances at the recording studio to bring him—is Ronnie exaggerating here?—chicken soup!)[24] express these men's desire to align themselves with or appropriate what they perceive as the tastes, distastes, and desires of black men. Although sexual politics play a crucial role in this nexus of identity formation, I am not making Mailer's argument for sexual envy delineated in his analysis of the white hipster. What is at stake is, rather, a far more poignant and complicated desire to maintain a vibrant outsiderhood in a living, viable artistic and social community.

Because of the mediary nature of Jewish American ethnicity, these conflicts and resolutions proliferate among the Jewish men I am examining here. Mezz, a member of a wealthy family that owned a chain of drugstores in Chicago, reacted vehemently against Jewish solidarity among other popular musicians like Al Jolson and Sophie Tucker: "I didn't go for that jive at all; being a Jew didn't mean a thing to me. Around the poolroom I defended the guys I felt were my real brothers, the colored musicians who made music that sent me. . . . I could never dig the phony idea of a race—if we were a 'race'—sticking together all the way."[25] Phil Spector was a millionaire whose mother infuriated him by bringing chicken soup to the recording studio. Both turned to a kind of essentialized African Americanness to salvage their integrity. In the mostly male world of jazz, the appeal of skilled and challenging music and musicianship and the attractiveness of African American race pride acted as magnets, drawing non-African American men into the musical idiom, culture, and language of jazz.

Perhaps the most interestingly ambiguous formulation of this complex mimesis of alterity is to be found in my third case, Lenny Bruce's signature *shpritz*, in which he reverses the terms. Instead of Jewish men being honorary blacks, black people, especially black musicians, become honorary Jews in his famous anti-essentialist, "neologizing" routine. Most Jewish hipsters identified African American culture as a stable alternative, the nostalgic embodiment of the earthiness and vitality that threatened to get bleached out of secular and assimilated Jewish culture in the

New World. They turned to it in part to provide themselves with a fixed reference point for their own changing identities: blackness and soul were unambiguously synonymous for them, and the closer they could associate themselves with black culture, the more soulful they were. Lenny Bruce pulls the switch: it is Jewishness that stands as the reference point for all that is spontaneously creative, earthy, and other. Like Mezzrow and Spector, Bruce also undertakes his ethnic self-creation in the realm of language and utterance, freely mixing "the jargon of the hipster, the argot of the underworld [or more properly, show business], and Yiddish."[26] Lenny Bruce was a vaudeville kid with intellectual aspirations who managed to both displace and assert himself in every milieu he moved in: the show-biz world, the ethnic Jewish world, the world of the intellectual hipster. What Bruce the ultimate Jewish hipster does, in this instance of positing Jewish identity as primarily hybrid by moving through all other identities, is to hippify Yiddish by mixing it in with the already identifiably hip idiom of jive. Like Mezz, Bruce married within his professional milieu—but he married "white." Like Jolson and Goodman, he married a "shikse goddess"—but this one was a stripper of lowly pedigree. Hot Honey Harlow, in terms of class if not caste, was arguably as far from Vanderbilthood (Benny Goodman, for example, married a Vanderbilt) as Bessie Smith. Honey's divinity lay in her beauty rather than in her social status. Though his perspective does not offer much in the way of emancipatory gender politics per se, Bruce is perceptive enough to satirize his own "looksism": in the skit "A Black Black Woman and a White White Woman," he challenges his assumed male audience to choose between a "black black woman and a white white woman"—who turn out to be, respectively, Lena Horne and Kate Smith; then he adds, having made that point, "so now we're discriminating against ugly people."[27]

Like my father, these three men married outside their Jewish culture. On the Jewish side of my family, it is assumed that my father's choice of life partner was symptomatic of his distaste for all things Jewish, most especially his family members. But exogamy does not always reflect self-hatred; it can be an attempt to achieve the fulfillment of a truer sense of oneself, to correspond more fully to what one feels one ought to be or in some sense already is. If Mezz feels that Jews have abdicated their special status as outsiders under social pressure to assimilate upward, he would feel that the status of blacks in the United States offers a truer reflection of the ideal position of Jews and that it makes him more of a *mensh* to move into a black idiom. "African American" is a historical category into which these men as Jewish Americans do not fit. But one generation previously, not at all far back in memory, their European Jewish forebears did occupy a position structurally analogous: as national underclass, as mythic other, as sequestered populations. An element of nostalgia and mourning, and a perceived opportunity for self-regeneration for Jews as creative non-participants in mainstream culture, tinge this identification with another oppressed ethnic group. "They" are more "us" than "we" have become. This is a convoluted form of projection, yearning, essentialism that actually corresponds more closely to Lenny Bruce's model ("Jewishness" as the signifier for soulfulness) than is initially apparent.

At the same time, it does not quite correspond to the paradigm suggested by Toni Morrison: that blacks and black culture serve as vehicles, catalysts, for white self-recognition. In her model, blackness appears either as a moment of extreme otherness that allows a breakthrough or challenge to an original but problematic white self-concept or as an oppositional background against which the white individual constructs his or her identity.[28] Mezz is no Jolson and speaks of him, in fact, with contempt—precisely for trying to force a "phony" Jewish solidarity within the entertainment world. African Americans do not figure as other in Mezz's aspirations, as they clearly did for both Jolson and Benny Goodman, both of whom married up, into the Anglo socialite world. The problem of essentialism is not Mezz's, perhaps, but mine. Who am I to say that he did not, after all, "become a colored musician" when he grew up? To insist that Mezz was really Jewish but thought he became black would reinforce an arbitrary racialization. Being *gemisht* makes me sensitive to this arbitrariness: Jewish law says I'm not Jewish because my mother isn't; under the Third Reich, on the other hand, I would have qualified as genetically Jewish; I define myself as culturally Jewish, unlike my siblings, who do not identify as Jewish at all. Why not extend the same leeway to Mezz?

In a period in which many Jewish Americans believed they were faced with a choice between continued loyalty to working-class anonymity and immigrant "greenhornism," on the one hand, and upward social mobility cum assimilation on the other, Jewish men perceived in the jazz world an alternative community in which difference and individualism were affirmed as virtues. Jazz offered a perfect community of individuals. Nonconformism to traditional familial (and racial) relations and the cultural sophistication of the jazz world made it, moreover, a site for an alternative construction of masculinity that eschewed, on the one hand, the Jewish image of the boorish and insensitive Anglo *sheygitz* and, on the other hand, the emerging stereotype of the passive, scholarly, but ineffectual Jewish man. It was an arena in which one could succeed, and even attract considerable attention to oneself, but not in ways that appeared to spell compromise and assimilation. The jazz world offered a model of masculinity for Jewish men, in other words, that enabled difference without weakness. In contrast to Fanon's "black skin, white mask" paradigm of mimesis and alterity, in which the white mask, assumed to camouflage alterity, corrodes the psychic health of its wearer and must be wrenched off, this is a mimesis that flaunts otherness and putatively permits solidarity between people recently emerging from a context of oppression and people whose oppression is ongoing in the American context.

Nonetheless, these gestures at solidarity were fraught with problematic contradictions. Black musicians did not necessarily perceive their relationship to Jewish music people as one of fraternal understanding. Although the integrity of people like impresario Norman Granz, booking agent Ben Bart, and musicians Artie Shaw and Red Rodney is acknowledged, others are taken to task for their exploitive association with black musicians. Duke Ellington's autobiography signifies heavily on the subject of Louis Armstrong's producer Joe Glaser (Armstrong was "a living monument to the magnificent career of Joe Glaser"),[29] as well as his own early producer Irving Mills ("In spite of how much he made on me, I still respected the way he operated").[30] Likewise, Diz's characterization of Granz as encouraging competition for entrepreneurial gain varies in spirit if not factually from Granz's own portrait of himself as someone deeply dedicated to breaking the race barrier.[31] James Brown chronicles his stormy association with Syd Nathan of King Records, who tried to bury "Please Please Please"—Brown's first million-seller—and who initially gave him "half a cent a side for writer's royalties and maybe another half a cent for performance."[32] Benny Goodman was sporadically insensitive to matters of racial prejudice, using the line "You know, I have problems too. I can't belong to this or that club because I'm Jewish" to avoid the responsibility of sticking up for his black sidemen when they encountered discrimination on the road.[33] When these musicians speak of being exploited they do not attribute this exploitation to their managers' Jewishness but address it as a labor-management or black-white dynamic.

Goodman used black music and musicians to get what he wanted: music of a high quality, prestige, material comfort, and upward social mobility. Mezzrow didn't need or respect blackface; in his own eyes, he was black. His search for a position of critique that was simultaneously located within a community led this upper-class Jewish Chicagoan to identify wholesale as a black musician. Bruce never pretended to be other than what he was, a renegade Euro American Jew with an attitude, a proto-punk, using whatever verbal and cultural ammunition lay at hand for his relentless exposé of social hypocrisy and human weakness; the most trenchant and effective tool he could wrap his tongue around and let fly was the current jazz argot. It held everything he valued: subversiveness, speed, wit, artistry, originality, flexibility, room for improvisation, flamboyance, and social critique without party lines or platforms.

How might Italian, Irish, and black people respond to Bruce's call to the soul of Jewishness? Would Count Basie, Ray Charles (to whose "Aramaic cantillations" Allen Ginsberg owes partial inspiration for the rhythms of his poem "Kaddish"),[34] and Dylan Thomas (a Welshman who makes it into Bruce's catalog) claim this honorary tribal status with as much zest as Mezz adopted blackness? Billy Eckstine's (white) managers wanted to sign his name X-stine "(for fear someone might think he was Jewish?)."[35] Likewise, Billie Holiday's autobiography stresses the fact that her lover John Levy was black rather than Jewish (as one might assume from his name) and that the papers ran pictures of him after their arrest to prove it.[36]

Bruce himself was acutely aware of the fact that he wasn't black. In his routine "How to Relax Your Colored Friends at Parties," the drunken white Christian guest clumsily tries to bond with the black guest by mumbling anti-Semitic slurs against their mutual hosts and attempts to compliment the guest by saying, "You look like a white Jew to me," signifying on the designation of Jews as "white Negroes." Bruce's complex routines undermine the stability of identity more than those of Mezz, who was quick to deny his Jewishness, or those of Spector, whose undignified antics reveal a shallow understanding of the concept of identity even though his musical exploits indicate a sensitivity to the special ethnicity of the sound he wanted to capture. Bruce wasn't trying to pass for other than he was; he didn't engage in Goodman's disingenuous me-tooism as a way of exculpating himself, and he certainly wasn't a booster of conventional Judaism. At no point, however, does Bruce deny his Jewishness; rather, he adds to it textured layers of argotic richness and performative personae. For these reasons, as well as his talent, his jazzlike use of improvisation, and his verbal ability to create abstract "extensions of realism, as opposed to realism in a representational form," Bruce was widely respected among black jazz musicians.[37] It has been argued, also, that Bruce's shticks correspond to traditional Jewish jeremiads and his "message" to Jewish ethics[38]; he sprinkled his monologues with Jewish words like *rachmones* (compassion) and punctuated his punch lines with *Emmes* (truth), as well as *cool* and *dig*—jive terms. So Bruce fits most closely the argument I have tried to weave loosely around these textual gems: that attraction to African American culture among Jewish men emblematizes and helps actualize some kind of positive nostalgia for the meaningful aspects of traditional Jewish life. He is the most self-conscious and self-critical of the Jewish artists I have discussed here.

It is not surprising to find an enthusiasm for the richness, immediacy, and hermeticism of African American speech acts among disaffected Jews. Jive functions in the United States as Yiddish functioned in Europe but had ceased to function in America—that is, as an infinitely inventive and renewable medium for cultural survival. Mezz, for instance, uses jive as a code of initiation. The Citadel edition of his book opens with a passage in jive—which Mezz exuberantly defines as "a polyglot patois [that is] not only a strange linguistic mixture of dream and deed . . . it's a whole new attitude toward life"—accompanied by an endnote, "See pages 354–360 for a translation of this jive." One of the proudest moments of his life is finding his name, "Mezz," in a jive dictionary, defined as the finest marijuana available. Phil Spector believes that *amen* is the signal word that will confirm his status as "not just any white guy." Note the difference between these two perceptions of African American language. Although Mezz turns to the African American idiom as the wellspring of spontaneous authenticity, he knows that its power lies in its infinite mutability and nuanced subtlety, its un-pindownability, and thus its ability to undermine its own cachet of authenticity. Deciding in his early teens that he "was going to be a colored musician" when he grew up, Mezz did not so much appropriate the idiom as apprentice himself to it, with a full appreciation of the poetry, dynamism, and social importance of this "four-dimensional surrealist patter."[39] The transformation took years. Spector, on the other hand, believed that a quick gimmicky disguise and the ejaculation of a few stereotyped phrases, balanced by the gun and the bodyguards, would safeguard his passage and even impress the congregated African Americans.

Way Out: Mad Cops

When Mezz was arrested for dealing, the police questioned his living situation with his wife, Johnnie Mae, and their son, Milton. "Was I colored. No, Russian Jew, American-born. How in hell did I come to be living with a 'spade'? Well I had this screwy idea that when you loved a girl you married her without consulting a color chart."[40] Though the last few paragraphs of Mezz's opus insist that "I only hope they spell my name right in *Who's Who*, and get the dates of my prison record straight, and don't forget to say 'Race, Negro,'"[41] he is not above reverting to his ethnicity of origin—if it'll make the cops mad.

3 Triangulated Desire and Tactical Silences in the Beat Hipscape

Bob Kaufman and Others

THIS ESSAY HAS THREE STRANDS: that is, it is about three things, and these three things are not autonomous but interwoven; discussion of each illuminates the others. It is about the historical intersection of Beat, gay, and racially minoritized writers and cultures in San Francisco in the late 1950s. It is also about a black poet, Bob Kaufman, who figures pivotally in the nexus of sexual, racial, and gendered tensions in a homosocial and homoerotic poets' triangle. Third, it is about a poem by Kaufman that purports to document these tensions in the "scene" he lived in but is strikingly silent about the queer presence that was so visible, and so much a part of his life.

Bob Kaufman's Disappearing Acts

In other essays I have tried to show how "Bagel Shop Jazz" illuminates the tensions and attractions between the three groups described in the three stanzas that comprise the poem's substance: the nonethnoracialized "Beat chicks," the presumed-male "white ethnic" Beats, and the presumed-male hip African Americans (black Beats).[1] The poem is a beautifully succinct tableau depicting, in somewhat static terms, the ways in which the women, through their preoccupation with love and sex, mediate between the "secret hurts" of the black, jazz-oriented men and the "dream world" of "high rent, Bartok," and "the pot shortage" that characterizes the "blackhaired[,] . . . Caesar-jawed" guys with "synagogue eyes"—that is, Jewish, Italian, and other liminally white Mediterranean immigrants. By "liminal" I mean that these white men can be specifically identified by the reader, through Kaufman's mention of their ethnicity, as threshold cases: both Jews and Italians had to work to establish their whiteness on first arriving in the United States, and they did so by distinguishing themselves from—that is, repudiating their possible alliances with—African Americans.[2] And indeed, in the recent revival of interest in the Beats, the discovery of the full participation of women and blacks in a white male–dominated counterculture should be encouraged. The poem elaborates on the presence, even in as hip a counterculture as the Beats', of the triangulated paradigm in which men express their desire for each other, and each other's status, through a feminized third element that is a conduit (rather than a third point properly speaking) of their mutual desire. The white ethnics envy what they perceive as their black comrades' authenticity and soulfulness, without specific knowledge of the "secret terrible hurts" that have shaped these outsider subjectivities and that they themselves can only intuit; likewise, they covet their groundedness and hipness. The black men in turn desire the power and privilege it takes to live in the "dream world" so blithely occupied by their white comrades.

However, there is another triangle operating here that a too narrow focus on "the poem itself" obscures, and it is important to tease it out of hiding, because the two areas of revisionist Beat scholarship that meet with the most resistance among fans of Beat literature are, first, a critique of the "romantic racism"—the appropriative strain in white Beat desire for black culture—and second, the homoerotics of Beat culture, beyond a somewhat fetishized notion of Ginsberg and Burroughs as iconoclasts because they were sexually non-normative and used obscenities in their writing. That is, just as an enthusiasm for jazz is taken as a sign of white Beats' openness to black people (and not just aspects of black culture), Ginsberg's and Burroughs's homosexuality is consumed as decontextualized, as if there were no gay culture in which these men participated (or didn't), and as if this status as lonely other served merely to enhance their glamour for a straight white counterculture. In fact, as both John D'Emilio's pioneering work on gay history[3] and the biography of the poet Jack Spicer make abundantly clear, Beat culture, especially in San Francisco but also in New York, lived in close and overlapping proximity with a burgeoning gay male community that had a cultural but as yet no political visibility.[4] Studies of Beat culture have tended either to condemn the Beat movement as wholly noxious in its exploitations or to exonerate (and indeed lionize) the "white negroes" for their individually flamboyant dissidence, rather than seeing a nuanced picture of competing and collaborating subject positions inhabited, to be sure, by subjects holding unequal social power. Thus, as Hettie Jones[5] and Amiri Baraka[6] note in their respective autobiographies, although Beat culture was deeply flawed, it offered certain possibilities in a world that appeared increasingly shut down, conformist, and eviscerated of creative, original thinking and cultural expression.

Bob Kaufman, born in New Orleans to a high-achieving middle-class black Catholic family (his mother was a schoolteacher, his father possibly a Pullman porter, a waiter in a high-end restaurant, or a bar owner), was active in the Merchant Marines from his eighteenth birthday until his leftist union activities came under suspicion in the early 1950s. When the AFL merged with the CIO, the more radical union members, including Kaufman, were purged; he was later expelled from the Communist Party and was characterized in his FBI files as a "drifter." He reemerged in the late 1950s as a Beat poet in San Francisco (New York had been the site of most of his union activities), where he cofounded *Beatitude*, a seminal journal of Beat culture, and published the broadside *The Abomunist Manifesto*, which was considered, along with Ginsberg's "Howl," to be a Beat manifesto. (It is the reading material of the wasted-looking young man in the famous *Life* magazine photo accompanying its article on the Beats that has become the touchstone of every Beat revival lecture in the past decades.)

There are multiple and conflicting accounts of Kaufman's genealogy, biography, and other relevant aspects of his life and work. Was he, as many accounts suggest, raised by an Orthodox Jewish German father and a Martiniquan "voodoo" mother? (No.) Was he in fact enrolled in the Merchant Marines or the National Maritime Union? (Yes.) Just like scholarship on Bob Kaufman, Beat scholarship keeps shifting as more is revealed and as details about homoeroticism, racial and ethnic tensions, and biographical minutiae become permissible public discourse. However, Beat scholarship will never stand on incontrovertibly firm ground because legend, hyperbole, and a scorn for official forms of documentation have constituted primary elements in the Beat aura. Further, Beat scholarship is coming to legitimacy precisely in the era when indeterminacy is an intellectual value rather than a liability. However, Kaufman's disappearance from literary annals is more extreme even than that of some other Beats who have achieved semicanonical notoriety, though Beat work as such is still new to the established curriculum. "Bagel Shop Jazz" itself is all about silence and obfuscation, though ostensibly it is all about talking, talking, talking. The veneer of hyperverbal poseurism hides what for many minoritized Beats was a life of "secret terrible hurts" that will never be known because the principals are dead, and they covered their tracks astonishingly well. An even thicker cloud of mystery, for instance, surrounds the figure of Stephen Jonas, a black Bostonian poet who moved in queer/Beat circles. Turning yet again to "Bagel Shop Jazz," one can find still more material for rectifying (setting unstraight, queering, "reNegrifying," in the words of one colleague) the Beat record. Here, juxtaposing the poem with other documents of the time, I investigate another silence.

The triangle I consider here, then, is not that of black and white men's desire for what each sees as the other's privilege, mediated by love-starved Beat chicks, but Beat and gay worlds (as they were imagined at that time) mediated by the figure of the black man, an object of desire (and fear) for gay white men, and an object of fear (and desire) for straight white men. Like the presumed maleness of the black and Jewish or Italian Beats, we find a presumed straightness in the figure of the black hipster who serves as fantasy vehicle for gay and straight men of the Bohemian counterculture. The countertext to "Bagel Shop Jazz" is the still unpublished diary of Russell FitzGerald, a young artist whose infatuation with Bob Kaufman during the course of his live-in relationship with gay poet Jack Spicer dramatizes some of the conflicts of Beat/queer life in eloquent, anguished, and highly disturbing terms. The diary chronicles not only FitzGerald's obsession with Kaufman but also his attempts to work that obsession into an overall artistic and metaphysical ethos in which spiritual yearnings, artistic expression, and physical/erotic desire are harmoniously lived and theorized. The rigor and purposefulness with which the young artist attempts to make sense of his emotional life, and the immediacy with which he experiences as contradictory the very forces he is trying to harmonize, foreground the pain of Beat utopian aspirations. (He is often, for example, driven by the torment of a physical desire he perceives as both exalting and debasing and that casts him simultaneously as victim and predator.)

For the Beat project was nothing if not utopian, and Kaufman's poem attempts to document this by showing the range of inhabitants who lived in the sealed-off and culturally marked-as-different Co-Existence Bagel Shop: it is interracial, it is hip, it is emancipated from the tedium of the workplace and its schedules because it has beautiful, sexually available young women who will work a day job proofreading or writing ad copy to support you. One of the goals of Beat utopia was this kind of cross-racial democracy, in the sense of identifying with the "fellaheen," as Kerouac called them—the down and out, the anonymous workers, and so forth. But, as the examples of both Athenian and American democracies have shown, equality and fraternity are usually purchased at someone else's expense. As much as "Bagel Shop Jazz" describes an insider-outsider society marked by its freewheeling valuation of coexistence, it also describes a tense negotiation between nonequals, who, drawn together by mutual yearning for a new society, have had to put up a united front against the "guilty police"—the normative world. As Richard Cándida Smith[7] elaborates in *Utopia and Dissent*, the vision of a working harmony between and among community (democracy, alternative domestic arrangements and sexual options), cultural expression, and everyday life was one that the

Beats shared with other art communities, among them the gay poets of San Francisco, who also shared with them an embattled position in respect to mainstream culture. But their respective democratic visions were somewhat in tension with the queer writers more drawn to a Platonic ideal of an elite intelligentsia. The Beats were more wholeheartedly enamored of the lower echelons of both cultural and economic registers, though they still held the figure of the artist in special reverence. The shining example of Walt Whitman was the great mediator for both groups. He was taken up by gay writers as one of them as he championed loving male friendships. He was taken up by the Beat writers because of his expansive, all-embracing vision of American life. And he was taken up by both because of his long poetic line, daring both formally and in its inclusion of all and any material as suitably poetic.

The relationship of the queer 1950s counterculture to Whitmanian-American democracy and Athenian political and philosophical thought is complex and (at least) double-edged; there was, among gay writers, affection for Plato's writings, especially the *Symposium*, because it offered an overt expression of homoerotic love at a time when that form of love was considered the highest human affective bond. At the same time, there was a consciousness of Plato's disdain for the physical world in relation to the ideal world, which they alternately found consoling and oppressive. That is, on the one hand, there is another reality hidden behind the cruelties of the world we live in, and we can take some comfort and joy in cultivating that realm. On the other hand, the social contempt for the physical and sexual so prevalent in American puritan society, especially in the 1950s, intensifies the prejudice against homosexuality, since it is not necessary for procreation and thus cannot be sanctioned within state institutions. This contempt justifies the criminalization of homosexual behavior or even inclinations.[8] Although the gay writers of the San Francisco Renaissance, among them Jack Spicer, Robert Duncan, Robin Blaser, George Stanley, and Stan Persky, sometimes invoked a revised version of Plato's *Republic* as an ideal (following the Austrian poet Stefan George, they referred to themselves as "poet-kings" of their own republic of poetry, even though Plato's "philosopher-kings" had exiled poetry in the classical work), they were torn between Plato's and George's belief in an elitist cult of the initiated, on the one hand, and Whitman's more democratic notion of brotherly erotic love on the other. Even in the split between the ideal and the immanent, which in some ways was a painful and self-denying ethos and which translated into "we wear the mask" or "we are not what we appear to be" (we are gay, but must pretend to be straight in this social closet), there was a kind of art, finesse, and sophistication involved in living double lives, or in having to keep one's life compartmentalized—this part could be public, that part had to be kept private. As gay historian George Chauncey has pointed out, while the circumstances of such double living were incontrovertibly oppressive, there was respect for the grace and skill with which the life was handled. Its practitioners did not necessarily consider themselves victims, or that they were victimized by their own skills. The ideology of ethnoracial or gay authenticity was not to become publicly or theoretically significant until the late 1960s, when minoritized ethnic, racial, gendered, and sexual communities based political movements on unitary identities.

It was the Beat era, however, that helped midwife that ideology of authenticity into being. What the Beats did for the gay community was goad it into visibility—a visibility that would eventually become politicized—by exemplifying flamboyant resistance to an oppressive norm. What the gay culture did for the Beats was to offer them a model for fluid relationships, outlaw culture and a high regard for the relatively apolitical politics of "lifestyle" (though the latter word was not coined until the 1970s). More than the queers, who had an ambivalent stake in the high art and philosophy of the Platonic tradition, the Beats insisted on making the signifier fit the signified. They tried to collapse the distance between the "private" and "public" selves, insisting that such a division was a form of social mutilation. So the Beats were, on the whole, less ambivalently anti-Platonic in their desire to refuse the gap between the Ideal and Immanent, the spiritual and the physical, the soul and the body. And they had no reason to be loyal to the cult of philosopher-kings, poet-kings, or any other type of cultural elite. They were unambiguously Whitman's heirs rather than Stefan George's or Plato's. The various Europes their parents had fled had treated them with cruelty and contempt and had visited upon them extreme economic privation as well as state-sanctioned class and ethnic prejudice. They associated high European art with their class enemies, though as Kaufman's poem demonstrates ("paint talk ... Bartok"[9]), they were attracted to the newer elements of classical art that drew on the "folkish." We need only look at the difference between Allen Ginsberg's and Jack Spicer's poetics, poetry, and personal comportments to see a glaringly dramatic embodiment of the dissonance between the Beats and the queers: Ginsberg is all-embracing, raw, confessional, intent on destroying the dualism between the sacred and the degraded. Spicer is resolutely private, hermetic, devoted to keeping his personality out of his work in the service of a higher entity, poetry. We can see the potential and the ugliness of both forms of democracy.

Nonetheless, this very anguish and urgency of the Beats to tear down the illusory wall separating them from themselves, from "reality," from an authentic life that expressed and externalized their spiritual yearnings, speaks to a complicity with patterns of inside versus outside, authenticity versus falsity, the "guilty police" versus the "beautiful shadows." Although they did reverse the hierarchy of those binarisms, putting the police in the "guilty" slot and themselves as the deviant but innocent victims, Beat culture (if not the work of specific Beat writers, such as William Burroughs) reified rather than dissolved the binary bind of life in the 1950s. And it did so using black culture as the lightning rod that conducted the meeting of Heaven and Hell. Furthermore, what has come to us as Platonic wisdom, like what has come to us as a united Beat front against the straight world, is far more complex and interesting than binarized (queer vs. Beat) generalizations can convey. The narrative complexity and poetic beauty of Platonic writing, for example, which does not tell a straightforward story celebrating an idealized spiritual love, allows us to see the dynamic intelligence and flamboyant, often conflicting ideologies, personalities, and styles at work in the construction of what, as good poststructuralist scholars or Beat aficionados, we know and mistrust as the Athenian roots of Western philosophy. Likewise, we can appreciate the nuances of the 1950s counterculture; its complicated internal alliances and schisms require close attention to counter glib, unqualified celebrations of a certain glorified caricature of Beat culture as emancipatory, on the one hand, and unqualified condemnations of Beat culture as exploitive and vulgar on the other. In remapping onto both the Beat past and the historicizing-Beat present these dramas laced with lacunae and loud absences and present silences, it is not hard to see what has been left out of the official Beat text and, to the degree that there was one, the official queer text. Missing in action from the official Beat scene: gay men. Women, insofar as they were foundational rather than decorative. People of color, insofar as they were foundationally interactive with it rather than merely inspirational, apparitional, or allegorical reference points.

The scene described by "Bagel Shop Jazz," a static and haunting tableau vivant, is prepackaged for historicization: you want to know who we were in the 1950s North Beach? Here we are: (nonracialized) women, white ethnics (men), and blacks (men). This, at least, is the substance of the poem's content. However, the door opens to a more comprehensive reading when we admit that the poem enacts its own aporia—its own blind spot. By today's standards, not only is it ragingly heteronormative (if complexly so), but when the researcher investigates Kaufman's actual biography, the milieu he traveled in and the company he kept, the absences are even more dramatic and can be ascribed to a purposeful (if mediated by convention) elision. It is not the case that queers were simply part of a vague backdrop of undifferentiated Bohemia. Kaufman was actively enmeshed in a triangle involving queer men; he was their friend, he engaged them as queens in public if playful verbal sparring. The queer scene to which he lived in such close proximity (in light of his protracted flirtation with Russell FitzGerald), with its far more believable and regular bar busts and its coded communications, its shadow existence, its secret terrible hurts, and its fantasies of love, forms the world that this Bagel Shop world protects the Beats against as much as it does against the police. The queens did not congregate at the Co-Existence Bagel Shop as a queer space, though as individuals they may have been customers. They congregated at certain bars which themselves had different flavors (the drag show bars as distinct from the intelligentsia's bars, for instance) and some of which, like The Place, did in fact cater to a broader group of Bohemians. The queer side of Bob Kaufman, such as it was, and of the Beat scene, is dramatically excised from the bagel shop poem, which is framed precisely to exclude the formal presence of queers as a group that makes up the counterculture. There is no queer content in the poem except insofar as the homosocial economy of desire that flows between white men and black men, mediated by women as presumed property of the other or as object of desire, can be considered queer. (It is emphatically not my objective here to claim a closeted homosexual or gay identity for Kaufman but rather to point out that certain experiences and elements that textured everyday Beat life have been suppressed in the record, both in this poem and in other Beat documents, such as *On the Road* and other of Kerouac's romans á clef, which suppress not only Dean/Neal's homosexual encounters but also those of Kerouac and even those of Ginsberg, the out homosexual.)

The Beat scene was one in which ethnic and subcultural styles were readily borrowed, experimented with, and consumed in the crassest sense of thoughtless appropriation. Kerouac's purple prose about jazz and its musicians is everyone's (both Kerouac bashers' and Kerouac aficionados') favorite example, in which his obvious enthusiasm cannot hide, though it mitigates a wholly negative and dismissive judgment about, his callow misunderstandings. Kaufman's poem, quite different from Kerouac's rhapsodic prose, captures with a kind of distant compassion the dynamics of this mutual exploitation—the currency-sex (women), high modernist culture (Jews/Italians), and the cool, stoic authenticity of hip black men that hides the depth of their suffering—that each party brings to the table in stereotyped profiles. The poem is also, of course, about how fragile these negotiations are, how tenuous this counterculture's sense of itself is. The unspeakable, queerness, constitutes the scene's hipness. However countercultural these bagel shoppers are, however much heat their conversation generates against the cold war raging outside, the triangle of other faces they present to the straight world relies on queer silence.

Despite the larger silence it enacts, though, this poem's manifest content should itself be seen as an anomalous breakthrough in Beat discourse because it disturbs the silence surrounding the tension between various members of the scene's constituency. In particular, Beat discourse (especially by white male Beats) about black men is generally characterized by an admiring, hyperbolic description of heteromachismo or preternatural musical talent. Often this rhetoric includes envious anecdotes about how much easier it was for black men to pick up cute chicks than it was for the writer. Black men, in these accounts, are either saintly musicians or hustlers on the prowl. This latter view is epitomized by Norman Mailer's notorious "The White Negro"(1959), which claims to be about how the white man envies the black man's sexuality and thus tries to emulate his style, but whose subtext is about how the Jewish man envies and wants to emulate the Gentile man's sexuality but can't say so. One of the contributions "Bagel Shop Jazz" makes to the Beat legacy is that it complicates this static outside-in view of black masculinity and attributes to African American men a textured, dignified interiority born of a collective experience of tragedy. Nowhere are the men, "white ethnic" or black, seen as preying on women; they are each preoccupied with troubles emblematic of their culture, be it high modernist or street-smart. Instead, sexuality, which in the writing of white Beat men is projected onto black men, is here projected onto women. And it is an extraordinarily naive version of sexuality that Kaufman imputes to the women: the stereotypically gendered syndrome of one-night stands en route to the search for true love is sympathetically if superficially rendered. The gay scene, which was a living, palpable presence in the North Beach counterculture, is effaced. Though to be sure the men are not indicated as specifically heterosexual, the women are, and the men, by being unspecified, are subsumed into a normative standard that need not speak its name—that is, heterosexuality.

Vice Versa

Not surprisingly, the gay community's public discourse did to Kaufman what he did to them in "Bagel Shop Jazz." In that public discourse we find what we might expect with regard to the black poet, that is, he is invisible, and to the degree that he is acknowledged at all, he is hypersexualized or seen as emblematic of the physical body, or its abstract and ambiguously positive analogue, the "folk." If he is black, in other words, he can't be a poet. Just as Kaufman dismissed them as soulless, precious intellectuals, they wrote him off as a vulgar, undisciplined populist. He was excluded from foundational anthologies such as Donald Allen's *The New American Poetry* (1960), and he did not participate in the informal workshops that coalesced around writers with serious literary aspirations, such as Spicer. It is, however, difficult to make absolute generalizations about the mixture of negrophilia and racism, or the way the two function in tandem in gay writing of the time, because the politics of identity functioned differently from those of today. It was possible for Gentiles, whites, and men to have warm, collegial friendships with Jews, blacks, and women in which they interacted on a daily basis, while simultaneously unself-consciously and publicly subscribing to strict prejudices at the abstract level.

For example, we find a blend of misogyny and comradeship in references to women. Women are reviled by Jack Spicer in his greeting to Denise Levertov (a poem he wrote on the occasion of her visit to San Francisco opens with the lines, "People who don't like the smell of faggot vomit / Will never understand why men don't like women"), but Robert Duncan wrote frequently about his affection for and being inspired by Levertov, clearly a comrade in aesthetic mission. Blacks figured in the gay poets' work mostly in comparatist contexts, where the social marginalization of gay men is juxtaposed to that of blacks—sometimes in gestures of solidarity, sometimes in gestures of dismissal, sometimes simply as a jumping-off point for the consideration of gay oppression, a topic much less publicly discussed than racial oppression. Robert Duncan, for example, opens his 1944 groundbreaking essay "The Homosexual in Society" thus:

> Something in James Agee's recent approach to the Negro pseudo-folk (*Partisan Review* Spring 1944) is the background of the notes which I propose in discussing yet another group whose only salvation is in the struggle of all humanity for freedom and individual integrity; who have suffered in modern society persecution, excommunication; and whose "intellectuals," whose most articulate members, have been willing to desert that primary struggle, to beg, to gain at the price if need be of any sort of prostitution, privilege for themselves, however ephemeral.[10]

Duncan had at that time also written a poem, "African Elegy," which he had submitted to John Crowe Ransom at the *Kenyon Review* and which, after the publication of "The Homosexual in Society," was returned after an initial acceptance because Ransom could no longer overlook the homoerotic content. The poem combines negrophilia and homoeroticism in a joyous though stereotypical fantasy of bondage and magic. Note the drug reference: African Americans were perceived by their white counterparts to be sophisticated initiates into the esoterica of drug use. And we may note also the ambiguous degree to which Duncan takes responsibility, in the last few lines of the passage below, for his own fantasizing. He knows he is projecting wondrous and titillating scenarios onto Africa, Africans, and African Americans and, as a white writer and gay man, claiming solidarity with them through the "darkness" of his own forbidden desires (it is important to remember, when we inquire into the projective nature of Beat writers' negrophilia, that miscegenation was illegal):

> Negroes, negroes, all those princes,
> . . . holding to their mouths like Death
> the cups of rhino bone,
> were there to burn my hands and feet,
> divine the limit of the bone and with their magic
> tie and twist me like a rope. I know
> no other continent of Africa more
> dark than this dark continent of my breast.[11]

John Wieners, another queer white Beat, whose writing can usefully be studied alongside Kaufman's for a similar approach to poetics and the role of the poet in society, also attributes a sense of aliveness and dynamism to "Negroes" (though less flamboyantly)—a dynamism he finds lacking in other segments of 1950s society. In describing an evening in San Francisco in 1959, he writes:

> Streetwalkers, showgirls, perverts, late businessmen, clerks, schoolboys, tourists, from the healthy country . . . poets with pale faces, girls dressed in black beside them . . . parade by on silent errands. There is seldom laughter except in the neighborhood and negro districts.[12]

Jack Spicer's campy dismissal of camp as authentic queer culture in "Excerpt from the Diaries of Oliver Charming" highlights the differences and similarities he perceives among black, Jewish, and homosexual "identity" insofar as the search for an authentic culture is concerned. He writes that camp is "a perpetual Jewish vaudeville joke—or at the very best, a minstrel show impeccably played by Negros in blackface."[13] He dwells on the differences between the three groups (assumed, in his paradigm, to be mutually exclusive and exclusively male) in precept 12 of the "Unvert Manifesto" (possibly an inspiration for Kaufman's *Abomunist Manifesto*?): "Jews and Negros are not allowed to be unverts. The Jew will never understand unversion and the Negro understands it all too well."[14] Unverts are metasexual homosexuals—that is, as far as I can tell, celibate or beyond the reach of the usual pleasures, and intimately familiar with the erotic pain that makes "platonic love" an experience that transfigures suffering into purified poetic material. By attributing to black and gay men the depth and soulfulness needed to undergo such alchemical sublimation, and by denying that possibility to Jews (presumably because, according to the stereotypes of the day, they were overly materialistic), Spicer is both participating in a Poundian legacy joining anti-Semitism with avant-garde poetics and declaring a kinship with black Americans' putatively superior spiritual capabilities, forged in the fire of extreme social suffering.

Here we can circle back to the notion of a Platonic symposium as a loose, floating trope for homosocial, homoerotic, and intellectual community. In his magisterial presence in the North Beach countercultural poetry scene, in his espousal of a doctrine of extreme dualism (the spiritual versus material split), and in his ruthless pursuit of purity in thought, conduct, and poetry, Spicer plays Socrates in this drama. His collegial friendship with apocryphally black poet Stephen Jonas notwithstanding (and Jonas, too, espoused an extreme skepticism toward fleshly pleasures and the comforts of identity-based communities of suffering, as well as a diehard Poundianism that included anti-Semitism), Spicer, uncompromising on all fronts, is no more forgiving on the subject of race than he is on the subject of, say, gayness, or poetry. As in Kaufman's exclusionary "Bagel Shop Jazz," there's no hint of the proximity of black presence in Spicer's work except in his "Song for Bird and Myself" (poems for Charlie Parker were practically de rigueur in hipster culture), in which a pun creates a shared sense of aesthetic commitment ("And are we angels, Bird?" / "That's what we're trying to tell 'em, Jack / There aren't any angels except when / You and me blow 'em"[15]). While Spicer did not consider himself a Beat poet, and he and his circle are not usually considered Beats, they were equally a part of the San Francisco Renaissance, constituted by the rich and nuanced intermeshing and dissonances between both (overlapping) scenes.

One could, in fact, easily read the entire works of Spicer and Kaufman and never realize that they moved in the same circles, drank in the same bars, slept with the same man. The document that gives the lie to these mutual silencings is the beautifully anguished, as yet unpublished diary of Russell FitzGerald, the young painter-poet who was the object of Jack Spicer's affection and who, even while he lived with Spicer and loved him as a mentor, pursued Kaufman wildly, famously, and hopelessly all over North Beach. In this drama Spicer is again Socrates, but not Socrates the powerful, wise philosopher; rather, he is the Socrates whose buttons get pushed by his own desire for the beautiful wild boy. FitzGerald, the wayward genius Alcibiades, teases Socrates, and undoes his claim to platonic disinterest. Kaufman is . . . Eros itself? Poetry itself, the object of obsessive desire that is talked into being by the community of lovers, philosophers, poets? Perhaps, but Kaufman, as a black man, also represents, in FitzGerald's negrophiliac imagination, the temptations of the physical rather than the balm of the spiritual. At one point in the diary, "Bobby" is spelled "Bo(d) by," and comes to represent in FitzGerald's feverishly conflicted imagination the pull of the physical, the erotic, the sinful. For all that the Beats tried to marry heaven and hell, both they and members of the *Spicerkreis* were heavily invested in that marriage as a crazy juncture of distinct opposites. "Bob is wonderful, a living poem," gushes FitzGerald,[16] charmed by Kaufman's high-spirited, endearing, falling-down-drunk monologues in which he castigates the "queers" for being inauthentic and spiritually impoverished, compared to his own richness in "soul." FitzGerald admires Kaufman's lack of social inhibition and the spontaneity of his playful invective.

Spicer and FitzGerald discuss Kaufman so much that he has more of a textual or discursive presence than an actual presence in FitzGerald's life. The "Kaufman situation," that is, the Spicer-FitzGerald-Kaufman love triangle, becomes more real to the infatuated young painter than Kaufman himself, who is busy having a life of his own that comes to include a (second) wife, Eileen, and a son, Parker. Kaufman becomes, literally, an icon in FitzGerald's passionate spiritual mythography: a recent, serious, and anguished convert to Catholicism at the time of his move to North Beach, FitzGerald executed a series of religious paintings, "14 Stations of the Cross," featuring Kaufman as Christ—a connection made throughout Kaufman's life and posthumously, when eulogies like A. D. Winans's "Black Jesus of the 50s" appeared on the storefront doors of North Beach. Kaufman himself played on this identification in a number of his earlier poems, including *The Abomunist Manifesto*, which features hilarious passages from the diary of Christ, figured as a hip-lingo-slinging Beat poet, and "Afterwards, They Shall Dance," in which he "sings the nail-in-the-foot song."[17]

While talk about Kaufman entirely permeates FitzGerald's journal and gives it an urgently poetic quality of erotic longing, Kaufman's voice is negligibly recorded. The moments that are documented, however, are significant, because they capture the improvisatory high spirits for which Kaufman was known before lapsing into his legendary silence, which lasted, with a few notable departures into writing or speaking again, from 1963 until the end of his life in 1986. In one such passage Kaufman jokingly excoriates Spicer's table at the bar, accusing the intellectuals of being soulless faggots. In another he quips, stringing FitzGerald along, "I have to sleep with women to keep from sleeping with men." Finally, after months of cat-and-mouse, games, FitzGerald goes down on Kaufman, who has "managed to pass out"[18] in a seedy hotel room. FitzGerald is promptly disgusted by his own behavior: "Even the smell on my hands seemed sickening."[19] This demystifying culmination of their intimacy doesn't quell his ardor, however, and for a year or more the two continue their game, enraging Spicer so much that he scribbles "nigger" across Russell's copy of Kaufman's *Abomunist Manifesto*, which Spicer knows Kaufman will see. FitzGerald's continual and addictive private vows not to objectify Kaufman are poignant, repellent—and unkeepable. "I swear I will never again conjure his body to feed my imaginary lust. . . . Dark brother, I free you from my legend, I love you real. No more masturbating, no more black magic. Oh my love forgive me. Oh God, grant me all the fire I need."[20] The purple prose is both sincerely agonized and laughably over the top, histrionically self-deluded. Meanwhile, Kaufman wears a ring FitzGerald gave him when the former sucked the blood from a self-inflicted wound on FitzGerald's hand and then "drew and held the admiration of everyone in the [Coffee] Gallery with one of his free-wheeling monologues denouncing the faggot table."[21]

In the midst of this swirling evidence of some investment on Kaufman's part in being adored by a man, it seems safe to say that Kaufman's performance of homophobia was a double-edged matter: his charm and charisma went a long way toward mitigating what may have been partial self-mockery as well. Typical of societies that try to blend utopian democracy with a respect for charismatic flamboyance, actions and speech veer every which way in this boys' world bohemia, complementing and canceling each other out until everyone is living with his back against the wall. Kaufman may have been willing to tolerate some objectification because he recognized the social stigma that queerness incurred. In "Unhistorical Events" he records some of the "secret terrible hurts" suffered by the anonymous poor, including himself and one of his former shipmates: "Apollinaire / never sailed with riffraff Rolf / who was rich in California, but / had to flee because he was queer . . . Apollinaire / never slept all night in an icehouse . . ." (1968, 30–31; the last line refers to Kaufman's having been, as a teenager, suspended by his thumbs in an icehouse overnight by Klansmen.) Also, as actor Ben Vereen has pointed out, the ills of racism have some minor benefits, including privacy to do and be as one wishes while whites believe that one is stupid, insensitive, or unaware of one's objectification. Thus, being reified by Russell FitzGerald allowed Kaufman a measure of freedom: he was never called on to reveal himself, to put his cards on the table as it were, since he was presumed to have no interiority.[22] However, it must also finally be recognized that Kaufman could be said to have *submitted to* FitzGerald's pressure—especially the night when FitzGerald exploited his unconsciousness—because the relationship was, ultimately, one between structurally unequal subjects. Although FitzGerald experiences himself as victimized by Kaufman's attractiveness and thus feels degraded in pursuit, we know that structurally, this is untrue. Although FitzGerald experiences Kaufman as a merciless tease and himself as abject, he is an enfranchised citizen; Kaufman is not. In 1950s United States, even in a social bohemia, where Kaufman's colleagues could hurl racial epithets at him with no more consequence than a bitter laugh on his part, what choices did he have? In becoming a full-fledged member of the triangle, Kaufman could be said to exhibit grace under pressure, even compassion. These scenes are strikingly absent from "Bagel Shop Jazz"; their absence could signal either an aporia on Kaufman's part, which is how I have constructed it in my reading of the poem, or a way of "writing back": we will love each other, we will silence each other. The third possibility is that this is too traumatic to address.

Biographically, there is no happy ending, but there is evidence of tenacity, creativity, and persistence against the odds. In 1960 Kaufman eventually embarked with his new family for New York City—a trip that resulted in Kaufman's return to San Francisco, three years later, a bitterly disillusioned amphetamine addict who would rise only occasionally to his former wildly antic, creative heights. "I want Bob Kaufman back," he was known to say from so far within his disappointment that his language became private and cryptic where it had been publicly, wittily accessible. When FitzGerald followed him east, some months later, he succumbed to heroin addiction, into which he drifted as a way of entering the world of black men. Eventually his wife (he had, in the midst of this infatuation, eloped with Dora Dull and her twin daughters) took him to Vancouver, where he kicked heroin and became a gourmet cook, dying of alcoholism in his early forties. His magnum opus, "The Stations of the Cross," testimony to the roles of Kaufman and Catholicism (heaven and hell) in his life, was irreparably damaged by flooding in Vancouver, but his journal's vividness enables us to reconstruct much of its passionate context. Jack Spicer too died of alcoholism at forty, uttering legendary last words to his friend Robin Blaser: "My vocabulary did this to me; your love will let you go on"[23]—a cautionary self-reflection on a life lived, perhaps, too purely and exactingly devoted to the real in poetry. Kaufman outlived his cotriangulants, dying in 1986 at age sixty of emphysema and cirrhosis in a Catholic rest home in the Western Addition, a black section of San Francisco. Wit and foresight characterized his last words, whispered to his girlfriend, Lynne Wildey: "If you're ever in the neighborhood, drop by—."[24]

4 Displaysias

Writing Social Science and Ethnicity in Gertrude Stein and Certain Others

IN OCTOBER 1995, language poet Charles Bernstein and I participated by telephone in a Gertrude Stein hour on WBAI-FM's *Beyond the Pale*, organized by Jews for Racial and Economic Justice (the gay and lesbian activist wing of the group had requested Stein as subject of their designated special show, which choice itself was extremely interesting to me, since, while there is no consensus on Stein's positions on racial and economic justice, it indicated the degree to which she has herself become a figure of political resonance in queer circles). Charles and I came in on the second half of the hourlong show and discussed first how we did or didn't see questions of identity arising in Stein's work, and how Stein's interrogation of identity through language play (as well as thematically) could itself be seen as a strong current in the Jewish intellectual tradition. Then came the question of her politics, her survival of World War II under the auspices of Bernard Faÿ in the Vichy government. The moderator challenged any designation of Stein and Alice B. Toklas as radical since they owed their survival to friendship with an anti-Semite whom they refused to repudiate even after Faÿ's disgrace in the wake of Allied victory. Charles and I bristled. Would it have been better that she not survive? She didn't betray anybody. People did what they had to. The whole village knew they were Jewish and protected them. I'd seen their wartime I.D. photos at the Beinecke, and they were terrified little old Jewish ladies (my notes say "suffering, aging, patient, angry and very intelligent"), not callous race-traitors. And so forth. Our vehement defense was cut off by the hour's expiration. Thanks, but that's all the time we have. Our disembodied, miscreant Jewish voices snipped, our absence doubled. The non-Jewish artists and the political Jew wrapped it up in person.

Though Stein's and Toklas's gratitude and loyalty vis-à-vis Bernard Faÿ is understandable, it's pointless to exonerate Stein's

French ID card photographs for Gertrude Stein (left) and Alice Toklas (right). Courtesy of Yale Collection of American Literature, Beinecke Rare Book and Manuscript Library.

occasional displays of colossal political naiveté, most spectacularly her support for Marechal Pétain as the savior of France. Rather, I argue for the ways in which Stein, in spite of her sometimes dubious enthusiasms (such as her early excitement about Otto Weininger), actively participated in the debates surrounding the scientization of ethnocultural characteristics and did so in a way not wholly reducible either to a simple repudiation of her Jewishness or to an affirmation thereof in conventionally recognizable terms. In fact, the complex relationship of Stein, as a proto-postmodernist, to Jewishness and to Jewish history anticipates current debates about the emancipationist or dangerously apolitical potentials of postmodern writing practice and poststructuralist, language-oriented philosophies.

The Jewish social scientist's inquiry into systems of character, physical type, and mental processes may reflect an attempt to understand the origins of his or her socially perceived difference, and to affirm that difference. However, the inquiry may also indicate an attempt to control by intellectual mastery a system of exclusion; the anxiety of "passing" generates a search for systemic order in which one can find one's own safety zone. Gertrude Stein's early novelistic experiments with African American language, for example, and the novel *Q.E.D.*, in which each person of the plot's lesbian love triangle typifies a different "national" temperament, constitute a similarly problematic move to study (the otherness of) oneself by attending to the otherness of an/other other. Stein's move to Europe, in which she plunged herself into a culture alien yet somehow evocative of an older, familiar world ("we [singulars, queer people] fly to the kindly comfort of an older world accustomed to take all manner of strange forms to its bosom"[1]), constitutes a kind of sociolinguistic fieldwork in which the real subject of study (as in most ethnographies) is herself. The writing Stein produced in France, though less thematically concerned with types and character, became a practice in which language itself, in a process of experiment, undertakes and undergoes a dissolution of category.

Since until recently it has been assumed that an inquiry into someone's ethnicity involves establishing how she herself "felt" about being x or y, Steinians have maintained that Stein's radical anti-identitarianism foreclosed such inquiry, except to assert that "it simply wasn't important to her"; this foreclosure is exacerbated by the ongoing debates about whether Judaism/Jewishness is a religion, an ethnicity, a culture, and so on. It seems indecorous to "out" Stein as a Jew, as it is not clear what that means for someone who was not religiously observant, did not observe dietary laws (Toklas's cookbook is full of pork and shellfish recipes), and had no interest in Zionism. On the other side, staunchly culturally identified, nonreligious Jews like the WBAI-FM moderator from Jews for Racial and Economic Justice take issue with Stein's lack of public solidarity with other Jews, seeing her as an assimilationist of a worse type than the secular Jews Freud, Marx, and Emma Goldmann, the latter two of whom qualify as (JFREJ-type) Jews through their political engagements. Claims such as mine—that Stein's Jewishness is, arguably, a language practice—can sound vaguely essentialistic, in the vein of Otto Weininger's thought, discussed below (preview: he's one of the villains in what follows, despite a certain pathos in the configurations of his particular *dementia Judaica*). Thus, Stein's Jewishness is a topic that is best approached obliquely, as she herself does; with narrative tentativeness; with an openness toward the inclusion of fragments—clues and minutiae—free-floating through her work like sidereal flotsam, as well as toward broad disciplinary inquiries into the status of the social sciences at the turn of the century and other such currents of humanistic cliché that, when pressed, relinquish their apparent predictability and turn into discoveries maybe intuited but nonetheless finally surprising. For many, it is not a topic whose viability is immediately self-evident; a scholar of Jewish women poets told me, "If you can find Jewishness in Stein you can find it anywhere." Moreover, the editors of an encyclopedia of Jewish American playwrights and poets almost excluded Stein, but for the insistence of one of the project's advisers. Likewise, although the useful *Jews and Gender: Responses to Otto Weininger*, edited by Nancy Harrowitz and Barbara Hyams, refers correctly to Weininger's influence on Stein,[2] no essay on this subject appears in the book, which deals extensively with Weininger and Joyce (fully three essays dedicated to this topic), as well as with Apollinaire, Heine, and German novels in general. Split into strict halves, the book addresses first the "scientific," social context aspect of its thorny subject—Weininger as a Viennese, as a liberal, Weininger and Freud, Lombroso and Wittgenstein, respectively; the second half comprises the literary essays enumerated above. And where, indeed, given the scope of Stein's inquiry, would one place such an essay? Anyone wanting to investigate Stein's relationship to the forms and styles of Jewishness that prevailed during her long life needs to be, as she believed herself to be, both social scientist and artist. These make a specious binarism, of course; they also express the becoming-oxymoron of the "social scientist" as that disciplinary identity took shape during Stein's era.

It is precisely this binarism to which Otto Weininger appeals in the introduction to his notorious *Sex and Character* (1903), a volume inaugurating (according to the German publisher's preface to the posthumous, post-suicide, authorized edition) the psychophilosophical science of characterology. Briefly, Weininger, working out of a European tradition of first religious and then scientific anti-Semitism and misogyny, proposes that genius—that is, the capacity to develop to the fullest extent the rational, humanistic spirituality necessary to become a fully actualized (as contemporary New Agers might say) individual—is the sole province of the Aryan male and is inaccessible to (Aryan) women and (male) Jews. This is because characterologically (character being a combination of biological, moral, and intellectual temperament), Jews and women are incapable of self-sufficiency; that is, they have no "center," no soul, no being-in-themselves; they are reactive and parasitic, concerned only with physical survival. Weininger stresses that he is not concerned, in his scheme, with literal Jews and Aryans, with literal men and women; these are "platonic" conceptions,[3] which in some measure are manifested in real individuals but function more nearly as tendencies; all Jews and Christians are combinations of Jew and Christian, all men and women are properly bisexual, with a tendency toward one pole or the other. Thus, for example, the crowning achievement of Jesus, the act that represented his genius, was that, although he was Jewish, he killed the Jew in him to found Christianity.[4] For Weininger, this example provides the only possible solution to the Jewish question. The individual Jew must, through "steady resolution, united to the highest self-respect,"[5] overcome, like Jesus, his own Judaism.

76

Zionism is out of the question, for it does not save the Jew, it merely isolates him.

Weininger's insistence on a wholistic, rational and moral individualism and on the perfectibility of society in a clear-cut and narrow teleology of values through the self-initiated perfectibility of the individual constitutes his liberalism. The belief in human progress along individual lines, but conforming nonetheless to a universally applicable ideal, is at the heart of liberalism. Steven Beller has drawn a useful distinction between "intolerant" and "tolerant" liberalism; pluralism is intrinsic to the latter, but has no place in the former (we see this distinction played out in debates about multiculturalism: will "difference" strengthen or weaken national unity? The question liberalism cannot ask is, why should national unity be the bottom line?). Weininger clearly falls into the former camp; human rationality is defined as a single style of thinking, that of the Aryan/Christian male; human morality has one universal code, that of the Aryan/Christian male. One can also see the nature of Weininger's assimilationism, which was a strange twist on the progressive thought of his time. While many liberal Jews, sociologist Maurice Fishberg among them, advocated assimilation under the aegis of a pluralistic tolerance (that is, Jews should not be forced to be other than Jews, but they should enjoy full and egalitarian contact with the Gentile mainstream—short of intermarriage in which the offspring became non-Jewish—and have full access to rights and opportunities enjoyed by Gentiles), Weininger's solution resonates with an older model of assimilation, that is, conversion. But it is not so much a religious conversion as a characterological one, and it must, of course, be voluntary, individually undertaken, and profound, not cosmetic, the result of rigorous soul-searching and ruthless introspective asceticism. Weininger brings the Protestant work ethic, and Kant's categorical imperative, to bear on the self-help project of Jewish assimilation. However, this linear logic, meant to save Western civilization, doomed him to suicide. Trapped in a system of thinking in which he believed himself to have found the answer but unable to actualize it in the world (in his own being), he was condemned to a self-canceling telos.

The overdeterminism of Weininger's binarisms—Jew versus Aryan, woman versus man, Hebraism versus Christianity, body versus soul—articulate an almost decadently extreme dialectic, the endpoint of modernism, perhaps, a line of reasoning atrophied from inbreeding. Weininger does in fact advocate letting the human race perish rather than perpetrate the immorality of coitus—immorality because it requires that man partake of woman's lack of identity by objectifying her; though she is in fact nothing but an object of man's projections, his moral integrity rests on him treating her *as if she were* capable of humanity.[6] It is not hard to see how Stein may have found Weininger's ethically argued distaste for heterosexual coitus reassuring (Charlotte Perkins Gilman, an American feminist and economist, was also taken with his work); likewise, his theory of universal bisexuality, which Freud later adopted, gave philosophical permission for sexual minorities to locate themselves on a continuum of social normativity. What is fascinating is how Stein's early enthusiasm for this straightforwardly misogynistic, anti-Semitic tract is later reworked; she revises its uncompromisingly unilinear premise of progress (Weininger argues that at least in theory, all people can and must kill the woman and the Jew in them to become the supreme individual, the Aryan male) into an emergent dialogic, one that finds emancipationist possibilities in precisely the putatively unwholesome elements of character, speech, and thought in woman and Jew for which Weininger had only contempt.

Like Stein, other Jewish contemporaries of Weininger's, such as Freud, Theodore Reik, and Maurice Fishberg (*The Jews: A Study in Race and Environment*, 1911), also studied the "problem" of Jewishness as social scientists (Freud, unlike Fishberg, tending also toward an essayistic, humanistic model of exposition) in ways that affirmed rather than denounced the Jews' perceived specialness as an ethnic group. Stein, too, in her very challenge to the concept or desirability of identity, in her very claim that identity is relational rather than innate and autonomous, enacted and affirmed a kind of Jewishness that eschewed fixed categories and unilinear ways of thinking, thus instantiating Weininger's charges of Jews' faulty reasoning cum being-in-the-world while championing that psychic style as valid, liberating, and intellectually and aesthetically rewarding.

Sander Gilman has thoroughly documented how Weininger's ideas grow out of a history of first religious, then scientific anti-Semitism in Europe, in which stock indices of Jewish difference were codified into a normative discourse that influenced Jewish social scientists such as Cesare Lombroso, Arthur Schnitzler, Joseph Jacobs, Maurice Fishberg, and Freud, as well as their gentile colleagues. Jewish creativity, insofar as it existed at all (Weininger thought not), was intertwined with Jewish madness and melancholia, Jewish sexuality with Jewish pathology. Jewish inauthenticity was considered either innate (Weininger) or a result of millennia of oppression, and so on. Gilman bluntly asserts biographical detail as crucial to understanding these men's intellectual formations, and conversely reads intellectual treatises as barely veiled autobiographical position papers: "The self-hating Jew Otto Weininger . . . was both a baptized Jew and a repressed homosexual"[7]; "Like the Jew in Viennese society [that is, Freud, whose theory of creativity and sublimation Gilman is recapitulating], the creative figure must deny his essence to become what he can become."[8] Gilman's own projections give permission to see Stein's oeuvre, if not representationally autobiographical (though that, too, in some pieces), at least firmly situated within the context of debates about Jewishness that were part of the psycho-philosophical backdrop of modernist (theories and practices of) creativity.

As Gilman, again, has argued (in *Jewish Self-Hatred*), the opening of the twentieth century marked the emergence not only of European and American Jews and women as political actors on their own behalf but of a host of sciences designed in part to contain these insurgencies through the establishment of racial, ethnic, and gender characteristics that determined immutable differences between demographic groups. For Jews placing themselves in mainstream intellectual life of the twentieth century, the challenge was to position themselves in relation to these sociobiological, psychological, sexological, and anthropological systems in a way that did not subordinate them to these discourses of classification and control but rather enabled them to participate affirmatively in the process of social (self-)definition. Unlike Weininger, many did not repudiate their own Jewishness but rather used the concept of ethnic classification to affirm what they felt to be special about their culture. Gilman has shown that Freud goes farther than simple affirmation; his theory of creativity disentangles what had been articulated (by Cesare Lombroso and others) as the nexus of creativity and madness characterizing the Jewish psyche. In Freud's view, creativity is part of everyday life and everyone's working consciousness and unconscious, rather than the special and pathological purview of one race; madness is recast as psychopathology, a current running through everyday life, part of, one might say, everybody's autobiography. Freud, in other words, takes what is other and universalizes it, not as a way of robbing Jews (we "others") of their (our) specialness but instead, as the Jewish orchestrator of theory, to give the Jewish gift (noblesse oblige, a bit) to the world, alerting it to its own unplumbed resources of wit, imagination, and magical logic.

Chronologically, Gertrude Stein wrote the works collected posthumously as *Painted Lace and Other Pieces: 1914–1937* between the eras of Weininger's wild popularity and the postwar reckoning of the humanistic sciences and the Jews who participated in them.[9] Though written well after the period of her early enthusiasm for Weininger's book (which was published when she was still living in Baltimore), and after she had definitively left the field of psychology, *Painted Lace* evinces a preoccupation with nationalism, race, religion, ethnicity, gender, and sexuality, and most important, the way writing and language can inform or "unmean" these social categories. The volume's governing metaphor, painted lace, serves as a slightly defamiliarized image of alphabetic writing on a page, calling to mind Derrida's well-known essay "The Violence of the Letter," which centrally features the juxtaposed images of a tribal chief "writing" in imitation of his Western visitors and the traditional linear cross-hatchings and other designs on the indigenously made ceramic pots, asserting that the latter is to be considered writing as much or more so than the former. Why not recognize the latter as a form of writing that predates the arrival of Western culture with its "corrupting" (read, literate) influence? Why not recognize "painted lace"—esoteric, "precious" or eccentric, "corrupt," "Jewish," "womanish"—modes of inscription as worthy emblems of expressive culture alongside and permeating those of the Aryan male speaking and writing?

I have learned that one dear colleague, whose anthropological work treats American Jews, characterizes my work as addressing "Jews who are hated by other Jews." "Bad" Jews? Like Gertrude Stein, Lenny Bruce, myself, and my dear elusive father the head-measurer? Like Weininger? I have no love for the latter, so rest assured, though the pathos of his tragic vision and life have a chrysalis-like cachet that seals him from the utter contempt he'd have merited had he successfully "transcended" his Jewishness. But the pathos that constitutes his one saving grace (in addition, perhaps, to his theory of universal bisexuality, which Freud made famous) meets its match in Gertrude Stein's assertive appropriation of his damning characteristics of Jewish men and all women; though Stein's Jewishness has many times been dismissed as a minor aspect of her life and work, and her qualifications as a "good Jew" many times challenged, it simply cannot be argued that she was ashamed or conflicted about her status as a Jew, though often her work questions what exactly being a Jew means. That she, like Freud and Weininger, was a secular Jew is quite obvious; that she, like Freud and Weininger, held a (then considered liberal) assimilationist position could be argued for or against; that she, like Freud and unlike Weininger, enjoyed being Jewish is palpably demonstrable.

I have written elsewhere of Stein's affirmative if only symbolic use of Yiddish ("Yet Dish") as a metaphor for modernist language use and sensibility: "only symbolic" because Stein, as a German Jew, never spoke Yiddish (though Alice, as a Hungarian Jew, may have; Stein called her "my little Hebrew," indicating that she felt Alice to be "more Jewish" than herself), and she certainly doesn't use Yiddish phrases in her work; she uses, rather, the *idea* of Yiddish as a flexible, makeshift emergency condition collage-n that stretches across homelands and host lands, history and geography. To conflate Czeslaw Milosz's phrase that "language is the only

homeland" and Heinrich Heine's familiar image of the book as a portable
homeland, Stein creates makeshift homelands in books comprised of language that itself is not stable but portable, mobile, motile. In other words, language for Stein is not the safe haven it may be for Milosz, but enacts the instability that necessarily informs a Jewish notion of home.

Through this practice, Stein valorizes verbal styles—repetition, circularity, "imprecision," unconventional syntactic and semantic constructions—that were despised as primitive, and that were literally thought to mark the speaker or writer as less than fully human. Daniel Boyarin has written that pushing language—both the production and the interpretation thereof—to its limits is a religious obligation in Jewish intellectual tradition. While Stein is not religious, her practice demonstrates the secularization of this tenet with regard to production; Freud's and Walter Benjamin's oeuvres amply instantiate its interpretive aspect. (In Q.E.D., Stein's persona asserts, "I have the failing of my tribe. I believe in the sacred right of conversation even when it is a monologue."[10]) Also, she championed the Old Testament as a model for new (experimental) American writing because of its stylistic tendency toward parataxis in "Lecture II: Narration." Erich Auerbach makes the same point in *Mimesis*, which is generally accepted as a response to the Holocaust he was surviving in Turkey—and, interestingly, complicity is not a charge commonly leveled at him as it is at Stein, who pled for the Hebrew Bible's centrality to Western culture in 1935.

At the same time, however, Stein's apprehension of the instability of language (and of her concerted experiments in language use) and of domicile does not have the catastrophizing angst of a Weininger, who understood psycholinguistic flux, polyvocality, multiple identity, and diffuse proliferation as atavistic and profoundly detrimental to the progress of a rational humanity. "The psychological contents of the Jewish mind are always double or multiple," writes Weininger. "There are always before him two or many possibilities, where the Aryan, although he sees as widely, feels himself limited in his choice. The idea of Judaism consists in this want of reality, this absence of any fundamental relation to the thing-in-and-for-itself. He can never make himself one with anything—never enter into any real relationships."[11] For him this was tragic; Jews (and women) were the ultimate negation of all that man could and should be, and this nadir of human potential was bodied forth in language use, the medium of exchange in human relations. For Stein, the instability of identity, or its illusory nature, permitted community, social being-in-flux, and relationality to flourish and create new ways of apprehending reality as nonpossessive: "I am I because my little dog knows me. The figure wanders on alone. . . . The person and the dog are there and the dog is there and the person is there and where oh where is their identity, is the identity there anywhere."[12] Knowing that for Stein, "thereness" is a suspect category, one can understand this as a challenge rather than a plaint; the poem, the first sentence of which functions as a kind of talisman sentence for Stein, becomes a treatise on the difference between entity (the unfixability of an apprehended other/object/being) and identity, a need to be fixed, recognized, and given meaning by an other. For Stein, making oneself one with anything, recognizing something in and for itself (whatever that may be), would be the kiss of death, as it was for Weininger.

It would bespeak a naive need for absolutes, however, to impute callousness to Stein's ludic writing; one need only look at work produced during the Third Reich to see that she and other secularized Jews were acutely tuned to the underside of displacement and instability. The tinge of melancholy in, say, *Paris France* or Walter Benjamin's "A Berlin Chronicle" (a piece that makes clear Benjamin's felt relationship between urban *flanerie* and global uprootedness) is not impelled by a thwarted faith in origins but rather by the thwarted desire (to be encouraged) to explore through memory and language the processes of memory, language, and human being itself. This exploration had been these writers' most compelling raison d'être. The wistful meanderings of these works in style and content—tentative here, sure there; sketchy and aphoristic here, humorously detailed and obsessively developed there—enacts a nonidentitarian, historically contingent "Jewish" writing practice that is most beautiful and exemplary where (and when) it is most under the gun. The fear in Stein's and Toklas's I.D. photos for wartime travel and the excessive absurdity of Benjamin's unnecessary suicide indicate both the fragility and resilience of this living-in-style, this lived style, this writing life.

Dis   playst Readings

The phrase "Painted Lace," the title of volume 5 of Stein's unpublished writings produced during and after World War I, and much affected by it, is also the title of a short work in that volume. The phrase offers a marvelous metaphor for the sense of redundancy-that-is-not-redundant, gilding the lily, "independent embroidery" (the title of another poem in the volume), a sense of performative excess that is, nonetheless, not expendable. Yet another title in that volume, "Emp Lace," combines the two phrases and simultaneously fractures the word "emplace(ment/meant)," whose militaristic positionality is untenable in a nomadic, free-range exilic language style implied by lace, by "independent embroidery." What can "emp lace" mean? Caveat emptor: language as commodity, as excuse for world warfare, is being "unmeant," emp-tied and untied, loosened like lace that lets the light through, like a writing we can't read straight and shouldn't, if we want in on the shaggy dog joke, the endless yarns spun by an amused, Fate/fé/friend-of-Faÿ/lady-fairy who never cuts that thread after all. In the art of lace, threads derive their aesthetic power from interplay with negative space, emptiness (which Weininger claims to be the essence, insofar as there is one, of both Jews—"the absolute Jew is devoid of a soul"[13]—and women), just as Steinian non-sense derives its power to "unmean" from the rigidly semantic context of most discursive forms, including that of social science (our special concern here) and its relation to the Jewish question.

Likewise, "Painted Lace" splits, opens, enlaces, and aerates "place" by interjecting a space and the extra lace of "ainted" letters. "Ainted" elaborates and negates ungrammatically in a stage aside (p-lace is still there, though displaced); Stein is "Arthur/author(ing) a Grammar" (*How to Write*). Decentered? You bet. Weininger's worst fears flaunted: himself, the Jewish homosexual, in drag, camping it up, reveling in his/her defects. "I'm a Jew, how 'bout u?" Stein teases Wein's ghost, by performing her tainted JEWOMANISH writing in calm, experimental tones. "What happens," the Jewoman scientist asks," when we separate these two letters p-l?" Oy, such cold experimentation, treating language as if it were dead matter: Jews excel in the field of chemistry, says Weininger, because "they cling naturally to matter, and expect to find the solution of everything in its properties."[14] Unlike Goethe's, the greatest genius of Weininger's imagining, Stein's work is not about feelings, not about individual self-consciousness developing ethically. Vey iz mir! It doesn't track like the transparent thoughts of the male Aryan, oh mighty hunter he, following the lettered spoor of the Great Idea to its Godly punctum, a humble manger that is the origin of all meaning. Instead, the fat lady's text winds around and around, has no beginning and no end, not even any middle or edge. It's all marginalia to itself, Talmudic bordering on borders, embroidery that has taken off from an always-already infinite regress of no regrets and plenty of RSVPs.

As its name suggests, the section of "Painted Lace" entitled "Voice Lessons and Calligraphy" addresses, among other subjects, writing style, composition, the relationship between orality and graphology, domesticity, and the "feminine" arts. By presenting both media (speaking and writing) in terms of refined, mannered mastery of a relatively old-fashioned (and thus cosmetic, frivolous) finishing-school type of art, Stein foregrounds the artificiality, the *madeness* (constructedness, as we might say now), of both speech and writing, anticipating the Derridean controversy and placing herself in the stream of the latter's argument, that is, in accord with his challenge to the supremacy and presumed anteriority of "the Voice." The section opens with "Independent Embroidery," which phrase operates, as suggested above, as a kind of governing trope for "Jewomanish" language use: diffuse, elaborative, inauthentic and defective, according to Weiningerian Austro-liberal values. Within this section, a short poem called "The Reverie of the Zionist" concludes:

> I saw [say?] all this to prove that Judaism should be a question of religion.
> Don't talk about race. Race is disgusting if you don't love your country.
> I don't want to go to Zion.
> This is an expression of Shem.[15]

Insofar as Jews are racialized, race should be uncoupled from nationalism; the notion that countries should be the provenance or teleological punctum of particular ethnicities was abhorrent to Stein, who loved living in France and also, from a distance, at least claimed to love America, but had no similar feelings about Zion. Some have read this piece as Stein's repudiation of her Jewishness; however, the argument that Jews did not constitute a "race" was a popular one among progressive Jews, anthropologists Franz Boas and Melville Herskovitz among them, in the interbellum period. Concerned about the anti-Semitic repercussions of how National Socialism had scientized (racialized) the Jewish question, they took the position that Jews should not be persecuted on the basis of race, and, in order to argue this, attempted to demonstrate that Jews were not a racial group. Moreover, in line with these secular Jews, who on the one hand were not particularly observant but on the other hand did not want to be perceived or persecuted as a race, the last line suggests that the foregoing ought to be a legitimate opinion to hold *as a Jew*. The piece appears to be shot through with contradictions; the "reverie" of the Zionist is anti-Zionist, Stein deliberately distances herself from some Jews ("Can we believe that all Jews are these") while claiming the right to speak as a Jew, and so forth. It must be remembered that the word *reverie* may have had negative overtones for Stein, who stubbornly resisted any charges of mysticism in her work and who saw herself as a phenomenological empiricist, tracking the minutiae of the changes of human mind for the pleasure of it—a disinterested scientist. Thus the Zionist is indulging in pipe dreams; Zionism is the opiate of the Jewish masses. The piece also betrays some anxiety. How to rationalize a situation whose irrationality threatens to (and nearly did) overwhelm and exterminate an entire people? The apparent contradictions also enact the internal heterogeneity, the contentious pluralism that comprises the Jewish interpretive community. These concerns about the nature of race and its relation to geography run throughout the rest of the volume, particularly in "Landscapes and Geography: 1925–1934," in which the words "natural" and "national" are juxtaposed,[16] and in which the ideological manipulation of social categories such as matrilineality, difference, and race or religion are subject to inquiry:

> Can a Christian father have a Christian mother.
> Yes.
> Can a Christian mother have a Christian father.
> Yes.[17]

> It is very necessary that natural phenomena are usual. It is very much it is very much used it is used very much in that way.
> There are three Negroes they do not at all resemble one another.
> Moreover there are three Negroes Negroes and women five of them and they do not at all resemble one another. It is not at all astonishing that one seeing them and seeing them knows very well then that it is another thing.[18]

When Stein writes, "Authorize natural phenomena,"[19] natural phenomena are understood to be that which can be written, that is, constructed creatively, as in "arthur a grammar." Nationalism and claims of naturalism are both systems of meaning created by and not anterior to the human mind, "never having been meant to be Natural Phenomena"[20] as commonly understood—that is, as bio-essential hard-wiring. However, "Natural Phenomena" is also queer girl sex: "Aroused and dedicated to natural phenomena . . . pearly and seized."[21] What has been declared deviant by racial nationalist logic is as natural a phenomenon as landscapes, geography, and writing. That is, it is all authored, all emptied, all painted lace, a vocal exercise.

One could say that even progressive anthropologists espouse Weiningerian teleology when they appeal to the twin virtues of hard science and humane citizenship, that Enlightenment legacy that ended, as they knew but did not want to know, in Auschwitz. While there is, obviously, a vast difference between racist and antiracist anthropology (and its cousins philosophy, "characterology," psychology, sociology), they share some ideology. Stein's language experiments eviscerate the truth claims of the modern(ist) achievements—rationalism and liberal morality—that the philosophers and scientists noted here continue to cling to. This evisceration carries with it a different set of risks, which are becoming apparent in a world where, for example, Jean Baudrillard could claim there was no Gulf War. Stein's work, however, neither collapses into despairing self-immolation nor issues prescriptives in a tinny, would-be heroic resistance to history. Relatively early in her career, it seems, Stein abandoned the idea of progress to which her coreligionists were tightly bound, but she did not do so in a gesture of nihilism. And while thematically her writing continues to participate in their concerns—concerns about her own survival—her writing process and practice have already created an escape route, a "line of flight." Her work doesn't strive to get "there"—no landscape, nation, or race except in words, and even those words are not a place but a naughty, knotty   emp   lace.

5 Imp/penetrable Archive

Adeena Karasick's Wall of Sound

And, as the welcome of a welcome,
(incarcerated or deported, persecuted, traumatized
and obsessed), i am writing a writing that opens from its own
threshold, erupts in withdrawal in carnal-soaked
codes, naked liaisons rapt with all that is trivial,
tragic suffocating

and oppressive. all that is sacred and
elliptic resting in jagged syntax breeks
irrupts

—ADEENA KARASICK, *adeenakarasick.com*

Nothing that has ever happened should be regarded as lost for
history.

—WALTER BENJAMIN,

"THESES ON THE PHILOSOPHY OF HISTORY"

Kitsch allow[s] us to look outward from within objects.

—WALTER BENJAMIN,

"SOME REMARKS ON FOLK ART"

IN THE 1960S (the Jewish) Phil Spector pioneered his famous
Wall of Sound, which he employed to greatest effect with his
equally famous girl groups, most notably the Ronettes and Tina
Turner, but also the Righteous Brothers, the Beatles, and the
Ramones. The Wall of Sound was an effect of thick, sonorous
resonance, an echoic "fat sound" achieved through dense layer-
ings of orchestration, often featuring unusual instrumentation
for pop music, against which a powerful vocal soloist would hold

her own. The technique was this: many musicians on diverse instruments, ranging from standard rock-and-roll fare (drums, electric guitars, bass) to the symphonic (violins, harp) to icons of other genres (acoustic guitars), would crowd into Spector's small studio and turn it into an enormous, reverberating echo chamber. All playing the same melody, the instruments would nonetheless subtly retain their differences in timbre, effect, and affect, as well as their minute differences in timing, thus creating a polyvocal dis/unity that is at the same time a fretful, multidimensional swirl of unrest and self-difference that stimulates, simulates, represents, and embodies emotional charge, which, given the banality of most of the song lyrics, is necessary to add texture and interest, as do the singers' vocal qualities, which are often rough or complexly appealing (Tina Turner, Veronica Bennett). The hum of the (human) universe can be discerned in the Wall of Sound, and, though compelling, it ain't necessarily pretty. The oceanic expansiveness of the sound, acclaimed for its super-resonance, also evokes dissonance, terror, displacement, and loss that is "river deep, mountain high."

A few not-so-digressive notes on this loss: listen to Tina Turner's "River Deep, Mountain High," a paradigmatic instance of the Wall of Sound. In the opening lines of each verse Spector wrote, "When I was a little girl I had a rag doll / the only doll I ever owned," and "When you were a young boy did you have a puppy / who always followed you around?" The voice ascends from lower pitch to higher registers at the words, "If I lost you, would I cry?" as if whipping itself from fear to assertiveness, from vulnerability to toughness, from childhood to premature adulthood that palinodically (*we're not orphaned children anymore*) reinvests transitional objects with animistic life (*oh yes we are*). Turner's voice is mournful, palpably full of tears over the loss of . . . childhood, innocence, love, self, home? As the verses progress, Turner's voice achieves her signature rough howl; her protests of the depth and height—the insurmountability and submersive dangers—not only of her own emotions but those of diasporic histories (the Red Sea, the Middle Passage, Mt. Sinai, the River Jordan, the mountaintop from which freedom can be glimpsed though the prophet may not get there . . .). According to rock-'n'-roll legend, Tina Turner became so overwrought in the recording booth that she tore her shirt open as the song reached its climax. More fundamental to the entire sonic empire edifice of the "first teenaged tycoon" (a common epithet for Spector at the time of his emergence), the title of Spector's big hit, "To Know Him Is to Love Him," was his father's epitaph; Benjamin Spector, a Russian emigré, committed suicide due to financial difficulties in 1949, when Spector was eight years old. Further, as Paul Gilroy has analyzed in a discussion of the gender standoff in popular African American musical idioms, the violence visited upon diasporic family structures reinscribes itself as self-mutilating gender relations in a displacement of these communal and familial traumas. Both Tina Turner's and Ronnie Bennett Spector's memoirs detail the physical and emotional abuse they suffered at the hands of their musical genius husbands; Phil Spector, now seventy, is serving nineteen years to life for killing actress Lana Clarkson.

Thus one can read the Wall of Sound as an aural cenotaph for those lost in diasporic lines of frightflight, submerged in "all that is trivial," to cite my first epigraph—in this case, the many near-kitschy recorded artifacts of a brilliant though troubled career of a popular music producer and his star musicians, who were more often than not people of color. The Wall of Sound is an instance of diasporic excess, an instance in which the creator cannot bear to leave anything out, cannot let anything that has ever happened be lost for history, which in this case is acknowledged through the sonorous temporality that is part cacophony, part melodious unification of effect: a secular, popular cultural, multivocal Jewish counterpart to the subaural registers of the cathedral organ that are said to induce visual and visceral feelings of oceanic awe in listeners of Reformation church music. This subaural force is so powerful it is believed to cause, if not actual visual hallucinations, at least a strong sense of a spatial and spectral presence, a visitation from a being who is/is not there, the transitional objects of "River Deep Mountain High"—rag doll, puppy—banal in themselves but the focal points of desperate attachment for the orphaned that stand in for an intuited but ungraspable and irreparably lost state of wholeness.

Spector's aesthetic legacy finds resonance in the creative world and work of Jewish Canadian feminist Kabbalah scholar and poet Adeena Karasick, especially the tour de force "The Wall," the centerpiece of her book *Dyssemia Sleaze* (2000). Like Spector's pop masterpieces, "The Wall" (like all of Karasick's work) teems and swarms with excess; in this case, an excess of history, sonically (as well as architecturally and visually) embodied in the ambiguously female "voice," not only the poet's but the Wall's itself, as it represents a similarly ambiguously feminine principle. "The Wall," in which the Western Wall of Jerusalem becomes, like every other apparent topic toward which Karasick turns her deconstructive imagination, a trope for Jewish female relationship to language, history, and spirituality, is, like Spector's Wall of Sound, an oxymoronically spectral monolith, a seemingly solid edifice that on exploration and closer experience reveals fissures and discontinuities, roughly striated and textured differences, competing threads of narrative, dissonant sound, and conflicted history, an archive of turbulent feelings delivered in a maelstrom of kitschy grandiosity and dazzling style. Perhaps the Wall/poem is more than a trope; it is a space that Karasick's imagination inhabits, as one inhabits an animated spiritual object in order to see how it contains the entire cosmos. One can look outward from within its animated (coded feminine) interiority. If not one scrap of history is to be lost, as Walter Benjamin implored his intellectual heirs on the eve of his death, the habitués of this echoic world, like Veronica Bennett and her cousins singing outward from within the raggle-taggle orchestra's overwhelming buzz, must be *scrappy*: tough/vulnerable, street/glamorous, gamine/gamy, derivative/authentic survivors making life strategies out of exaggerated eye makeup and beehive hairdos and voices as grainy as they are melodic. This fractured, bubbly compendiousness, as well as the sense that one is being spoken to from within a condition of overwrought (hysterical, coded female, teetering on the banal) expressiveness, characterizes all of Karasick's work (not to mention Spector's): a title like *Dyssemia Sleaze* and the cover of *Même Wars* (itself a mockery of the self-disclosing genre associated with feminine mass culture), which shows Karasick with her face half-concealed by illuminated letters, in boxing stance and gloves, amply carry forth the combined urgency and triviality of a postdiasporic, feminine Jewish logomania. The "structure of feeling" of her performative persona and of the volumes of poetry is, to repeat, *scrappy*: simultaneously earnest and ersatz.

A semiotic analysis cum poetic paean addressing the many issues embedded in and performed by Jerusalem's Western Wall, the piece collects the detritus of almost two thousand years of diasporic history (and, of course, a much longer history as a people in more or less a place, albeit a history that includes slavery, exile, and what is now termed internal displacement, though that term suggests, anachronistically, that there is an "externality") and sets it in stormy relationship with and within itself; the poem is itself a "storm from paradise," even as its topic is the pile of wreckage upon wreckage, the putatively monolithic Wall caught in the storm. As the embodiment/dwelling of the Shekhinah, the indwelling spirit of whispering and listening, the Wall is the pile of self-different wreckage, the roaring windstorm, and also the angel of history it is buffeting away into the future.[1] The poem "The Wall" itself, of course, is all these things as well: a tsunamic wall of words and images bearing down on the reader, a chaotic pile of junk, a roaring whirl and whisper, a messenger frightened of its prophetic task approaching the future butt-first, Chaplinesque.

Yes: what if Benjamin's angel of history, Paul Klee's drawing *Angelus Novus*, were, in fact, ambiguously female: the Shekhinah as comic gamine? What would be the ramifications of recognizing the angel of history as the breath of life, of language, of poetry, in a feminine principle that is not strictly speaking female? For while images of bound and gagged or open-mouthed women and praying men fill the pages of "The Wall," and *Dyssemia Sleaze* more generally, the opening passage of the former reminds us, in cut-out, punk, ransom-note lettering, that the binding/sacrificing and family violence foundational to Judaism is not only not restricted to women but takes the form of cruelty to children and fratricide:

ACCORDINGTOANCIENTISRAELITE

TRADITIONSTHEWESTERNWALL

STANDSINFORTHEBINDINGOF

ISAAKAKEDATYITZHAK

ACCORDINGTOMAIMONIDES

ITISALSOTHESITEOFARAVNAHS

THRESHINGFLOORISTHEPLACE

WHEREABRAHAMBUILTANALTAR

TOSACRIFICEHISSONISAACAND

WHERENOAHEMERGEDFROMHISARK

WHERECAINANDABLE[SIC]OFFERED

SACRIFICEISTHESITEOFTHEARKOFTHE

COVENANTANDTHE

SYMBOLOFTHEDWELLINGPLACE

OFTHEDIVINEPRESENCE[2]

Gender is a central concern for Karasick, but not in a binaristic way that would simplify the history our angel represents, any more than the Shekhinah, a universal capacity (as everyone has indwelling spirit) that is figured as female, is present only for or in women. Angels are ungendered but generally presumed to be male; Benjamin's comment on the ephemerality of a print journal of his time suggested that angels are ephemeral as well: "according to a legend from the Talmud, even the angels are created—new ones at every moment and in countless hosts—simply to sing their hymns before God, then to cease to be and disappear into nothingness."[3] It should not be impossible to shift the perspective, then, and imagine an ungendered but feminine-inflected counterpart to this tragicomic figure: Chaplin's gamine, like him a scrap of expendable humanity in the eyes of an instrumentalist majority culture. If the Wall is a pile of rubble, the wreckage of the past, it is necessarily an archive; the angel, also, is this archive, this mountain of refuse away from which s/he is being driven by the whirlwind. A whirlwind, by the way, within which there is no still small voice but a babel of cacophonous girl-grouped dys/harmonies: a whirlwind that is a Wall of Sound. The poem is likewise a cacophony of fonts, formats, and voices, illegible print superimposed on photographs, visual and verbal puns, prayers, send-ups, and equivocations.

Of all the things the Western Wall and this poem about it are, the archive is a useful if somewhat arbitrary metaphoric point of entry. An archive, as we all know, is a repository of significant documents and meanings, importantly centralized as its etymology—*government, town hall, rulership*—implies: any historical edifice saturated with cultural significance could be called an archive—this Wall, for instance. An archive is also, as we also know, and as we wish government and rulership were, a site continually productive of knowledge; it swarms with activity; it is an arch-hive. Its business—its feverish buzziness, one could say—is impressive, vibrant with both regally official document and semiodetritus ranging from the quotidian to the eccentric, from the mundane to the otherworldly, from the constant to the ephemeral. This Wall that doubles as a hive is full of, erotically athrob with, plant and animal life, as well as its more famously noted spiritual and national life, and the attendant affective, literary, and expressive aspects of Jewish life; one page of the poem shows, in a repeating image symmetrically organized, doves perched on the ridges of the stone blocks making up the wall, over which a Star of David is superimposed; tufts of grass growing from between the Wall's cracks, and the unevenness of the stones themselves, cast shadows that look like writing.

In Karasick's A.D.D.-MTV-ish world, it's hard to distinguish movement from stasis, organicity from inorganic material, human writing from accidental tracery, the significant from the less so. What counts as knowledge, what counts as a "find" in an archival quest, in a descent into the teeming underworld of source material? Which of the myriad competing factoids or docu-fragments in the rubble heap of information and human culture is the philosopher's stone, the holy grail, the nectar of the fountain of youth, knowledge or redemption, the centrifugal funhouse map of the through-the-looking-glass promised land? We make it up as we go along; knowledge on this path through uncertain space—the poem, the sound, the Wall—is always becoming. Each of these archives is a divine and human comedy and each has its multiple points and paths of entry, its orifices, its tunnels of love, its birth canals.

The stepping-stones on one of its paths of access are the letters of the alphabet, that great, mystical, dynamic ecosystem that has held us in its web since premodern times; every letter is an archive of feeling, of meaning, of specific spiritual insight, as the Kabbalists have elaborated. The interaction between the archivist and the contents of the archive (or here,

the orant orifice and the oracular edifice: the page facing the dove–Star
of David Wall is entirely taken up by an enormous, wide open, sensu-
ally lipsticked female mouth—Sandra Bernhardt's—both aggressive and
vulnerable) speaking to each other across time within the "container" of
materials is productive and continual, and changes the materials and the
container as it changes the archivist. The body likewise is an archive continually reproducing itself, a repository repositioning itself at every turn, a
body in performance remade, remaking itself in poeisis and autopoeisis in
every context. The Wall, with its multitude of cracks and fissures stuffed
or unstuffed with paper, reads like a female body whose orifices have
been dammed up with a range of never-quite-effective "feminine hygiene
products" intended to ward off danger both internal and external precisely
in that liminal space where blood emerges, where speech emerges, where
seed and succor penetrate. (On the other side of the Wall, of course, is the
Dome of the Rock, a political danger in the nationalist narrative but also
a graceful, hovering image of androgynous architecture.)

The female performance poet (Karasick, but also Ronnie/Veronica
Bennett with her *beehive* hairdo, and with her multiple ethnicities in constant conversation within the Wall of Sound) embodies all of these: the
archive, the interactive site, the (coded-female) reproductive body spew-
shpritz-ing verb effluence as if it were a bodily fluid (which it is), all that
material set in diasporic orbit around the flailing, stuttering body, a world
unto itself but sited among other worlds in chaotic interdependence,
transience, and tangency: Adeena Karasick, Jewish Canadian feminist
performance poet and author of *this* "Wall," a chaotic, palimpsestic meditation plastered on the see-through semiotics of the Western Wall (all
over it, as we say, like a cheap suit), is an arch-ark-hive of activity whose
manic mellifluid production fuels this inquiry into the beehive-archive,
the honey in the cavern, the crevices of walls honeycombed with writing,
the queen of the drone of barely distinguishable syllables bubbling malleable as beeswax. In this postmodern performative medium and with this
premodern thematic material, modernism is archived by being sand-
wiched between the pre- and post-cursors to which it has given its name;
it is the content that announces itself as substance ripe for redefinition,
ready to be put in its place (twixt the twin walls of pre and post), though
that place is noplace. (Nationalized Jewishness as modernism sandwich?)
In fact, Karasick's overstuffed archive could be figured not only as sandwich spilling over with organic matter but also as a teenage girl's jewelry
box, chaotically ajumble with bright baubles and genuine treasure, kitsch
transfigured by sheer juxtaposition and effect, a shimmering disorganiza-
tion of syllables and letters vibrating against each other in a pageant of

Collage from "The Wall" in the book *Dyssemia Sleaze* by Adeena Karasick. Courtesy of the artist and Talon Books.

According to the Temple traditions, one of the major reasons the Western Wall was considered to be so sacred is because historically, it is where the Ark of the Covenant had stood, and therefore houses the Shekhinah. Each stone, fissure, crevice emanates what historically has been deemed as female presence-non presence. But perhaps "female" should be re-read in this context as a perverse dynamic which houses a multiplicity of identities that have been marginalized – a trope for all who embrace the ambiguity of a culturally produced identity – a performative s/cite for mobilizing the exigency of différance.

Derived from *SHKN*, "to dwell", the word *Shekhinah* was used by Rabbis in the 1st C. TO INDICATE God's presence in the world. Commonly read as the *female* principle, the term itself is never actually employed in the *TORAH BUT IS ALLUDED TO IN A VARIETY* of other related forms: such as *Mishkan* (TABERNACLE: ALTER OF SACRIFICE), *Mashkon* (surety, indebtedness), *Shkhena* or *Shachane* (neighbour), *Shekhivah* or *Shakhantie* (to lie, rest, dwell amongst), and *Mashka* [(skin as in "spread your wings over me and cover *ME WITH SKIN*")].

However, though *Shekhinah* is most often referred to as *female*, according to the *Zohar*, the *Shekhinah* is described as "...sometimes male and sometimes female". Referencing both **"the erectile organ of the vulva"**, **the scission, the cut, THE WOUND** and the *ateret berit*, the corona of the phallus, s/he thus questions, interrogates, **any possibility of a strict** sublimity that is, at the same time, "touchingly primitive." You name it, she can trope it.

Since the year 70 c.e., the date of the burning and destruction of the Second Temple (rebuilt on the site of the first, which had also previously been destroyed), the Western Wall—or, more colloquially (but disavowed by formal definitions as tinged with anti-Semitism), the Wailing Wall—is the primary site around which the Jewish history of displacement and diaspora is organized; it is the sole remnant of that rebuilt temple and hence both a simulacrum and a token of an "authentic" past, a past that encompasses Isaac and Abraham, Cain and Abel, Noah's ark. The Wall comprises premodern forms of writing whose cultural significance was established during the modern era using the narrative strategies of modernity (the rise and fall of great civilizations, the coming to consciousness of individuals against that backdrop, the "right to a homeland," and so on). Now in a postmodern deconstruction/demonstration, those forms of writing become postmodern. The forms of writing that constitute the Wall, a bricolage and border of eras, civilizations, religions, materials (grass, stone, mortar, paper, animal life, and the shreds of paper containing prayers in many languages that are stuffed so pastiche-ishly into those crevices and fissures that are within human reach) also are the elements of Karasick's performances. The Wall appears to be static, a stable referent, a literal monolith in that it is built of stone, and it has certainly been a symbol around which acute if belated (perhaps particularly anguished and acute *because* belated) battles of nationalism have been pitched, just as millennia earlier, violently destructive battles of imperial and religious rivalry and dominance created the absence that is now filled with a plenitude of melancholia, resentment, and other toxins, as well as serving as the wellspring of grief, sustenance, consolation, and meaning that have been attributed to it. Karasick offers a version of Jewishness and of the Wall that provides something of an alternative (though also ambivalently continuous) narrative to the scene of permanent exile and/or desperate and/or triumphant return to a point of origin, a teleological trajectory that ratifies the modernist tale of rising and falling, coming and going and going and coming, and, in the case of Jewish nationalism as ratified in 1946, always too late (pace Mel Brooks).

Instead, Karasick proposes, or intuits in Jewish thought and particularly in its mystical underpinnings as made explicit in the Kabbalah, a form of diaspora that remembers but does not fetishize a point of origin, that entertains the possibility of an originary moment or site but does not posit one as fact, that recognizes such a hypothetical point of origin as useful and dangerous a fiction as all others, and that sees language itself, rather than a lithic edifice, as the terrain in which this flux of departure, return, circumvolution, orbit, diasporic fragmentation, and fables of origin and exile performs itself: "all that is sacred and elliptic resting in jagged syntax." The Wall is itself a linguistic structure, and language itself is multilithic. Not only has the Wall's importance been narrated into being, but its crevices and crannies are literally filled with tiny bits of writing, scraps of paper on which supplicants have confessed their deepest desires, which are then shoved into the Wall to literalize a verbal offering—which is both gift and request—to the God whose absence and presence are embodied and negated in this porous, penetrable rockface. Language can be lithic and static, as we see in the nationalist narratives that have dominated the modern era and that are trying so hard for a last-ditch comeback right now; Karasick's job is to unbuild it, to reinject it with short-fuse phrase fragments and swirls of expressive deliquescence, to limber it up and dismantle its aggressive mask of rooted stasis to show the (s)warm inside its archival aliveness, its anarchival, rhizomic exuberance. Karasick aims for an ex-stasis, the ecstatic outside of, within and beyond formal fixity, an ex-ile or ex-ilium, repudiating isolation (island) and Ilium, the Trojan war that set in motion, through exile and diaspora, a narrative of empire that enslaved the Jews.

For Karasick, the Wall is also an archive of ethnoracialized religion and culture, etc., gender, sexuality, nation—as Jewishness and its relation to space, place, time, and the broad and narrow socii it has been embedded in have been variously figured over the millennia of its emergence and evolution; her task is to demonstrate, to perform through both the multimedia text and her own performative style, that is, through her body, its instability and downright volatility, its permeability, its corporeal and theoretical vulnerability. Karasick's descriptions of the Wall as a fluidly interlinking series of systems, including as a regulatory mechanism of knowledge, a psychic system of memory and forgetting, a governing figure of subjectivity, and a space of embodied experience, have enlivened some of the possible ways in which we might conceive of hypernationalized, hyperpoliticized, hyperspiritualized, hypertextualized locations in relation to cultural critique. At the same time, her exploration of its significance in contemporary culture in its social, political, historical, and material contexts raises vexing questions about the Wall as a set of practices, as an apparatus, and as a discursive network (ho hum!).

This notion of language spatialized, which can't help but assume political dimensions, is forecast in an earlier Karasick video poem, *Alphabet City*, which dramatizes the gridded lettering of Manhattan's Lower East Side, or Loïsaida, as it is known by its largely Spanglish-speaking population. Home to the Nuyorican Poets' Café, Alphabet City is currently the site of great verbal and artistic creativity as well as urban ethnic hybridity. Though this grid of Avenues A, B, C, and D constitutes, at first glance, an entirely different kind of space, historically, aesthetically, and culturally, from Jerusalem's Western Wall, Karasick finds in both sites a rich, fluid wellspring for lingual poiesis, down to the level of letters themselves, a poiesis that she in turn mediates through her bodily, textual, and oral performance as she herself claims a space as a wellspring for poiesis, not as Author, capital A, but more as focal point for irruption, as the dramatic narrowing of a flowing body of water increases its power and spectacularity. Likewise, *Mumbai Ya*, another video poem, plays with over-the-top silly puns and opulent images of South Asian/Hindi kitsch: "Hello Dahli," "kiss my sari ass," and so forth, in a disorienting and shape-shifting send-up or performance of orientalist identification. Her performances, as well as some of the visuals in her printed work, enact aggressive displays of sensuous femininity—fashionable, borderline commodifiable but joyously assertive in their foxiness—reminiscent, perhaps, of Ronnie Spector née Bennett in the Ronettes' heyday as Spectorized spectacle as well as auracle, and certainly of Tina Turner, with an umbral edge of diasporic tragedy. Like the Ronettes and the post-Ike, 1980s comeback Tina Turner, Karasick uses her hair to construct a relationship with her audience; in her case, her face, in both the video and book-cover photographs, is never fully visible. The look is alluring rather than shy, because the one visible eye is looking directly into the viewers'; the human veil is a turn-on, what Alfred North Whitehead has called a proposition: a "lure of feeling," coaxing the reader or viewer into direct engagement. A bodily performance must make an investment in the aestheticized self that is generatively open—generously risk-taking. The danger of "falling flat," always present in such corporealized work, lends it some of its interest, as in (I can only hope) the overload of corny puns with which I sometimes freight my essays. The willingness to incur charges of excessive self-regard a woman faces when she performs her looks, her body, her need to be seen, to be read, indicates a certain urgency and vulnerability; the visceral discomfort it can engender in an audience is often one of identification gone awry, a skewed empathy that reacts against itself as judgment of the other. While much of her work is undisguisedly Jewish in content and methodology (as she has put it, Kaballah is not defined by its religious content; it is an interpretive strategy), her performances, which draw on a heavily Brooklynese spoken-word intonation, and her video poems, which do not address Jewishness directly but rather use linguistic and performative strategies of displacement and cultural-geographic transformation, nonetheless undermine assumptions that there is a Jewish essence, identity, or quality that preexists the act of writing (even the major argument of "The Wall" is that the most holy site of Judaism is an ongoing self-construction that "writes" itself in the historically layered words of its supplicants, celebrants, and critics). Her performance in *Mumbai Ya*, moreover, intimates that ethnicity is no, uh, forgive the expression, sacred cow; that is, Jewishness itself might be characterized by "an aversion to identification—. . . a practice of dialogue and . . . an openness to the unfolding performance of the everyday."

From *Alphabet City* to "The Wall," Karasick returns narratives about space and place embedded in material sites to the linguistic realm, be it sonic or visual, disorienting the concept of sitedness in the meanwhile. Is a Jew a traveling, corporealized archive functioning in modernity to preserve the premodern and foretell the postmodern? Or, to rewrite my earlier trope, is a modern Jew a modernism sandwich in reverse, all modernism on the outside that protects (I first wrote "protests") an inner anachrony, a defiant simultaneity that gives the lie to the neat linearity embedded in the "pre-nonprefixed-post" continuum whereby we arrange our relationship to time? Whatever; perhaps this modern Jewish exhibitionist/self-concealer is our Angelus Novus, our celestial trampette blown backward, robe billowing in Marilyn-manquée clumsiness cum grace. Of course, a Jew is no more simultaneous than any other person—anyone can be an archive!—but Jewish thought and the current Jewish cultural studies can bring a useful perspective to these contemporary musings. At the least, Karasick's work multiplies how "Jewishness" might look, sound, act, and interact; how it might be *read*.

Moreover, the notion of architecturalized lettering is a distinctly Kabbalistic one, with a deep exegetical tradition and the special place occupied therein by textual materials in the most literal sense; this tradition, compounded by the prohibition against pictorial representation, means that letters themselves become descriptors; they are their own illustrations. "A" doesn't stand for "apple"; "apple" stands for "A." Karasick's commitment to the materiality of language down to its smallest elements, letters and phonemes, is also at work in a later post-Wall project: an English-to-English homophonic translation of the *Sefer Yetzirah*, the first and oldest book of the Kabbalah, which has been published in her most recent volume, *The House That Hijack Built*. "Homophonic translation" is a seriocomic genre, formalized by Jewish American objectivist poet Louis Zukofsky, in which sound rather than meaning is the connection between source text and target text, or product. As the *Sefer Yetzirah* is the Book of Creation, it and Karasick's distressing of it (subjecting it to chemically transformative processes as Marc Jacobs might distress fine fabric for a punk-sleaze look)—her hijacking of this sacred text—constitute creatively deconstructive processes rather than merely products, a recreation of language and of the text that reveals new meaning (and hence new realities beyond those bound by ethnocultural specificity) through the slippages such homophony incurs. Thus one might use the term *poiesis* rather than poetics to emphasize the incompleteness, and the desirability of such incompleteness, of process. Hinting at the textually violent, mutilating aspects of the project as well, Karasick, in her words, "[carves] out ways in which this text could be dislodged from a socio-religious and historically-limiting hermeneutic." Thus, this morphously polyverse, self-inflicted, and seemingly purposeless—that is, an English-to-English homolinguistic "trans'elation," as she puts it—translator's task is actually a monumental, though demonumentalizing, undertaking of reworlding or unworlding, and one that stays true to the import of the book itself, as its "focus," as Karasick explains, "is on the 22 letters of the Hebrew alphabet" (how they were formed, how they interrelate, how they make meaning). The text itself is inscribed through slippage, elision, rupture, and undecidability, and language is foregrounded as "a continuum of letters, names, mathematical equations, gates of meaning." Here are the first several lines of the piece, with the "translation" in boldface above the already translated source-text:

With dirty tombs, sticky pathos official isms
With 32 mystical paths of wisdom
riveted, Yeah
engraved Yah
The Horde of Ghosts
the Lord of Hosts
a Grid of serial
the God of Israel
lifting, Gedichte
the living God
connaisses or verse
King of the universe
Of shady
El Shaddai
Mercy, flanged rations
Merciful and Gracious
Honeyed Exiles . . .
High and Exalted . . . [4]

If one did not know of Karasick's serious and longstanding commitment to Kabbalistic scholarship, one might take this as an attempt at sacrilege, but this intertextual rend(er)ing is an homage, albeit a feisty, cheeky, and daring one that takes eye-opening ludic liberties. It is also recreational activity in another sense as well: it is pleasure and eros. "I do it because it makes me feel good," Karasick says. "It soothes me." It is also a process of recreation as self-creation as doubling; we know from Gertrude Stein that English, or any language, is never the same when it is revisited: you can never utter the same word twice. English to English, ashes to ashes, sweets to the sweet, taste my honey honey, it's never the same anguish, the same lashes, the same master suite; and the archivist, the poet, is never the same poet as she was, will be, or even is. Archive and archivist, poet and poetry, angel and rubble heap change places and become each other fluidly, seeping into each other through active cerebral and bodily—bawdy—engagement. Kabbalistic study itself has been, for Karasick, an exercise in self-creation. When she began this self-initiated apprenticeship to her culturally specific language mysticism at age eighteen, no one would teach her, as Kabbalistic study is traditionally an activity reserved for men over the age of forty; the local yeshiva to which she turned for instruction offered her a diluted version. Since then, she has sought out teachers to work with her one-on-one and has cobbled together a diasporic patchwork of mentors and teachings in a praxis well in tune with her penchant for palimpsest and bricolage, and one mimetic of the Wall itself as it emerges in her altervision an architectural, historical, and textual crazy quilt (constructed by a swarm of quilting and spelling bees) whose bristling textemes and rough surface materialize letters, meaning, sound, and the word, testifying to their livingness, interdependent mutability, textilic/exilic multiplicity.

As beekeepers in an ark-hive of activity, it B-hooves us readers to understand something about the bee herself, that tiny, restless archive hovering tumultuously under the sign of bee-coming, who guards her living, glistening trove with maternal ferocity. The an/archive is alive with materials self-created by bees, its geometrically perfect walls dripping melopoeia. Approaching, we understand the danger to which our investigations commit us: all beekeepers die of anaphylactic shock sooner or later; instead of becoming immune one becomes more sensitive. You don't assimilate it; it assimilates you. Human becomes antihuman, inhuman, or posthuman as your allergic reaction is written on your body; hives and rashes, welts and archive fevers; page 54 of *Dyssemia Sleaze* shows Richard Avedon's eerie photograph of a naked man covered with bees and a line-drawn stringwig for maximum-creepoid X-Files effect. Marked as and by the archive, you *become* the archive, involuntarily at that; contrary to your original foraging intentions, you are the prey while the archival material is predator; the material becomes the archivist acting violently on you and you become its source material, the burning welt world words written on your flesh yielded up to be mined, explained, exploited. Lanced, your boils and welts ooze viscous language, a bodily fluid symptomatic of illness, invasion, corruption. Honey is gall to be retransubstantiated by any means necessary—through extrusion, expulsion, abjection, exile, reproduction, birth, mothering. Your archival sputum gums and gels into a language-web, that prison-house where you catch and are caught, the labyrinth of labial excretion that turns mortar into honey and walls into wombs, permeable and bruised, endlessly generative in their degenerative uncontrollability. The bee, a natural alchemist, excretes or secretes (sex-cretes?) its own gold, its own shelter, its own workshop, its own book as portable homeland where it conceals or reveals its own secret, "a secret that bleeds, is infected, swells and pu(l)ses in the gaps. Is always already a secret within a secret that only another secret can explain."[5]

Moreover, its beeswax commands a venerable place in the history of Western writing and domesticity as fuel, energy, sealing wax, writing, printing, unit of monetary exchange or tribute payment, modeling, casting and painting material. Wax itself, medium for earliest phonograph sound, has been invoked as a liminal material, a becoming-material, as in recent critical comparisons between wax museums and cinema, media that interface between animate and inanimate, creation and dissolution— transitional media that harden, soften, and then melt thoroughly, becoming in turn opaque, translucent, and wholly clarified. Playing out the relation between wax and cinema further, the dissolve shot in French is *fond enchaîné*, or sequential melting (enchained melting, a vividly erotic image); and we are reminded by its etymology that a "ghetto" is an archive and an ark-hive: a foundry (place of melting and casting) to which Jews were sequestered during the Italian Renaissance. Both a melting-place and a foundation (from *fundere* and *fundare*, respectively), the Wall and the body of the performing female poet are citational nonsites of transformation, exile, elixir, palimpsests, and gridded g/riddles where heat solidifies and liquefies. The techniques of the essay poem "The Wall" also enact the dissolve shot in the sense that there are close-ups so close that their details become grainy or fuzzy; layered sequences of medium and meaning melt into or through another (one could say they "bleed" into each other, emphasizing a family resemblance between wax and blood that foregrounds the female abject).

Honey, need it be said, on the other end of the abject-idealized continuum from wax, is a primary metaphor for eros, treasure, beauty, sensory delight both internal (taste) and external (visual pleasure)—as we learn most notably from the Song of Songs, the holiest book of the Hebrew Bible for the Kabbalists. Honey wine, or mead, is the premodern Anglo-Saxon kenning for poetry: it is the mead of Odin, who stole it from a giant, who stole it from an elf, who killed a nomadic sage made from the combined spit of gods and men, mixed into honey his blood, which became mead, the poetic mother-lode. (In other words, the feminine abjection theorized by Kristeva the Bulgarian Jew would not differ so dramatically from the divine poetry of the hypermacho Nordic gods, if history did not teach otherwise.) In contemporary as well as premodern and modern Ethiopia, as in pre-Christian Norse culture, where poetry was known as "Odin's mead," copious consumption of mead and honey beer accompanies poetic cutting sessions, where spontaneous oral poetics are spun by competitive cognoscenti. To speak with honeyed tongue, though, honey, simultaneously suggests deception, dissimulation, as in disingenuous simulacrum and danger, as poetry, a gift, is also a toxin (gift being, etymologically, poison); the bee's venom is indistinguishable, at some register, from its honeyed legacy, its exilic elixir. Honey, venom, and wax range along a transubstantial continuum saturated with anthropophagomorphemic signification. Forgive the Christian vocabulary (transub., etc.); Spector's Wall of Sound was also crafted to resonate with a "Gospel" sound, sneaking a diasporic Jewishness in under the heavy cloak of sonic buzz as the stranger, in Edmond Jabès's title, smuggles into his host city a "tiny book" in the crook of his arm. Perhaps an appeal to the Kristevan body fluid resonances of these viscous materials—sound, honey, venom, gall (gift as sacred potion/poison)—would be more appropriate, but I hit on the orality and consuming/devouring notes of this transub/succubus bouquet as well. These sticky substances are produced in the ark-hive, house of the bee and home of the scripture, beit, the letter "b," the bosom of family valuables.

And further: we need, in this belle-letteraturistic Kabbalistic world we enter when we enter Karasick's honeycomb, to understand B, Beit, the little house of the second letter, the tiny arkhive residing in mysterious fulsomeness under the sign of B-coming, the shelter (the ark) that clothes and covers the sacred words of history and spirit. Though it is the second letter of the alphabet, Beit is the Bginning, as it is the first letter of the Torah; with this letter God created the world. The belatedness of B, its deferral, implies a second-rate standing, woman created from man, or a B-grade movie; Karasick implicitly participates in a feminist project at the most atomized level when she elevates the standing of the B in her oeuvre.

While Alef, the first letter, is silent, encompassing all sounds, Beit as a consonant introduces form without which all would be chaos; it is thus a domesticating, Apollonian, aesthetic ordering principle, just as the Wall signifies in its materiality a world of affect, history, time and space unmoored. Like an arch-hive, Beit is an arched structure or a shelter, like the absent temple, already the Second Temple, a replica of the first, at which the Wall's partiality gestures, and like the Dome of the Rock "behind" it, a graceful haunting present shored up by the pastness of the Wall; the B references a structure which is not there, like an ultimate signified or an inaccessible, invented and infinitely inventable and inventive, past—one wall of the Beit is missing, creating an opening for full circulation of the universe or, in other terms, of the Real; that wall, one could say, is next year, that is, never and always already the wall in Jerusalem.

Having thus taken to heart Benjamin's exhortative description of/to the historian that s/he leave not a scrap of the past uncollected, Karasick exults in scraps and detritus, verbal, material, and otherwise, and unbuilds a wall by showing how scrappy and disheveled the Wall actually is, made up of shards and debris, a collage of verbal ghosts and letters to God, love letters to letters of the *alef beit*, every alphabet an archive, every letter within that alphabet an archive that is, among other things, a space of embodied experience, so that words written in stone are not fixed but just as fulsome and living, as ghostly and shimmering, as ephemeral and elusively persistent as words inscribed on flesh, wind, water, or other physical elements, as sound; stone is as permeable and vulnerable as flesh, as skin, as spirit or other animal or human elements; history as malleable, evanescently alive, and performative as culture, as art, as dreams or any other imaginative zone or body of activity.

> And, just as the stones of the Wall (layers upon layers) are not whole, but broken, cracked and weathered, they are structured like a language (mimic the ideological cracks in the surface of a complex and inaccessible, non-linear grammar). A language marked by fractures, contaminations, durational spaces, chronic mochery, crutches, leeches, ruptures.[6]

Fond enchaîné indeed: the photographs in the poem dissolve harshness into grainy softness, staunchness into permeability, stone into paper which trumps rock which trumps scissors which trumps. . . . In an interview conducted before the work's publication, Karasick explains how this artifact of origin and fixity becomes a kind of sacred, ritualistic girl-child's play, feminized and kinked up through its means of production and reproduction. She describes the then work in progress as an extensive full colour poetic essay on how the Wall (the Wailing Wall) is structured like a language. And I find that working with different typefaces, fonts, layering letters upon letters in a very physical way . . . foreground[s] language as a material body. . . . And, all the collages, assemblages, graphic intrusions are all constructed with purple gluestick, manicure scissors & transparencies. Some people go to fetish bars. I go to Kinko's.[7]

As suggested at the outset of this dyssemic oddessay, part of what animates this recovery of the Wall as multiform unconscious, as a site of polymorphemic and heteroglossolalic per- and multiversity, is the coded-feminine Shekinah: breath and poetic inspiration; our Holy Ghost, our kitschy muse with manicure scissors in hand, an animating visitation associated with the interior, with air, wind, and fire, with feminized (interior) pink bedroom space, but also with the adolescent angel-tough voices lofted by the Wall of Sound. Ronnie Bennett Spector as (non-Jewish) Shekhinah as angel of history? This realm of culture is the B-side, the B-girl, the B-lated archival matrix, Eve the second human, in which nexus nests and rests the next rest of the language and all verbal imp/possibility. The beehive Adeena herself—the "poem itself"—the Wall itself—becomes B-Eve, that tatterdemallion in shattered medallions garnered from the war of bleeding words; like a Joanie-come-lately of Ark she leads the holy war against forgetting and language loss, the restoration and preservation of all archives, all bodies which are archives which is all bodies.

Though Jewish linguistic tradition is at the center of this investigation and practice, the above description of a gaminesque liberty-lady of language (Wall as Statuesque Libertine?) should not be understood as the sole domain of any one group of people, ethnically or otherwise determined. Multiple ironies abound that cannot be lost on anyone reading this book—anyone, that is, invested in poetics, pre- and postmodernity, Jewish cultural life, radical, secular, and so forth. Not only was the 2002 invasion of Iraq (arguably the birthplace of modern alphabetic writing), undertaken with an eye toward "stabilizing the Middle East," accompanied by archival destruction that beggars description, but the uncertainty and conflicting reports about what archaeological, artistic, and textual treasures were lost or retrieved are themselves symptomatic of conflicting desires to forget, remember, destroy, retrieve, remake, declare solidarity, repudiate connection. Not intending an indecorous aestheticization of serious and volatile political matters, I note the weird way that, at the time, archive fever seemed to grip the *New York Times* and other major mainstream U.S. news venues over the looting of Baghdad archives and museums while less was said about the loss of Iraqi life, medical supplies, water, food, civil and civic life and infrastructure, more. (Years later, though anxiety about archival damage has been much allayed, the focus continues to be on lost American life as the main tragic outcome of the war.) A new wall has appeared in Israel/Palestine, harshly political, cordoning off and reifying nationalist intentions, interfering with Palestinian daily life, underscoring and shoring up a duality (us/them) on which modernity has already foundered. There are urgent and immediately contemporary political undertones to be deciphered from the Wall, though one can read them without going there. While other pieces in *Dyssemia Sleaze* touch on the political suffering of Israel's current others-within, especially "Mehaneh Yehuda" (Jewish Market, site of a Hamas bombing in Jerusalem in 1997) in which the word "HAMAS" is multiply glossed, "The Wall" stays inside a Jewish context; eruptions and challenges come from within, from feminism, from a diasporic take on place and space, rather than from an investigation into the Wall's precarious proximity to Muslim worship, its role in sustaining physically a holy site of Islam, and what that Janus role might say about current anguish on the other side. Perhaps Karasick's dual approach—an intentionally dysfunctional hyperglossic outpouring combined with lovingly careful attention to the minutiae of the letters to which *Dyssemia Sleaze* is dedicated

(. . . these letters which t/ravel together,
mysteriously united, one stretched towards
the other, one emerging from the other's side, one
suckling the other; folding in on these letters i belong to
that carry me and dance both within the pages
of this text and as social, historical
effects of reference)[8]

—can offer tools for processing all of these losses, and perhaps this essay is a tiny bioverbal thread pulsating, penetrating, and interlacing the constitutive body of freedom (an Invisible Wall), working athwart its political closure, running sonic sustenance across the lines. Perhaps, and more likely, this is wishful thinking; a radical poetic practice within the world of "Radical Jewish Poetics," "The Wall," not allowed an oppressive materiality, does not explicitly extend beyond or behind the Wall to embrace that Wall's political, linguistic, sonic others, *nos semblables, nos soeurs*, trapped behind a Wall of Sound.

Part 2

Poetics for a Postliterary America

6 Kinetic Exultations

Postliterary Poetry, Counterperformance, and Micropoetries

> Yes, pappy, i went to kollage, but what the Hell has that to do with poetry?[1]

> Should I sing a requiem as the trap closes?
> Perhaps it is more fitting to shout nonsense.[2]

> Jokingly invoking the death of Jimi Hendrix
> I find myself vomiting all over my copy
> of the *Princeton Encyclopedia of Poetry and Poetics*.[3]

CREATING NEW INTERLOCUTORS in and out of the academy is an apt description of what we do when we teach: in the academy—at the graduate level, since at least in theory many of our students are training for an academic life; out of the academy—at the undergraduate level, since, at least in the public land grant institution I'm in, our students are bound by and large for lives of bare and secular survival (as, in fact, we and our graduates are as well in these anti-intellectual times). If they can carry into those bare survivalist lives a kinetic memory of exultation occasioned by the poetic and by exercising their own apperceptive faculties at large, and if they can find resonating experiences in their intimate, public or professional lives, the revolution in poetic language can claim another victory by stealth, however subtle, diffuse, and even invisible to the instrumentalist eye. "We must multiply poetic subjects and objects," wrote Guy Debord, and this serves as an incisive mandate for the poetry/pedagogy enterprise.[4]

The inarticulable poetic experience I want to facilitate in students has everything to do with empowering citizenry, though what this citizenry does with its power must remain open even to anarchistic impulses, as that's often where new societies are envisioned. Thus, the word "citizenry" here does not index what Stanley Aronowitz warns against in his essay, "Is a Democracy Possible?"—the argument made by Jefferson, Dewey, and Walter Lippman that a people imbued with high culture through a formal education constitute the entirety of those fit to govern.[5] On the contrary, as my examples demonstrate, the poetry that inspires this putatively charged citizenry does not have to be academic or even the product of educated literacy, and in fact, this "citizenry" overlaps with what Rachel Buff terms "denizenry," a looser term that implies the ambiguously embodied/illicit/disempowered socius that may not reach the visibility of the "citizen."[6] I hope to create in the academy an environment where these expressions can be understood and reflected on *as* poetry. That is, the ill-literate, extraliterary, alter-literary, or postliterary need to train the conventionally literate in new ways of hearing, reading, seeing, experiencing, making the transparent opaque and the opaque transparent. New knowledge travels from the ground upward and outward.

And one more necessary element in this discussion is not a revision (many of us understand the following as axiomatic) but an *emphasis* on the audience (listenership) as cocreator, as makers, as poets. Such audiences provide new interlocutors, new conversations, emergent communities of urgency, that can't necessarily, as Giorgio Agamben has observed, correspond to any current understanding we now have of the word "community."[7] Not that newness is new; newness itself is infinitely renewable. *De Vulgari Eloquentia*, written almost a millennium ago, is rewritten by every avant-garde and every ideology of salvation, only to be recuperated and rearticulated, and each time with threads that can't be woven neatly into the juggernaut of normative text; shreds of resistance, of quirky paths out of centricity, hang off the edges and await our enjoyment and engagement.[8]

Everybody's going on about pedagogy, from rigorous left-radical theorists to the No Child Left Behinders, with the in-between liberal touchy-feelies weighing in as well. The reason is clear: with the shrinking of a meaningful public sphere that includes an operative democracy, people turn to the classroom as the putative site of nonviolent conflict and change (minor disclaimer: antiglobalization demonstrations are trying to reassert the power of street action). The problem with this model, however, is that it is already nondemocratic. Etymologically, *pedagogy* betrays a discourse founded on condescension, to which even those of us who work with adults over eighteen can fall prey. The word is used compulsively and unreflectively in graduate programs that require teaching as a form of intellectual labor, in practica and other such workshops (though some

POETICS FOR A POSTLITERARY AMERICA

nontraditional programs have introduced the term "androgogy" into their discourse). One troubling aspect of "pedagogy" is that when it comes to poetry and I suspect most other things, it has the idea backward: "we" teach/lead "them." This "we lead/teach them" thinking is a dead end. Instead, as poet Jack Spicer wrote, "Poetry comes to us through the young . . . and that is why we need them."[9] Young people in general (and one could usefully expand this category to include other disenfranchised people), as well as our students, who are our structural if not chronological juniors, are producers, conduits, and rapt consumers of the poetic. As such, they lead us and sharpen our sensibilities. Sometimes they are us. They're the ones constructing and instantiating new publics, new republics that will tease Plato's shy poetry out of hiding beyond the walls of *Republic XIII* and make it, or him, Plato, queen of the garden. They are themselves a defense of poetry.

Postliterary Poetry

I will start by delineating the contours of "postliterary" poetries and "counterperformance." In so doing I have several intentions, including showcasing artifacts from these realms of gold: video stills and transcriptions of Bob Kaufman, and of some performers at a Minneapolis poetry slam: Adam H, aka Blac-Q, aka lbn Mujaheed, a freshman at Macalester College when the tape was made; and TW, a member of the Twin Cities recovery community and participant in a neighborhood poetry slam. It is hard to convey in perfunctorily made videos of live performances (the Loft, one of Minnesota's literary organizations, taped the slams to prove to their funders that the events had indeed taken place) the passion one can feel from and for language that bridges the vernacular and the literary. Nonetheless, I want to turn my workplace, the academy, into a place where this language is valued. And part of this project, as it has been for other subjects under revision such as gender (rearticulated as "gendered" or "sexed") and race (reimagined as "racialized"), means challenging the category of poetry itself, and how poetry is conceived of in a liberal humanist context—rewritten here and multiplied as "poeticized material," "poetic activity," "poetic events." Again, the situationists' take on the subject of the poetic, which entails a revision of the conventional meaning of the word "poetry," is: "The domain we mean to replace and fulfill is poetry . . . realizing poetry means nothing less than simultaneously and inseparably creating events and their languages. The moment of true poetry brings all the unsettled debts of history back into play."[10] We might also say, with potter M. C. Richards, "Poets are not the only poets."[11]

My epigraphs are also artifacts. The first two are from poets who, despite the relatively decorous diction of these particular lines, were not decorous poets: they were street poets, whose stints in prison, the Merchant Marines, psychiatric hospitals, and the military gave their lives what institutional contours they had. In these epigraphs that are also epigrams, Jonas and Kaufman call into question the relationship between formalism, the academy, poetry, and the sense of urgency that compels that poetry. So does Ed Morales, a Nuyorican poet in both senses of the word (he is a New York Puerto Rican who writes poetry, and he is associated with the Lower East Side's Nuyorican Poets' Café), who did go to college but, as is obvious from this passage, maintains a fine sense of irony about its benefits. Perhaps it is more fitting to shout nonsense. What the hell's kollage (spelled collage with a "k") to do with poetry, indeed? This is a question that I, as a professor whose department has allotted me the field labeled contemporary poetry to graze in, face daily. My approach is not primarily formalistic, and academic poetry is pretty boring to me; yet  "the poetic," "poetry" itself, blazes through my waking sleeping mind like a comet so large my head can't hold it, my tongue can't tell it, and my body dies when I can't get it. So this chapter is someone's attempt to move into a new perceptual field unbounded by discipline, where we have all moved all along with muscles we may have forgotten but poetry hasn't. With respect to postliterary poetry, performing on the border means performing in the zone where vernacular meets academy, where disciplines are undone, where street and workshop are one.

Minus its Lacanian frame, John Beverley's *Against Literature*, whose subject is Latin American literature, offers a roadmap that gets close to what could be done for poetry in the United States.[12] Beverley investigates the ways in which nonliterary genres like *testimonio* and revolutionary poetry throw into crisis the tight and cofoundational relationship between official politics, nationalist self-representation, and literary production, even in as revolutionary a context as the Nicaraguan revolution, in which most of the key players were poets as well as military or political actors— their poetry and their understanding of what poetry (and all of literature) is was formed by a classically oriented literary education; and, paradoxically, Ernesto Cardenal's Solentiname experiment faced a crisis when these classically trained revolutionary literati couldn't handle the so-called crude poetics of the newly literate peasantry they had given their lives to uplift. Unlike in the Latin American situation, where literature has always been explicitly understood as a nation-building enterprise, Anglo American literature and its critical apparatus has posited itself at least in the last several generations as resolutely disinterested, apolitical, and esoteric (pace the Kennedy/Frost and Clinton/Angelou inaugural spectacles). To some extent, even those of us who came up intellectually in an era that proclaimed that everything was guided by a politics, this political influence or agenda was assumed to be tacit, especially when it came to poetry. The elitism and racism of the New Critics had to be teased out through attending to and eventually condemning their silences. Thus, we used the close reading skills we'd learned from the New Critics and Agrarian poets to flush out their unspoken or sotto voce faith in the hierarchies of class, gender, and race, which had given them a primary spot of dominion and privilege. This technique, of course, continues to validate a certain type of poetry, the type that needs "unpacking" or decoding. Even in the wake of the canon wars and poststructuralist and materialist critical incursions into the world of discourse, there remains an anachronistic reluctance to speak of poetry in other than formal or thematic terms. The narrative arts—novels or films—on the one hand and mass-produced mass culture on the other have been the beneficiaries of the innovations of politically charged cultural studies, while poetry—especially, I'm sorry to say, contemporary poetry—seems to still be encased in its golden cage, with the most adventurous work limited to close readings of heretofore neglected women poets, and "neglected" means that fewer poems of theirs than of their male coevals and friends appear in the standard teaching anthologies. There are, of course, exceptions, and I could list young scholars who are closing the gap (among them Zofia Burr, Joseph Harrington, Robert Kaufman, Eric Selinger, Jeff Derksen, Sianne Ngai, and Michael Chasar), and poetry journals such as *XCP: Cross Cultural Poetics* and *Poetics Journal* do include materialist critique, but it is still difficult to find (U.S.) writing about (U.S.) poetry that is not simply literary criticism rather than cultural critique.

And while in other circles the field of cultural studies is already mourned as having become trivialized, as having abandoned its class-based analysis and its political commitments in favor of Shakespeare-with-a-twist or the playful deconstruction performed by subaltern subject Imelda Marcos on the Filipino people, it has steered clear of poetry, leaving it until recently in the hands of the critically unengaged. That biographies of well-known modernist women poets, institutional histories of poetry studies, or critiques of anthologies are big news in the poetry world, that people still argue for the viability of the spoken word because of its mass popularity, and that Adrienne Rich is seen as either revolutionary (because of her politics) or retrograde (because of her roots in Boston formalism) are cases in point. An author-based, canonical version of cultural studies has been incorporated into poetry studies: "Homosociality among the Romantics," "Was T. S. Eliot really anti-Semitic?," "Reassessing the official Frost biography." The National Poetry Foundation's "decade" conferences (poets of the 1930s, 1950s, 1960s, and 1970s) are arranged largely by author (three or four panels on Ezra Pound in the 1950s!), as are the conferences of the American Literature Association, a coalition of author societies. Certainly these scholarly projects can be imaginative, rigorous, exciting, insightful, and profound. But in sum, they contribute to the existing matrix of either dominant literary texts or standard appreciative or critical practices rather than challenging them, reinforcing a static conception of what literary studies can be. The depoliticization of cultural studies as New Historicism (complete absorption into the normative textile of literary discourse, like a stain that didn't) provides a cautionary tale about the limits of disciplinarity.

In terms of aesthetic representation of nontraditional or heretofore noncanonical writers, the scene is no more promising. As for poets of color, if their work is formal and decorous in the lyric tradition, like Rita Dove or Michael Harper, their poetry is accepted as a token in this matrix of dominant literary texts. There was less black nationalist verse in the 1988 *Norton Anthology of Modern Poetry* and hence less black representation tout court than there was in the 1974 edition. The numbers are creeping back up again in more recent editions, but this dramatic enactment of the dictates of historical contingency constitutes a direct and unambiguous lesson in the politics of canon-building right there. As for vernacular poetry by people of color, that's called folklore. Even Henry Louis Gates, Jr.'s *Signifying Monkey*, which is a brilliant argument for the foundational significance of a piece of vernacular poetry, is primarily, in literary critical circles, cited for its insights into the already deemed literary work of Ishmael Reed and Zora Neale Hurston rather than for the theory of culture it posits in the earlier part of the volume.[13] Small wonder, for Gates frames his own work this way. Even his foray into the world of the spoken word (mass/popular culture's poetry castrated of the scary P-word) was tinged with a distant be- and a-mused professional condescension, as if vernacular remained a slightly guilty private pleasure rather than a front-and-center facet of literary life (the way my father regarded Yiddish); Gates wrote in the *New Yorker* on a certain orally delivered poem: "I don't see it making the *Norton Anthology*, but it has a certain vigor, and the crowd cheers and whistles its approval."[14] "*The Norton*" still reigns as arbiter for this ambivalent lover of vernacular. With the exception of a handful of texts that are dubbed folkloric or ethnographic (such as Steven Caton's and Lila Abu-Lughod's studies of poetry as social practice among Northern Yemeni men and Bedouin women, respectively), Barrett Watten's rigorously materialist critiques of his contemporaries, or refreshing anomalies such as Charles Bernstein's uncategorizable ur-shpritzes whose main characteristic is humor, poetry studies are mostly in the lite ages, up where the aether is pure; they cling to their isolation, as if that loneliness made them pure.[15] (The *ressentiment* that surrounds much writing on poetry, including this essay, is an effect thereof.)

It takes this isolation, in fact, as testimony to its specialized role as prophetic genre. For example, in an old interview, Jorie Graham discusses intelligently her most recent work at that time, which drew heavily on a rich polyvocal chorus of competing voices, including those of Wittgenstein, Benjamin, Plato, and Brecht. But then, refuting the claim that contemporary American poetry is "elitist":

> what can I say to that? A country becoming increasingly poorly educated, producing some of the most culturally illiterate children in the world a country willingly narcotizing itself via radio and television should pray desperately that some few crazed idealists might devote their lives (on behalf of the culture I might add . . .) to raising the consciousness, the aural and sensate capacities, of their culture. Or no, not raising it, but restoring gifts truly innate though repressed by corporate rapacity and the willingness of people to be raped.[16]

This is the quintessentially liberal plaint and appeal to high culture as socially salvific, of which Aronowitz complains in the essay alluded to earlier. It is possible to make the argument for poetry as counterdiscourse or antidiscourse without divorcing it from the concerns and practices of everyday life. The suggestion that people are willingly deprived of their oral and literary traditions overlooks the resistances that have been raised against co-optation, the flexibility and ingenuity of living traditions struggling to thrive in hostile circumstances, and, in fact, the social, communal, and often oral/performative traditions that make up even contemporary poetry's origins. TV, radio, and other public venues can indeed be stultifying, but they can also be reimagined as dynamic contributors to a social renaissance of poetry and poetic activity. As in the early poetry of Paul Beatty (now primarily a novelist), the media can become subject matter and suggest formal techniques (such as flow and rupture) for much brilliant verbal play.[17] The image of the anonymous masses, drugged by a debased culture and in need of rescue from themselves, suggests a narrow conception of what poetry, poets, and poetry scholars must be.

And for the most part, cultural studies in turn have written poetry off as a priori high cultural, ergo unrecuperable. This is due primarily to the conflation of "poetry" with "lyric," so that the Frankfurt School's critical theory addresses poetry as lyric at length, while the Birmingham School's cultural studies tend to eschew lyric and hence "poetry" as such almost entirely, although they do attend closely to the "poetics" of subcultural or subaltern dress, associational trends, affect and gestural style, even song lyrics, without conceding that there may be a relationship between these and "poetry" as conventionally understood. In its U.S. manifestation, the scenario is particularly ironic, because, far more than narrative written genres like novels or essays, poetry in the form of ritually charged incantation has been central to the cultural traditions of many subordinate people in the United States and elsewhere. Nonetheless, because of a perception that poetry belongs to an elite, as well as what Kurt Gegenhuber has aptly termed "poetry anxiety" on the part of professional literati, the stand-off between cultural studies and contemporary American poetry continues.[18] Given this situation, I hope to be forgiven some general, provocative-to-some, old-hat-to-others polemical statements, such as: Academic poetry is dead on arrival (when I gave this talk in my own department, 'twas considered a challenge; at SUNY–Albany, people yawned). Performance studies, cultural studies, postcolonial studies, and ethnic studies are more fitting arenas for the study of poetry. It *is* more fitting for academic intellectuals to shout nonsense, as Kaufman speculates, or at least to learn from trying to do so and feeling like idiots. In postliterary poetry studies, we'll be listening to the cries of infants with fetal alcohol syndrome and drug addiction; we'll be attending meetings of Persons With AIDS support groups and taking in personal narratives and anecdotes in settings where it's not permitted to record or transcribe them, or even repeat them to others outside those rooms; we'll be going to slams in bars and community centers, writing on housing project walls. And we'll be attending as participants, not simply as scholars who want to support, document, and study people who are not us. I feel the need to add, though it should be obvious, our investment in these practices is not simply for the aesthetic frisson these languages elicit but for what they can tell us about our own human situations; they will, in fact, be life sustenance for us not because we are "studying the other" but because we are ourselves those persons with AIDS and the parents of addicted infants. Many of us already engage in these life-sustaining verbal processes, protesting, as many of my students do, "but I don't *do* poetry," "but I can't *read* poetry." Well. We can shout nonsense, and if we can't yet, then we teach what we need to learn. This is an appeal to poetry studies, that we bring to it a new aesthetic infused with a sense of solidarity and commitment, that it be touched by an *engagé* cultural studies.

A postliterary poetry is comfortable with its own politicization, not necessarily thematically but in its production, distribution, and reception. Its producers will not necessarily receive MacArthur awards and NEA grants, though they may; there will not be one name on everyone's lips—"Oh, that's the postliterary poet." In a postliterary world, letters speak, and there is writing without words, sidewalks burn with language, textiles whisper names of the dead, and the wearers of mass-produced or "hand-crafted" garments hear these names in their sleep or as they walk, legs chafing in pants made in Singapore, the Phillipines, Macao, Eastern Europe. More modestly, the postliterary also includes orality, slams, 'zines, and open-mike readings with underground cachet and unpredictable energy. It can't be contained; there isn't a bordered field large enough to feed a world that hungers for poetry like bread. But on the borders there's poetry enough for everyone. Who knows how perpetually liminal utterance will sound or look? Poetry itself is revolutionary—the academy can only gain by loosening its bleeding grip on a thorny, withering bouquet.

Counterperformance

I want to look at the possibilities of counterperformance on several levels, especially as practiced by poets of marginalized groups in American culture: young people, black people, street people, and various combinations thereof (young black men and women, old black street poets, and so on); at how proper notions of public declamation are vitiated by the performance itself; and how performance signifies differently when the performing subject is a traditionally subjugated person. For example, the indigent Bob Kaufman's mumblings (he'd lost his teeth, and went intermittently without false teeth), monotone, and physical fragility contrast with the biting wit and lyrical control of his verse. His few public readings, which foregrounded his frailty and physical abjection, form a marked contrast to more conventionally dramatic renditions of his poems as recorded over the years by professional actors Ruby Dee, Ossie Davis, and Roscoe Lee Brown, instantiating different performances of "blackness." In another instance of performing blackness, BlacQ/Ibn Mujaheed/ Adam Harden and TW, among others, took the Twin Cities by storm in November 1993 to place as winner and finalist, respectively, in the series of poetry slams that accompanied the Nuyorican Poets' Café tour. The power of their performance lies variously in their unpolished styles, in the beauty (and yes, there is a place for this word in the postliterary, but that place is not static, or even a place) of their committed language, the timbre of their voices (untransmittable through this print medium), in the unorthodoxy of their presences.

Standard literary and liberal humanism values rhetorical clarity, whether the discourse is accessible language or linear argument, formal integrity or audibility—all these values speak to an ideal of sound mind in sound body and similar clichés. But Tricia Rose, among others, has written of black cultural forms such as rap that privilege distortion of normative aesthetics and muddiness of sound (for example, the hyperbass, which is allowed to "leak" into empty tracks of multitrack recording systems in order to achieve a "phat" or blurred sound) and whose aim is to break car stereo speakers.[19] Likewise, phantasmagorical dreams of completeness and coherence crumble in the face of Kaufman's performance. When Kaufman barely audibly mumbles, "Way out people know the way out," you know he's "way out there, never coming back," as he himself once observed about Van Gogh (one of his few possessions, in the last decade of his life, was a coffee-table book of Van Gogh reproductions). He performs unwellness, dis-ease and instability, physical frailty and incoherence, but at the same time, with a ceremonial dignity that aestheticizes him in the positive sense of the term as the ghost of the underclass disappointed, the ghost of dreams of the great society, civil rights and black nationalist gains; as a figure of disappointment and of beauty, he both empowers and terrifies. Now, this is problematic. What has been criticized as a misogynistic necrophilia of Western literature's love of the beautiful dying woman, or the patriarchal aesthetics of worshipping the muteness of the inspiring female figure, becomes here a classed and raced aestheticization of, in this case, a dying black man in pain. Granted the man is a poet, an actively self-conscious producer of meaning, but his mode of meaning-making is so different from the scripted role of the modernist iconoclast or the black power poet that to use this figure to recuperate him into a familiar type would be disingenuous. And granted, the poet is a man, but his masculinity is so different from the scripted roles of maleness, black or white, that to dismiss him as part of a patriarchal tradition would be pointless. Indigents are not supposed to have bodies. Their bodies are problems, targets for policing through policy and through physical abuse. And poets are not supposed to have bodies. Their words on the page, their words about their bodies, are supposed to transcend all that. Their disembodied job there on the page is to awaken feelings in the readers' bodies; hence the model of reading poetry as a solitary, charged adolescent experience. Bob Kaufman's fragile body, his mumbling, amphetamine sweat and disoriented mien, do not merely underwrite our trained pathos for the privileged but suffering (white) male poet whose body is shattered but whose voice is intact, or who, like Robert Lowell, fueled his poetic achievement with the pathos of his mental illness at war with his patrician legacy. Instead, the complete fragmentation of Kaufman's presentation denies any comfort, confronts the audience with the end results of poverty, addiction, and racism: that wasted mind that is the terrible thing, within an equally wasted body. Since much of his delivery is incomprehensible if not inaudible, showing this video can provide a signal opportunity for exploring with colleagues and students the possibilities of "hearing" at a different register from that hearing we bring to normatively intelligible discourse; to paraphrase George Lipsitz, one can learn to listen by listening to learn here.[20]

Adam Harden's/BlacQ's/Ibn Mujaheed says about his November 1993 poem, "This is the first piece that I wrote when I came out here to go to school."

> I sat down in my college lounge thinking I had made it, that I am free
> of the bullet spree,
> and it came to me.
> I look down at my young black body, no bullet scars can I see,
> but still, it came to me.
>
> I avoided the attraction back home.
> Many of my boyhood friends could not do the same.
> They walked the streets very much in vain,
> But they own those streets now.
> Pushing, surviving, living the only way they know how.
> I held onto my books, increasing in education that could not put gold around
>   my neck,
> gear on my back,
> or a gun on my hip, but they knew.
> My boys knew I was true.
> Mom said your time will come, son, be patient.
> And when graduation day arrived, Pop screamed, "I'm proud of you, son, you
>   did it!"
>
> And I did,
> yet it came to me.
>
> No longer do I lay myself down to sleep to the gunfire lullabies.
> No longer do I see my blue-uniformed enemy
> watching me

every other block I
thought I was free
when it came to me.

That paranoid state of living has stopped for a moment in this gentle college
    land
No longer do I walk the streets with my mother-fucking master plan
So I lay down this night thinking I just might read a little Walt Whitman,
    maybe some Keats
Might even get real deep and check out some
Baraka.
And so on my break I flipped on the TV
And this is when it came to me
Cops
Americas Most Wanted
And the countless half-assed shows of the like
What kind of fucking country is this when it showcases, plugs, and advertises
the violence it supposedly so despises?
Are my urban streets a made-for-tv circus for you fucking suburban clowns?
All you want to see is the crime
while the TV powers-that-be make their dime
and your white boys, well, they want to dance to my rhyme
Stop the madness, stop the exploitation,
stop showcasing what your government views as the plague of this nation.
It's amazing for me
to see
that the massah still runs the show.
Maybe now it's not his slave girl that he sees in his wet dreams as his playful
    little
'ho,
But our neighborhoods, our families, us.

And I thought I was free
But it got to me.

He killed me on the TV.[21]

When Walter Benjamin, in the late 1930s, protested that to give the
masses a chance to express themselves without giving them their rights
was the foundation for fascism, he was not, of course, speaking about the
contemporary multiculturalist vogue.[22] He was speaking about the rise of

POETICS FOR A POSTLITERARY AMERICA

Nazi Germany, and the self-expression of the masses against which he warned was mass rallies in which hatred caught fire. However, the extreme separation of the academy from the mainstream, and the naiveté of the academy's belief in itself as a standard-bearer of and shelter for progressive thought and free and diverse expression, portends a need for wariness about that academy's simultaneous fetishizing of and disdain for popular expression. Here is a poem that both formally and thematically addresses the academic humanities' role in enabling and disabling young people of colors' political and expressive aesthetic self-realization, that speaks to the simultaneous proximity and distance of the academy from the street. Blac Q's poem speaks to the violence of representation from which his new liberal arts home in the Midwest cannot protect him. Whitman, Keats, and even Baraka can't save him from the TV cops; in fact, as Harden's analysis suggests, the *TV Guide* is a parallel syllabus for Western Civ. Though education is his way to be himself, and though he turns to poetry as a salvific from the ravages of the cartoon-like violence that assails him at home and in the Macalester College dormitory lounge, there is no less violence in this world than the one in which his homeboys wear gold and patrol their turf. In terms of his physical presence, Adam Harden looked very young at the time of this performance, younger than his nineteen years; the embodiment of a live reading enhances the power of the words, the control and precision of delivery, the adolescent look and self-presentation. He is and is not literary, as his references indicate; referring to himself as a poet of experience, he enjoys critical feedback on formal matters. He values poetry slams in that they echo some of the old rap-off energy from the eighties. Though he resists the label "hip-hop poet," as have Paul Beatty and Tracie Morris, poets to whom that label has also been assigned, it is not hip-hop but labels that trouble them.[23] Like Duke Ellington, they find categories and the processes of categorizing to be grand canyons of bombast.[24] Blac Q's poetic analysis of the violence of representation and the representation of violence, the distance and the proximity of the academy to those representations, and the disorientation of participating in multiple spheres, demonstrates the power and insight of "student writing" from a young poet whose work bridges the academy and the street. He is, as all of us are, a multiply constructed subject whose several identities, conflicting and mutually sustaining, find their poetic expression formally in a vernacular modernism, and publicly at a series of poetry slams that helped to offset the doubt he expressed to his creative writing teacher, Cherokee poet Diane Glancy, that his writing was "really poetry," like the lyric verse of the other students in the class.[25] He introduced the poem by saying, "This poem's about the alcoholic in my home."

Walk with me Lord through my home
for there lives a disease I can't face alone
I'm imprisoned with confusion and my emotions are in cages
as fear will rise in my mind it reflects on these pages
I don't understand why I'm losing control
So much pain in my heart and despair in my soul
He's feeding a sickness that wants more and more
Incurable pain is beyond my front door
I press my face against the window to see my way out
But this disease called alcoholism has filled me with doubt
I am a voice with no name and no peace of mind
As my own co-dependencies are robbing me blind
So walk with me lord
through this lonely place
So I may survive on your will
And then on your grace.[26]

In a contentious *Critical Inquiry* essay some years ago, Timothy Brennan argued that rap should be analyzed aesthetically rather than sociologically, that is, as epiphenomenal to historical events such as the Los
Angeles uprisings and the quotidian economic disasters that define the
American experience for people of color.[27] This plea, iconoclastic in a limited sense, runs the danger of reinforcing the great and illusory divide
between aesthetics and history that has (accidentally on purpose) crippled
the academy's ambivalent desire to be of use. While literary humanists
debate the status of the political vis-à-vis the aesthetic, artistic and cultural work has outstripped this distinction, evolving forms that are not
recognizable as objects of this debate. TW's poem is one of these, a prayer,
closer to the *testimonio*, that originally Latin American genre indebted to
conventions of religious narrative, than to what we consider modernist
workshop poetry. The poem puts academic discourse about poetry, not
to mention academic poetry, into crisis. While its "formal perfection" or
"doggerelesque" adherence to rhyme is not entirely beside the point, more
compelling is its counterperformative aspect. Post-Foucauldian academic
embarrassment about "confession" is itself embarrassingly beside the point
here. It's inappropriate to run this event through vitiated critique mills, to
protest the use of a term like "co-dependencies" in a poem, or to urge the
writer to use images instead of stating her feelings. Modernist workshop
conventions are not up to the task; different "listening skills" are required.
Like Blac Q's poem, this one participates in several different traditions, but
it's also something new. The confluences of discourses here—twelve-step

philosophy, public prayer and black religious oratory, the dactylic tetram-
eter that by convention places it in a folk tradition, its delivery at a poetry
slam, a mock competition that brings everybody out (street poets, Sunday
poets, workshop poets, closet poets), and the poem's respectful reception
are all fodder for rich analysis. The poem is compelling to me (others have
virtually puked when I've shown it to them) because it performs at the
social, emotional, and aesthetic registers, effecting a felt change of consciousness on the part of the listener who is learning to hear.

Micropoetries

The study of micropoetries entails a dramatic revision of academic approaches to poetry, a turn away from formalism and canonicity in favor
of the microgenres that permeate everyday life. The question would be,
what cultural work does this artifact or this poetic event accomplish? It is
impossible to isolate event from context; they are implicated in each other
to the degree that insistence that poetic material "stand on its own" becomes meaningless. Micropoetries include graffiti, poetry written as ther-
apy, prison poetry, a relative's topical verse, fortune cookie doggerel, verse
using modernist conventions (line breaks, the sudden private aperçu) to
market corporate slogans lasered in gothic script onto wooden plaques,
preslam vernacular poetry, sounds that contribute to a texture of living in
forgotten places. I borrow the term from ethnomusicologist Mark Slobin,
whose study of "micromusics" brings to light new fields for intellectual
and emotional play, that is, research.[28] Among his roster of micromusics
one finds lullabies, counting ditties, family songs that locate an immigrant
family's town of origin generations later. Consider the opening of W.E.B.
Du Bois's "Of the Sorrow Songs," a meditation on a lullaby inherited
from his "grandfather's grandmother," the words of which he doesn't understand but faithfully transcribes syllable by syllable in order to propose
a theory of cultural transmission that constitutes an early and profound
analysis of the cultural, historical, and emotional work accomplished by
slave spirituals.[29]

Approaching these traces, these semiobytes of charged language, with
an attention that transgresses ethnographic, formalist, and materialist
agendas will tell us what we need to know about the hidden life of language, of bodies, of social relations. Studying these bodies of work is
important not because they're whimsical and eccentrically eclectic or
because such scholarship flushes the most obscure verbiage out of hiding (poetics scholarship as ethnoexotica tourism), but because it offers a
texture of reality to proclamations such as "poetry is social practice." As

George Lipsitz observes in "Popular Culture: This Ain't No Sideshow," what might appear to some as a quaint novelty is heavily saturated with meaning that richly rewards investigation.[30] Such investigative work creates an ever more lively and complete sense of the scene of creative activity at the grassroots level.

In my undergraduate poetry classes, two assignments have become the core of the students' encounter with poetry as experience. They must attend a poetry event and write about the cultural work the event accomplishes, and they must research and document a micropoetry. I have received many brilliant and some perfunctory papers. When I described this assignment to a poet friend, he remarked, "It seems as if you aim to increase your students' sensitivity to their sociolinguistic environments—but beyond that?" That is, how do I then make the bridge to the "real" poetry that he writes and publishes? How do I use that "increased sensitivity" to analyze more conventionally conceived of, though not necessarily linguistically or thematically conventional in themselves, "poems"? I guess I don't. Often, the students' records of these shards of language in which they find special meaning become poetically tinged themselves; the process of analysis becomes a creative moment transcending the strictures of an assignment.

Longish disclaimer: Again, I'm not attracted to these artifacts for merely ideological reasons, though often the content of micropoetries and their analyses note political issues such as class, labor, violence against women, and so forth. And of course, since words refer, content at the crudest level of comprehension can't *not* be the partial subject of a receptive analysis. Rather, like the intensity one feels from some music or from authentic conversation, a tonal quality of close attention and respect compels our audience, our careful respect for these resonant and audient performances. To listen to someone who's really listening—to *hear* people listening—initiates collaborative communities. The claim I'd like to make for certain texts that appear to be conventionally representational—and in some contexts in which I've presented them, they've been derided as crude social realism of the most falsely conscious stripe, which misses the point completely—is one that the language poets have foregrounded through their practice and some of their critical writings: it is a useful exercise to listen to these apparently semantically overdetermined texts attending to the degree to which, to paraphrase Bob Perelman's description of an early language poetry principle, "semantics are definitely soft-pedaled but not inaudible."[31] In trying to articulate some powerful apperceptive experience that does not reside in representation alone, or in sonic beauty in a conventionally lyrical sense, I risk invoking what in the sixties was called "authorial voice," a concept that has rightly been criticized as a mystification

POETICS FOR A POSTLITERARY AMERICA

of the writing process and a prescription for the subservience of reader to writer. My intention is rather to understand the degree to which all writing bears traces of a push against the limits of the rationally known, and to delineate, as gracelessly as a drunken boat afloat on the great poem of the sea of language, some thoughts on how to effect receptivity in ourselves, a receptivity to hearing that pushes against limits.

How can the poetic as a shared project illuminate our public and civic relations? The point of bringing poetry into discussions of the public sphere is precisely to counter usefully the divide-and-conquer practice of genre that would dictate poetry's irrelevance to the common good because of its subjectivist orientation. I would argue, following Nancy Fraser's call for more and internally heterogeneous publics in which differences are openly articulated, that because of poetry's *permission* for subjectivity or hermeticism, poetry becomes a completely appropriate venue for clarifying identities, evolving and devolving, that contribute to a rich, ahierarchic heterogeneity composing a thus far hypothetical democracy.[32] While Fraser's critique of Habermas's bourgeois public sphere, and most discussions thereof, do not take the aesthetic into account as a meaningful category, this exclusion is not necessary. Though I'm barely in a position at this point to elaborate the role of the aesthetic itself in articulating the academy to its secular counterpart and in enabling multiple, empowered publics, it seems intuitively obvious that the preceding examples embody such an articulation. These realms of gold are an alchemical ideal, utopian heterocracies empowered by charged talk language, but, like other alchemical heterotopias, they're also always already here.

7 When the Nuyoricans Came to Town

(Ex)Changing Poetics

> Once again we shall discover those motives of action still remembered by many societies and classes: the joy of giving in public, the delight in generous artistic expenditure, the pleasure of hospitality in the public or private feast. . . . We can visualize a society in which these principles obtain. . . . We should come out of ourselves and regard the duty of giving as a liberty, for in it there lies no risk.
>
> —MARCEL MAUSS

Nuyo/Rican

A naming controversy is haunting the Nuyorican Poets' Café—the controversy of Nuyoricanismo. Approaching my subject, the visit of the Nuyorican Poets' Café touring group to the Twin Cities in 1993, I dimly apprehend, behind my back but fast approaching, the wingèd chariot of this controversy swarming like a glorious headful of snakes around the Nuyorican Poets' Café and headed right for me. The fact that a multiethnic touring group, of which only one member was a "classic" Nuyorican—that is, a native New Yorker of Puerto Rican descent—raised some eyebrows in the Twin Cities, whose Puerto Rican population is itself negligible. The term "Nuyorican" arose in the 1970s as part of the politicization and specification of various ethnic, racial, and other populations historically subordinated by social category. According to some, the word came into usage through or simultaneous with the establishment of the Young Lords, a liberation and service organization for New York's Puerto Rican population analogous to the Black Panthers in Oakland. Thus it was from the start a politicized word, a neologism born out of political urgency, a coinage that arose out of a political need to be perceived as historically, geographically, ethnically specific—to be identifiable.

However—and this is an axiom often overlooked by critics of identity politics—the denominator "Nuyorican" was understood and assumed to contain multitudes. Puerto Rican history itself, with its Afro-Hispano-Caribbean indigenous interaction over many centuries and its fraught colonial relationship, first with Spain and then with the United States since the Spanish-American War, makes for a rich if conflictual mix of ethnic, nationalist, and political identities. Its topographical status as island, moreover, makes it a meeting place of transient naval travelers of all kinds and with many different purposes—hybridity in action. This already multiply signifying designator, "Puerto Rican," becomes increasingly internally heterogeneous when transplanted to New York City, a megalopolis consisting of several islands and countless racial, ethnic, social, and economic variables.

Nuyo/Minne-apple: Divergent Populisms

These issues of naming and poetic audience—one problematic among many raised by examination of poetry in the public sphere—come into dramatic focus in another instance of two poetic/social/regional communities in an intense and circumscribed encounter. When the Nuyorican Poets touring group came to Minneapolis–St. Paul, two distinct writing communities came into direct contact. Those two groups were the multiethnic, fast-talking, vernacular-rapping East Coast performance poets of color and the stoic, liberal, middle-class Minnesota writers of free-verse, confessional lyric, epitomized by the Twin Cities writing institution the Loft. These intersecting groups enabled a third group, which had been there all along but whose poetic achievements and potentials had received scant public attention, to come to the fore in the makeup of the cities' writing profile. That group was the urban poets of color, the teenagers and storytellers, the open-mike punks and hard-edged oral poets who had not found their modes of cultural expression sufficiently addressed or attended to by extant venues, be it local publishers, the Loft, the university (which was at the time trying to establish an MFA program in creative writing after years of internal opposition), or other local educational or cultural institutions. The long-term legacy for the Twin Cities, then, was a more overt split between the various writing institutions, which function on conflicting populist principles, and a healthy proliferation of grassroots literary activity. Fissures led to pluralistic growth. While the Nuyoricans were not the sole force that through the green fuse drove these flowers, their visit made manifest in dramatic and carnivalesque stagings the different constituencies of poetic production and consumption in a large

POETICS FOR A POSTLITERARY AMERICA

midwestern city known for its support of the arts, its social conscience (and consequently relatively good social services), its pro-education orientation—and also for its cultural and ethnic homogeneity. This particular urban culturescape is thus a notable backdrop for the scene of cultural exchange.

This event as cultural moment foregrounds the ways in which specific cultural, ethnic, or regional aesthetics that develop in one context travel to, germinate in, change, and are embraced or rebuffed in other locales, in the process facilitating or catalyzing movement and change in the host region's patterns of expressive culture. In traditional societies, cultural exchange helps to heal fissures or avert dramatic change and does not generally cause underrepresented portions of the socius to split from their community and form new groups. In the Nuyo-Minneapple case, however, the exchange did help fuel a change: several key players from the Loft and other venues established new writing and performing institutions, notably SASE (pronounced "sassy"): the Write Place, a more grassroots counterpart to the Loft (still going strong over a decade later); the broadside *Shout! A Community Arts Newspaper for Poets Storytellers and Performance Artists*, which folded after several years of consistent publication because the editor moved to San Francisco; Cacophony Chorus, a group involved in oral performances and poetry slams throughout the cities; and SlamMinnesota! and Minnesota Spoken Word Association, both healthy and thriving as of 2010. But am I establishing a false dichotomy between change and continuity here? Between traditional societies like the Tlingit or the Haida, where studies of cultural exchange have been conducted, and a modern city with an ethnically diverse population arranged in strict and predictable hierarchy? And what is the effect of poetry's being both the medium of exchange and the substance exchanged? How, in this case, were poetry and poetic discourse socially binding or socially fracturing?

Nuyorican poetry has been alive and well since the 1970s, when the anthology *Nuyorican Poetry: An Anthology of Puerto Rican Words and Feelings*[1] appeared not to initiate but to present to the respectable world of "publishable results" the already dynamic and thriving creativity of the combined forces of the "outlaw" poet and the laboring poor. Although at that time "Nuyorican" referred specifically to New Yorkers of Puerto Rican descent, a definition pointed up by the book's subtitle, and although several of the poems contain explicit Puerto Rican nationalist sentiment, Miguel Algarín's introduction advocates as a virtue the variety and mélange that comprise that identity. Algarín also points out the uniqueness of the Nuyorican situation and how it has enabled a rich hybrid language:

We come to the city as citizens and can retain the use of Spanish and include English. . . . [The] pressures of getting a job stimulate the need to master a minimal English usage. But really it is the English around you that seeps into your vocabulary. . . . The interchange between both yields new verbal possibilities, new images to deal with the stresses of living on tar and cement.[2]

All of the contributors were Nuyorican. As documented in the more recent anthology, *Aloud! Voices from the Nuyorican Poets Café*,[3] the cafe that had been primarily associated with founders Algarín and Miguel Piñero reopened as an homage to Piñero after his death in 1988. This time around, the ethnic focus was wider: while the Nuyorican neighborhood ("Alphabet City," an auspicious name for a poetic locale) continued to play host to the cafe, and while Algarín also maintained a high profile as editor, founder, emcee, impresario, and poet, the main body of poets who participated in cafe activities were not only Puerto Rican but African American, Euro American, other Latin ethnics, and whoever was willing and able to swing in the groove. Algarín attributes the cafe's phoenix-like resurrection and growth to its multiethnic, inclusive profile. While the era of cultural nationalism had given the café its start, this pride, while not abated, had metamorphosed. In a sense, this is not such a radical change, because Puerto Rico, like many Caribbean islands, already exemplifies multi-, post- and transnational postmodernity.[4] And Nuyoricans represent the diaspora of multiple diasporas. What better conditions for a postnationalist cultural venue to enable writers who participate in *many* oral, performative and poetic traditions? By the time a group of the café poets toured the country and stopped in Minneapolis in the fall of 1993, the café had published a book, Paul Beatty's *Big Bank Take Little Bank*; hosted weekly slams as well as frequent readings by featured poets; and was considered an integral and catalytic phenomenon in the spoken word movement. Only one of the six who came to Minneapolis, Edwin Torres, was an ethnic Nuyorican, but all were dazzling vernacular performers whose creativity had been nurtured in the panethnic warmth of the Nuyorican Poets' Café.

The Nuyoricans' visit to Minneapolis was kicked off by founding father Miguel Algarín, who hosted an inaugural slam at the Rogue, a now defunct nightclub in downtown Minneapolis. That slam brought to public attention several poets whose visibility continued for the next month and beyond. Among them were Blac Q, encountered in the previous chapter; Joanne DiMarco, a Native American who often sang an invocation before reciting her poetry; Pony Tail, a Euro American "poet of the people" who coped good-naturedly with his low scores; and Michael McAllister,

POETICS FOR A POSTLITERARY AMERICA

a young poet whose work rode the razor's edge of the perilous joys and beauties of gay urban experience. Blac Q, McAllister, and Diego Vasquez, who is primarily a prose writer, ended up sharing slam championship: they got to perform with the Nuyoricans on stage at the Walker Art Center, the Twin Cities' most prominent artistic establishment. After a month of Twin-City-wide slams, organized by Loft program director Carolyn Holbrook to take place in neighborhood venues such as bars, cafes, and drop-in centers, the troupe of Nuyoricans arrived: Paul Beatty, Dana Bryant, Bob Holman, Tracie Morris, Edwin Torres, and Mike Tyler. The Walker Art Center, which defines its mission and constituency more broadly than the Loft, was excited about the visit and extended an invitation to the Loft to cosponsor the event. However, with the exception of Holbrook, who was in the process of leaving the Loft, the Loft was somewhat skeptical and apprehensive about the Nuyoricans, fearing that sponsors and important founders would not support the New York style, that slams would prove unpopular in Minnesota (a feeling that to some extent has proven accurate), and that the Nuyoricans' guests would be perceived by the Loft's steady clientele as invading the quiet Midwest and making local spaces too loud. However, the Loft accepted, ambivalence notwithstanding.

This ambivalence, not peculiar to this institution, should be seen in context. The upper Midwest's historical populist pride is characterized by a respect for stoicism, silence, modesty, and inconspicuous competence rather than visible brilliance. For example, the University of Minnesota considers access a standard of its excellence, criticizing more selective state universities across the country for their elitism. Minnesotans call this modesty "Minnesota nice." But this catchall phrase, used by detractors and boosters alike to characterize the state's dominant sensibility, means, among other qualities, such as a concern for social justice and unpretentiousness, a bland appearance of acceptance that hides an emphatic rejection of difference. "Minnesota nice" is often contrasted with "New York in-your-face," along with which go "pushiness," "grabbiness," loudness, and general intrusiveness (it's not hard to read the ethnic subtext here); the contrast suggests that "nice" primarily refers to a diffident politeness rather than a pro-active helpfulness, friendliness, or willingness to engage.

The Loft exemplifies both the engaging and trying aspects of Minnesota nice. Founded in 1974 to serve the community with low-cost, high-quality writing classes and events, the Loft employs many local writers to teach seminars on topics ranging from how to get published to working with your dreams as material. It also brings in many national writers for readings or short-term mentoring projects in which the featured writers are connected to a carefully screened handful of local aspiring writers for several weeks. Editorials in the cities' largest newspapers have celebrated the Loft's achievement, citing its sixty workshops and seventy-five classes a year, and claiming that it had achieved its primary goal of combatting the isolation and solitude most writers feel.[5] The Loft has helped many local writers find community as well as employment, and it is one of the primary examples of Minnesotans' sense of commitment to public service, with a worthy record of nurturing writers and fostering careers that occasionally result in national recognition.

Many in the Twin Cities, however, feel frustrated with the Loft's limitations.[6] Its aesthetic is fairly conservative and conventional; rarely are courses offered that stress experimental poetic developments. Its espousal of what Charles Bernstein has called "official verse culture," combined with a constituency of mostly white, middle-class women and men interested in documenting their personal experiences, makes for a somewhat homogeneous atmosphere tinged with an earnestness untempered by verbal color or flamboyance: understated, nondisruptive confession.[7] "Stoic prairie stuff," was how one skeptic expressed it to me: "Why I started drinking again or why I quit drinking, take your pick, after I hit a deer on the highway." Another term for this genre is "prairie anecdotal."

In response to pressures to be more inclusive, the Loft revised its mission to explicitly include a multicultural imperative, initiating a program called Inroads, in which local writers of color (and later gay and lesbian writers) offer brief residencies to work with aspiring writers (also local) of that minoritized category. These have mixed success, as do the instances where nationally known writers of color serve as visiting mentors: on one memorable occasion, an I-hit-a-deer suburban local "mentoree" read about his wife's "warm, ample rear" on the same bill as the leather-jacketed, cosmopolitan diasporan Jessica Hagedorn wittily jibing at Imelda Marcos in the high-spirited code switching that characterizes her work. A heavily attended program against censorship featuring Kathy Acker, Amiri Baraka, and Nat Hentoff was deemed to be a failure because Baraka was "rude to the audience," Acker was pornographic, and Hentoff was, well, Hentoff. Likewise, the Nuyorican poets' visit, which most of the world considered a screaming success, was a loud intrusion that needed several years' disavowal through subsequent tepid programming. In general, then, there is much well-intentioned piety at the Loft (in one newspaper article on the Loft's mixed reputation the director, without irony, praised the institution by comparing its board meetings to Sunday church services), but because it understands its primary mission, to serve the local community, as acceding to that community's aesthetic sensibilities (as well as the tastes of the Loft's major donors), its programming is slow to incorporate the truly exciting aspects of contemporary poetics, most notably experimental ("language-centered") writing and performing that draws on (dissident) traditions other than personality-centered post-Romantic Western narrative, memoir, or lyric.

This combination of commitment to public service with a narrow view of acceptable cultural expression reflects the larger Minnesotan and upper midwestern value structure: a Scandinavian-inherited public-spiritedness and an orientation in favor of "the little people" (with the understanding that the latter are white Protestants), but also an intolerant liberalism rather than an inclusive one. That is, entitlement to equal rights is predicated on the assumption of shared goals and cultural values: plainspoken, modest conformity to an ethical norm. Cultures that celebrate vibrant, sensuous expressiveness, colorful clothing, highly embellished speech, or the enjoyment of leisure (and the corollary uncoupling of work from suffering) are profoundly mistrusted.

There are, of course, other writing cultures and expressive venues beyond the mainstream, and Minnesota is famous for its civic support of the arts. The Walker Art Center, which initiated the Nuyoricans' visit, is far more nationally ambitious than the Loft (whose first commitment is to the art of its own locale), and plays farther out on the edge. With Diane Glancy; the extended stay of Roberta Hill (Whiteman), an Oneida from Wisconsin, as a doctoral candidate at the University of Minnesota; and Jim Northrup, an Ojibwe poet who lives a traditional life on Fond du Lac Reservation several hours north of the Twin Cities; and with a large urban Native American population, there is a strong Native American presence in the mix. This Native presence is one of Minnesota's most powerful assets; however, it evokes some anxiety on the part of the white settler culture that dominates the state. In larger historical terms, one could read the "I hit a deer" genre as encoding "I shot an Indian." The politics of context govern how these local Native American artists interact with the mainstream art scene. "The outsider presence [of the Nuyoricans] threw all this into stark relief, because they have the glamour of the Big Apple, but the 'local wildnesses' bring up a history that [the settler culture] would prefer to exclude from the chat group."[8]

Moreover, a quartet of high-profile, nonprofit, small literary presses—Coffee House Press, New Rivers, Milkweed Editions, and Graywolf, which make a point of publishing local as well as national work—is undergirded by several highly regarded micropresses (Chax, Standing Stones, Detour Press) and a plethora of 'zines. The glossy magazine *Colors*, then in its fifth year of publication, was devoted to writings by Minnesotans of color; Mark Nowak's *XCP: Cross Cultural Poetics* blends left political imperatives with a lively aesthetic. Patrick's Cabaret, a monthly showcase for performance artists founded and hosted by queer HIV-activist and performer Patrick Scully, is another stage for alternative expressive culture. In addition, a number of bars and cafes regularly feature open readings. However, many of these sites of literary activity had little if any interaction.

Beside the tension between different aesthetics and their underlying differences in cultural tradition, a related tension often found in the Twin Cities' arts communities is that usually billed as national versus local. The assumption that these two are in a binary relationship can make it difficult to achieve real cultural mixing, which itself is a not a desirable goal for many Twin Citians concerned with the cities' own survival as a metropolis that combines a "small town atmosphere" with "big city excitement," as one billboard advertises the cities to themselves. (Much as the term "small town" appeals, it also should be understood as a code for white, and to resonate with the settler culture's defensive ambivalence toward more powerful, "central" metropolises, on the one hand, and toward the colonized, with whom it lives in close proximity, on the other). In some ways, moreover, the elision of "local" (poets living and practicing in the cities) and "regional" (which designates a sensibility) works to make urban writers of color or sexual minorities less visible, in that they are local but not regional in sensibility: they do not hymn the praises of the hard woodsy life or the moral complexities of hitting deer with cars or bullets, they are not overwhelmingly preoccupied with middle-aged reckonings with childhoods. Writers of color from elsewhere are occasionally brought in and lionized, and the "stoic prairie" confessionals of the Loft's constituency support each other through teaching and taking courses, but there is little space in legitimate venues for writers explicitly working in what Renato Rosaldo calls "dissident traditions" except as mentors or mentorees in the Inroads program, a designator that reinforces a centrist view of the disenfranchised as peripherals needing help to join the mainstream.

Interestingly, two of the most scathing reviews and comments on the Nuyoricans' visit came from local writers of color Diego Vasquez and Adrian C. Louis. The former's short opinion piece in *A View from the Loft* complained that, in contrast to the money showered on the out-of-towners, the local winners were unpaid except for the privilege of sharing a stage with "overpaid nitwits." Vasquez later contextualized these comments by reiterating his firmly held belief that to honor artists without paying them is no honor; moreover, as someone who has been warmly received in Minnesota, he feels it indecorous to fawn on coastal culture at the expense of one's home.[9] Louis also termed Tracie Morris and Bob Holman "nitwits"; in his case, it was for referring to themselves as Nuyorican, although the former "appears to be Black" and the latter "looks white, although from his garb and hairdo he could be from Mars"; for claiming that TV was more receptive to oral poetry than the literary community; and for claiming that performative gestures were a form of writing.

Because of this heavy conformism, an embattled sense of separatism gets projected onto and sometimes adopted by the alternative or traditionally subordinated communities; this is another dynamic that makes creative cross-pollination and hybrid artistic production difficult. The Inroads series, shaped around identity, is a case in point. A temporary transplant from the Bay Area, Djola Branner (fresh from the performance group Pomo Afro Homos), had a performance piece canceled because he wanted to hire a Latino director he admired, while the producer of the piece thought that the play needed an African American director who could understood that specific experience (both the producer and Branner are African American). Adrian Louis's concern that Bob Holman and Tracie Morris didn't look like Nuyoricans and that this impaired their credibility as artists could be understood in this context. Branner has observed that there's little sense of play here, and that artistic narratives by minorities are treated as and expected to conform to tales of victimhood. All the same, thriving institutions such as the Minneapolis American Indian Center, the African American Penumbra Theatre, Mixed Blood Theatre, and the newer consortium Asian American Renaissance are often, when they explicitly state their missions, accused by dominant-culture critics of divisiveness. (One such critique famously followed sometime St. Paulite August Wilson's call for a renewed need for African American theatrical institutions.) Partly because Minnesota is a more newly colonized space, its "settler culture" lags behind New York's and California's in its skills and resources for navigating between the Scylla of a necessarily overdetermined identity politics and the Charybdis of liberal, difference-denying "colorblindness" of a dominant Euro American culture threatened by uninhibited experiments in cultural difference. And for the same reason, communities and artists of color face different dilemmas with different investments in identity than their coastal counterparts.

Enter into this particular and also not altogether unusual set of political and aesthetic tensions, in the fall of of 1993, the Nuyorican Poets' Café touring group, word-dazzlers and cultural healers. The words of Bob Holman, one of the troupe, convey the tenor of their energy: "It was a Fellini marriage. It was all for Poetry and Poetry for All. We turned the town into the Café for a week, and we danced all night." Holman takes for granted, in ways that Minnesotans do not, the importance of breaking rules:

> The big plus though was penetration of the local communities. I remember getting the word early that Jamison Mahto [a Native American Beat-style poet] was going to boycott us (!) because the Loft had said that only a "limited number" would be allowed to participate in the Slam. I did a radio show at [KFAI], and used my time to make a personal appeal to Jamison, whom I'd never met, and told him we were cool and fuck the rules and really wanted him to turn up. So, guess what? The man was actually listening and the appeal worked. He showed, we raved and bonded. . . . Many Minneapolis poets who had felt excluded by Loft hierarchical programming managed somehow to overcome all that and found themselves entwined in Café poets vibe and entanglement agenda. The Slam Open was a totally raucous affair, with over 30 poets reading—the list just kept getting longer. Round 2, next night, was at the Walker Café, an inspired choice. Nothing like this had ever happened there, and when a Museum extends itself, really opens up to the populations, why, everybody wants to use the Museum! Museums should be our Grange Halls![10]

Holman goes on to document some of the personal pleasures of the trip, which led to further developments in his own projects as well as an appreciation of the contagion of the Nuyorican vision:

> For me though, it was Beni Matias driving me up to the Res near Duluth to meet Jim Northrup, and shoot him reading his poems there with Pat in their warm and cozy, where I really entered Jim's world. It resulted in Jim's appearing in *United States of Poetry* [a series Holman produced for television] . . . and Caroline [Holbrook] confessing to me that she wanted to start her OWN Café, like the Nuyorican, and by Gumbo, midst storm and gang, SASE did come into being, . . . and Mike "Spam" Hall getting props long overdue . . . and [disabled performance poet Elaine Shelley]. . . . [11]

Thinking It Through

Some insights from Marcel Mauss's classic *The Gift* seem useful here. Two groups, tribal units as it were, under the same general (national) rubric, come together to share, celebrate, and give away that which is dearest to them, poetry, in a set of spectacular displays, games, and gatherings whose purpose is not only to share but through sharing to bring honor and glory to the sharers. Accordingly, there is an undercurrent of rivalry in the display of hospitality and gift-giving. It was true that two different concepts of "people's poetry" got some airplay in a mock competitive staging (the slam, to which many Minnesotans had objections precisely because of its competitive aura), and that the exercise of bringing the Manhattanites to Minnesota involved an aesthetic challenge for both parties. Both hosts and guests understood that poetry is an "economy of the soul," that is, not an exchange economy but one of gift or theft. In the Maussian sense of self-interested extravagance, the cultures exchanged Nuyorican extravagance, entertainment, and poetry for earnest Minnesotan hospitality and piety. The elements of Twin Cities culture that resonated with Nuyorican panethnicity and social marginalization came alive in a larger public and basked in the cities' spotlight; the elements accustomed to seeing themselves as the givers, the bestowers of charity, were somewhat more puzzled and tentative in their reception.

There was also a healthy exchange beyond all the local politicking and regional anxiety: the Nuyoricans brought to Minneapolis a brilliantly carnivalesque display of verbal excess; the Twin Cities contributed its own talent, particularly that which had been underrepresented in mainstream quarters, its hospitality, and a warm reception that, à la Minnesota nice, veiled its diffidence. In a sense, the results were, as in Mauss's studies, a consolidation of each community through a homeopathic contact with the other: the Nuyorican poets, through their tour, constituted their national presence as cultural heavy-hitters; and through its lack of follow-up programming, the Loft renewed its commitment to its primary clientele's regional sensibility. However, a generative legacy came into view in the months and years that followed. A third, previously marginally represented, group of Twin Cities poets came to the fore, developing institutions and venues of its own: SASE, *SHOUT*, and the Cacophony Chorus, all of which have operated independently of the Loft and the Walker Art Center.

The newer institutions lost no time in following up on their contact with the Nuyoricans and other nationally recognized oral poets: SASE brought Bob Holman and Dana Bryant out to the Twin Cities the following year to serve its mentoring program, and *SHOUT!*, on a shoestring budget, published interviews with Quincy Troupe, Allen Ginsberg, and Jim Northrup in its first year. By contrast, it took several years for the Loft to bring Edwin Torres back for a residency in 1996, its only programming follow-up to the Nuyorican visit. Mauss's archaic model offers some analytical insights, even adapted to this postmodern potlatch in which coastal pre- and postmodern verbal traditions came into productive conflict with the Midwest's blend of third-generation modernist aesthetics and trenchant regionalism. However, though the hortatory epigraph of this essay, one of Mauss's conclusions, is a bracing wake-up call to Minnesotans to shed some of their protective diffidence, to embrace the joy of contestatory giving and taking, the colonial and postmodern subtext of the societies in question here limits the unqualified applicability of Mauss's insights.

Exchange has a somewhat different valence in Steven Caton's *"Peaks of Yemen I Summon": Poetry as Social Practice in a Northern Yemeni Tribe*, which delineates the function of poetry in representing and moving people through key social events like political showdowns or weddings.[12] In the socius he documents, exchange comprises poetic competition, which is used as a deflector or a sublimating medium for serious differences, but whose invention and declamation achieve real social effects (that is, the public poetry is not a palliative or an evasion of the matter at hand but rather a negotiation thereof). Similarly, competing styles of poetry and the exercise of this rivalry in public spaces, as well as local writing institutions and their interrelations, constitute Twin Citians' sense of themselves as literary creators, producers, and consumers. However, Caton describes practices that have deep roots in time and traditional society; many of the Twin Cities' institutions under discussion here are nascent and unstable, although the aesthetic traditions they perpetuate (post-Romantic lyric, African American oratory and inventive wordplay) are as venerable as modernist traditions can be.

Mary Louise Pratt's well-known "contact zone," reworked from Bakhtin and sociolinguistic research to examine travel literatures, ideologies of imperialism, and transculturation, might also come into play.[13] If the meeting between cultures constituted a "social [space] where highly disparate cultures [met, clashed, and grappled] with each other . . . [in] highly asymmetrical relations of domination and subordination," it was complicated by multiple layers of asymmetry: notably, the intermediary presences of a politically progressive white "settler culture," on the one hand, which prizes its humility over the moneyed arrogance of the coasts, and on the other, networks of local writers who have much in common with the Nuyoricans (shared histories of oppression, languages, aesthetic orientations), and who have had ambivalently supportive relations with local arts institutions. Pratt refers to "slavery, colonialism, or their aftermaths as they are lived out across the globe today" as primary instances of such asymmetrical relations. In coastal versus midwestern or urban versus rural encounters, many Minnesotans experience New York as colonizing the Midwest with intimidating displays of power, imposing its fast-talking flash on a culture where still waters run deep. However, to accuse the Nuyorican poets of colonialism would be to confuse style with social power:

POETICS FOR A POSTLITERARY AMERICA

cultures in which loud talk, interruption, competitive verbal games, and ritual displays of bright color and movement are often *not* socially empowered in places where the majority culture is of Northern European descent. The Nuyorican cosmopolitanism that intimidated mainstream Midwesterners resulted from histories of slavery and colonialism.

Pratt elsewhere describes the "strategies of innocence" of the European naturalist explorer, the apparently harmless fuddy-duddy whose sole interest in natural wonders distances him or her from charges of complicity with overtly militaristic or economically imperialist agendas. This concept helps to pressure the "big shots from New York" *ressentiment* that pervaded, however subtly, the dominant writing community's reception of the Nuyoricans. In Nietzsche's analysis, resentment becomes the basis for a justified domination: Christianity valorizes meekness as an aesthetic, ethical, and stylistic mask behind which to conduct its bid for global supremacy; homespun plainspokenness and stoicism become the downtrodden virtues justifying a regional aesthetic that discriminates against the joys of sophisticated alterity, that views with suspicion even the right to be different. (The word "different," applied with no normative standard for comparison, as in "That shirt is kind of different," has a particularly distancing, pejorative connotation in the upper Midwest.) It is possible to welcome spoken word imports from elsewhere as flashy bits of exotica while seeing the threat in too much too close to home; the Nuyoricans' visit became, for Minnesota's "official verse culture," a homeopathic warding off of local wildnesses, while for local non-normative artists, the visit inspired greater activity.

Worthy of deeper study also are the creative individuals and works that surfaced at this time. The strategies of thick description exemplified by Crapanzano's *Tuhami*, whose rich spiritual life is rendered in equally rich detail, and the essays in that portion of Lavie, Narayan, and Rosaldo's *Creativity/Anthropology* devoted to "creative individuals in cultural context" exemplify this approach. Here, the anthropologists exhibit their own creative gifts, their empathies with "folk" poets, performers, musicians, sculptors in extended interpretations of these individuals' relations to their traditions, societies, and artistic processes and of their body of artifacts—songs, poems, sculptures, and dances. Particularly moving for me were Adam Harden's poetry, which we encountered in an earlier chapter, as well as his name change from Blac Q, at the beginning of the month of slams, to Ibn Mujaheed ("son of war," "ready for battle") when he read on the stage of the Walker; the evolution from a question, a "stage name" that gestures toward the entertainment factor (cue ball) in the slam venue, to a committed word-warriorship that denotes a legacy ("son of").

The poem astutely analyzes the limitations of upward mobility through education, the faux security of the "gentle college land" of Macalester, one of the most heavily endowed private liberal arts colleges in the country, and its innocent complicity with the "blue-uniformed [blue-eyed?] enemy / watching me" even as he watches the cop shows on TV that target him, and young black men, inevitably, as national criminal cum entertainment. Harden read with conviction, but his voice was quiet and young; his oversized clothing hung on him, and the brim of his baseball cap shadowed his face in an enactment of the self-effacement Minnesotans admire, though it worked with effective ambivalence against the hard-hitting confidence of the verse. After winning the "slam shut," he pretty much disappeared from the local slam scene, unlike the other winners Michael McAllister, who later read at the Nuyorican Poets' Café, and Diego Vasquez, who, despite his anti-Nuyorican position at the time, subsequently won a grant to host six slams around the Twin Cities.

Another atypical poem commanded attention: "this poem's about the alcoholic in my home" described the predicament of a self-sabotaging relationship to alcoholism and alcoholics ("my own codependencies robbing me blind") while touching on the value of writing as self-healing ("I'm imprisoned with confusion and my emotions are in cages / as fear will rise in my mind it reflects on these pages"). Minnesota's recovery community, though nationally recognized ("land of ten thousand treatment centers," as the joke goes), is characterized by its dependency on clinics and the medical establishment rather than by an emphasis on the spiritual program laid out by Alcoholics Anonymous and other grassroots self-help networks, and it is stereotypically white. This poem is an artifact both of the publicness with which the region embraces the language of addictionology and of a departure from the mainstream in its reliance on spirituality rather than clinical, therapeutic, or transformative aesthetic expertise. One could invoke the tradition of African American oratory and public prayer, in which the slam audience was implicitly asked to witness the poet's committing herself to the care of a power greater than herself, as more formative of this poetic event than the conventions of medical addictionology or, certainly, of either the local slam-and-open-mike scene as it came out for the Nuyoricans, or the official verse culture that, while it permits and even advocates the "personal voice," shies away from such devotional directness in favor of an Eliotic distance and circumspect descriptive tone mediated by objective correlatives such as deer in the headlights, vegetables, and stark winter landscapes ("show, don't tell"). The poem and its understated presentation merged some of the concerns respected by the mainstream (female confession, twelve-step recovery) and the stylistic legacy of dissident traditions. The poem's author, like Harden, disappeared from public view after the month of slams.

Moreover, in the spirit of Howard Becker's *Art Worlds*, whose opening epigraph by Thackeray documents the crucial role his "manservant" played in the author's creative process by bringing him coffee every morning at 6:00 a.m., attention to the importance of the cultural workers who enabled the events should complement attention paid to the poets and their work: Carolyn Holbrook, who left the Loft to found SASE, a more grassroots, hands-on, interventionist writing organization that, among other things, runs programs for at-risk kids, aspires to generate writing and reading venues for the international diasporic communities of the Twin Cities (among them Hmong, Horn of Africa, and Filipino), and other equally ambitious projects; and Bob Gale, who as proprietor of the Bad Habit Café sponsored open mike readings for several years with no notice from larger writing institutions until slam month, and subsequently started *SHOUT!* and Cacophony Chorus, both of which later ceased operation owing to lack of community support.[14] As Gale points out in an interview with Michael Brown, an originary slammer from Chicago, slams were slow to take off in Minnesota compared to Boston, Ann Arbor, and San Francisco, although Chicago, the birthplace of slam, is geographically close to the Twin Cities.[15]

Minne-Confessional

This is clearly not a disinterested analysis. I hope that, erratic as it is, it may spark others to reflect on their own literary communities beyond simply constituting or recording them for posterity (as Ginsberg did for the Beat scene, and others are currently undertaking for the language poets). Rather than freeze-framing a scene, I want to understand the dynamics of *these* poetries in *this* public sphere. Though I was not a central player in the Nuyorican event, I participate in the literary culture under discussion. I teach American poetry at the university, which keeps its distance from such populist events (while I was consistently the only member of my department at the public events, I was immensely gratified to see, at the first Algarín-emceed slam, all the first-year doctoral students from the Program in American Studies sitting in the last row of the audience); I've served on the boards of or have collaborative friendships or cordial collegial relations with former and current members of the Loft, SASE, and Walker Art Center program staffs, as well as with the staffs of *Rain Taxi Review of Books*, *SHOUT!*, and *XCP: Cross Cultural Poetics*. I am also an audience member at many of these events and an off-and-on dues-paying member of the Loft, SASE, and the Walker Art Center. Since I live here, I have a stake in making the Twin Cities' literary culture one that is congenial to my tastes, and this essay is obviously not free from that agenda. However, partisan as I am, I cannot claim to have an embattled position, and I am not writing an "autoethnography" fueled by the same kind of urgency that gives rise to indigenous accounts of traditional life threatened by colonialism. (If anything, the university, because of its size and structure and the way it interprets its land grant mission, is more complacent than the institutions described here.) Nonetheless I am critical of certain aspects of this, my community, and want to hurry its changes along (thus justly risking the epithets "pushy," "outsider," "East Coast aggressive," and the like); this is as much a letter to that community as to my world of poetic and ethnographic scholars.

Poetry

To return to some of the questions raised earlier, what happens when poetry, poetic activity, or poetic discourse is keyed in as a major factor in these deliberations? What if, for example, poetry itself were considered the contact zone (a temporarily autonomous contact zone, at that, as in Hakim Bey's *TAZ*), the culture that travels and the medium of travel itself (Emily Dickinson: "when I want to travel I close my eyes"), the medium of exchange (as in playing the dozens, or as in folklorist Américo Paredes's description of the centrality of a particular corrido to the history of two rivalrous border families), the gift being given, the subject of autoethnography? Does the "outsideness" of poetry—its dubious though arguable antidiscursivity—give it special transformative properties to catalyze the process of meaning making that constitutes cultural self-creation and interpenetration? Undertaking such a perspective compels rapturous language to describe the performances of the Nuyoricans: Edwin Torres wowed the crowd with his hand movement performance for his "Indian Hand Poem" and sent us into poetry overdrive again and again with his linguistic deconstravaganzas of Spanglish and other supreme orphodelphic detritusyllables ("I represent, the chatta-zondatta of nonconformist complains . . . I, Puerto-REEK"); a slow scream arose from the crowd after his lyrical parry and philistine thrust:

When angels fall in love,
they place their halos over each other's chest
and let their hearts fall through.

. . .

The cloud you're in, is the heaven [I feel when I'm with you] . . ."
So I said, "Well, what do you mean by that?"[16]

You say you want heteroglossia? Semiotic flux and shimmy shimmy coco-pop? Roll over, Bakhtin, and tell Kristeva the news. Tracie Morris's astonishing gestural and verbal pyrotechnics as she imitated the "scratch" sound of hip-hop technology to Carmen McRae tone-songs! Bluesish and jazzish, the "queen of hip-hop poetry" was fully embodied, in the house, stand up and be counted, a quick tongue and tender wit, her gender-bending bragging poem, "Ten Men," aroused nervous if approving laughter at its honesty about the "anguished pleasures"[17] of smart black womanhood; "The Spot" castigated "superficial people everywhere" for wearing the X gear that marks the spot that should remind us what Malcolm died for; "Project Princess," a praise poem for girls who like herself grow up in the high-rise projects of Brooklyn and are its "black gold," its richest resource, hymned the tough sweetness of the young women ("multi-dimensional shrimp earrings [framing their cinnamon faces]") who blush at compliments but whose fists can "deck" a verbal transgressor, no problem.[18] Paul Beatty's hairpin-turn puns and relentless stream of race-bending cultural manifestos and disclosures of personal vulnerability that raced by so fast your ears had to double as wings to catch up. Dana Bryant's magisterial movements and Shange-with-a-traditionalist-twist womanhood soliloquies that made intimacy, grief, religion all alchemical matter for striking/making the aesthetic motherlode; Bob Holman's ebullient emcee style and Mike Tyler's physically contorted teen spirit standing ovation at the Walker's final wordbang meltdown meant that poetry had arrived, been recognized, accepted as the gift of a love supreme.

It doesn't get any better than this. For days the Twin Cities levitated over the rest of the prairie, supercharged with the dark light of WORDZZZZZZZZ from afar, good news of the planet's verbal health and resiliency despite history's ravages. Even the Mega Mall was paradise enow. (Well, almost.) But when the stardust of fragmented wordbits settled and the aura dissolved back into its constitutive elements. . . . Is it so? When the gods arrived laden with gifts, were we too busy looking at the floor to be more than passingly delighted? Too embarrassed about our rapt surrender and childish adulation? Needing to disavow that transdiscursive trance? Let's hope not. Deep under the deep freeze the heat, stirrings of new words.

8 Avant-garde or Border Guard

(Latino) Identity in Poetry

1949: In the room of the impoverished thug who dominates him sexually, the French petty criminal Jean Genet, on his knees undressing his abusive lover, hears the rustling of the newspaper that stands in permanently for a windowpane, and muses:
"It's a newspaper printed in Spanish," I said to myself again. "It's only natural that I don't understand the sound it's making." He goes on: "Then I really felt I was in exile, and my nervousness was going to make me permeable to what—for want of other words—I shall call poetry."

—JEAN GENET, *THE THIEF'S JOURNAL*

1952:
> The sound of words waits—
> a barbarian host at the borderline of sense.
> The enamored guards desert their posts.

—ROBERT DUNCAN,
"THE SONG OF THE BORDERGUARD"

1989: If we think of cultures as permeable . . . [they] may then be represented as zones of control or of abandonment, of recollection and of forgetting, of force or of dependence, of exclusiveness or of sharing, all taking place in the global history that is our element. Exile, immigration, and the crossing of boundaries are experiences that can therefore provide us with new narrative forms or . . . with other ways of telling.

—EDWARD SAID, "REPRESENTING THE COLONIZED"

1991:
> I grew up hearing two languages thinking they were one language
> so concluded that there was one language which you just made up
> yourself.

I hear things people haven't really said
It doesn't worry me, and I feel privileged
that I doo-n'tun-derstan .. D everything . . .

—EDWIN TORRES, *I HEAR THINGS*

PEOPLE HAVEN'T REALLY SAID

PoetiX/Poiesis

Poetry is an anxiety-provoking genre of discourse; Jonathan Monroe has referred to it as a "utopian genre,"[1] and Karlheinz Stierle has gone so far as to call it "essentially anti-discourse."[2] The borderline condition is one of constant anxiety-productive, creative tension, as well as destructive, soul-killing anxiety—a no-place utopia, limbo of nightmare and dream possibilities. "Restless serpents," Bernice Zamora calls her constant inner movement, her power undoing and redoing[3] José Saldívar, in *Border Matters: Remapping American Cultural Studies*, in turn calls Zamora's poems "desiring technologies" that create, direct, and undercut erotic flow from a specifically grounded Chicana subjectivity.[4] While poetry as a discourse enables subjectivist expression, this does not mean that people simply talk about their experiences but that they create experience and subjectivity in the process of meaning-making, of poiesis. This poetic process constitutes and enacts linguistic and collective subjectivity. Following some admittedly predictable generic conventions here, then, I would like to link poetry, as is common, with subjectivity, and then to suggest that for certain kinds of subjects (specifically, in the cases I examine here, Nuyorican and Chicano) who have not been conventionally honored as such because of their subordinated social locations, poetic-subjective language can and often does provide a sort of laboratory for experimentation with new forms, new consciousnesses, new communities. These forms, consciousnesses, and communities are not, however, mere acultural novelties but carry with them the traces and influences of many dissident or socially subordinated traditions as well as evolving new ones.

Because Saldívar gives poetry as conventionally understood a high profile in his exploration of postcontemporary border culture and its accompanying theory, in the form of homages to Américo Paredes, Bernice Zamora, and Alberto Ríos, I want to explore somewhat further the notions he sets forth regarding how poetry can generate and represent collective or at least historically and contextually grounded ethnoracial subjectivities. At the 1997 XCP: Cross Cultural Poetics conference, the question was raised whether poetry (highly charged or formalized literary expression) is a subset of poetics (the general practice of making culture),

POETICS FOR A POSTLITERARY AMERICA

or whether poetics (the analysis of verse or the strategies that comprise it) is a subset of poetry.[5] Although my subject is poetry as conventionally understood, my allegiance is with the first formulation of "poetics"; the activity surrounding and constituting the production and consumption of imaginative language ("poetry") is but one of many lenses through which to approach a general practice and analysis of expressive culture, or poiesis, a continual process of making and remaking. And Saldívar is not alone in this recognition: as his book documents, anthropologist Renato Rosaldo, as well as folklorists Paredes and José Limón, among others, have focused specifically on poetry as a site where cultural contestation is embodied. Juan Flores and George Yudice, in their *Social Text* essay, "Living Borders/ Buscando America: Languages of Latino Self-formation" (1990), bridge Puerto Rican, Nuyorican, Chicano, and other Latino/a issues by looking at poetry as enacting a process of "self-formation" that transgresses official borders between English and Spanish, Anglo and Latino/a.

Moreover, poetry enacts, sometimes in the space of a single word, how power relations are negotiated in and through language. This observation becomes more than a general truism when language itself, or the relationship between certain specific languages, is the object of and not just the medium for representing the struggle for power, representation, and expressive freedom. Interlingual punning, code switching, the coining of neologisms become means of dramatizing political at-homeness in the otherwise forbidding culturescape of the United States. In particular, Nuyorican poet Tato Laviera's pithy coinage "AmeRícan" ("I'm a 'Rican/American") foregrounds the strategy of bilingual punning and the affirmative assertion, not of a fixed national or ethnic identity, but of a survivalist verve that enables cultural flourishing in the spaces between languages and cultures, the inter- or transcultural zones where new identities are forged.[6] Another instance of this incisive neologistic play is, as Saldívar points out, Tish Hinojosa's "frontejas" music, as well as in the name of Chicano activist and Elvis impersonator stage persona "El Vez."[7] By all accounts, the borderlands' linguistic laboratory of poetic activity continues to provide signal opportunities for experimentation in production and analysis, theory and practice. One could conceivably argue that poetic vanguardism happens precisely, or that the conditions for poetic innovation are at a premium, in the interstices of geopolitical boundaries— in islands (Manhattan, Puerto Rico), on coasts (San Francisco Bay Area, Los Angeles), on national borders (the length of the Rio Grande)— characterized not only by cultural and linguistic heterogeneity but also by vast dissymmetries of power.[8] Poiesis thus can be construed as the making of a resistant (and simultaneously permeable) hybridity, the making of a border sensibility. Saldívar includes a broad range of literary, popular, and scholarly materials in his analysis of the deeply textured and multivalent creative process of border consciousness. Following his lead, I examine a couple of artifacts, poems that produce and delineate different kinds of in-betweenness, assertions of aesthetic and cultural power, and the right to complex expression.

As will become clear in the two poems discussed, Edwin Torres's extravagant language experiments do not tell of private angst or triumph. In fact, they avoid conventional narrative altogether; experience and history take place "*en mi boca*," in what he calls his "sound laboratory." Chicano poet Javier Piña's video poem, "Bilingual in a Cardboard Box," sharply dramatizes the power differential between English and Spanish and the split between public and private culture forced on bilingual subjects by a monolingual social system; he speaks of being in a wheelchair and living in a cardboard box, though the video shows him able-bodied and sitting on a bed (in other words, the poet is metaphorically crippled and homeless as a result of anti-Spanish legislation). Both poets address the problematics of bilinguality and interlinguality, of living in two languages that are in a highly volatile, politically charged relationship of domination and subordination.

Looking at and through these two poets' work permits one to foreground the following-unparallel-ly constructed explorations and observations: (1) The possible role of poetry, that stereotypically "private" and interior genre, in addressing and unraveling the border between private and public cultures. (2) The poems' exemplification of strategies for publicly and affirmatively using the Spanish language, whose embattled status in current U.S. politics has nothing to do with bilinguality per se but rather with the political and economic status of U.S. Latino/as and immigrants from Latin America and how that immigration reflects on U.S. foreign political, economic, and military policies. (Aside: monolinguals in the United States are tremendously impressed, for example, by European polyglots; I remember a lecture by Toril Moi that was prefaced by a breathless recitation of her multilingual fluency by the women's studies professor introducing her. And we all know the expensive programs our colleges and universities offer to go to exciting locales far away to learn Spanish when most of us could just go down the street a few miles by public transportation for a comparably authentic linguistic experience.) (3) The public acting out of a poiesis—a process of making—in which "artifacts" maintain their porousness, stay close to their material sources, resist a static artifactuality divorced from the poieses of identity, and enact as well as thematize critiques of government-imposed monolingualism.

Before going any farther I should point out that both these poetic events are part of the spoken word movement, which has sought to gather all kinds of vernacular and high-cultural poetries and market them at the mass-culture level. Edwin Torres, however, is now attracting the interest of poetry communities that would rather die than be associated with "spoken word" (which is basically a marketing term); Javier Piña is unknown on that particular experimental circuit, though his poem played on television screens nationwide. The high-art poetry circuit, and the anxious middle-brow even more so, scorn the gimmicks of mass culture, while the resources of the Public Broadcasting Corporation lavished on Piña's poem to make it accessible to monolinguals resulted in a powerfully choreographed representation of the "bilingual issue."

For Torres, language is not only a border but a home that is geopolitically noplace—that is, utopian—but still has a vibrant, locatable existence: in the migrant, morphic body and in the corporeal process of making sound, making up language, verbing nouns, and reworking negative stereotypes. He sends Anglogocentrism on a kamikaze mission toward an insulingual fiesta of detrisyllabic extravagance, defying both traditional notions of the (Eurocentric) avant-garde and a politically real linguistic borderguard:

> Born with the confidence that enables me to use my heritage . . . as a verb!
> Born with a cornucopia of linguistic peacocks en mi boca.
> Mi boca di Boricua.
> . . . I, hereby emperor my mouth into the ravines of Puerto-Stroika!
> . . . I represent, the chatta-zondatta of nonconformist cumpleaños . . .
> see-amma slow groove,
> Puerto Rican in the mud///
> I wonder, can I besa-mi cabeza if I cuerpo-po-po-po?
> Disparate, toe's-sonata . . . I, emperor WILDLY!!!
> . . . drunk from the trials of my toe-bulations.
> My this-little-piggy-that-little-piggy-bilation
> [. . .]
> I, Puerto-REEK: exis-stenching minutiae toe-nail sole-flats.
> [. . .]
> Barefoot of all chances . . . [9]
> [. . .]
> Puerto Rico—be my verb.
> Puerto Rico—be my tongue.
> Puerto Rico—be the word, that moves my poem, through its song.[10]

Torres, born in the Bronx, lived in Puerto Rico until the age of five or six, and has only returned once since then, for a year, as a teenager. Nonetheless, the island and the Spanish language remain sources of creativity for him, the origin and end content of his experiments. The name Puerto Rico embodies his creative process, a ground of expressive permission to expand limitlessly, to declare the world his linguistic domain:

> my playpen
>
> is the universe—
>
> inside
>
> my kind
>
> we use words
>
> dear neighbor
>
> we are the new ethnic
>
> our margins are beyond borders
>
> from where we stand our edges stretch
> the cranium, explode the heart— . . .
> between naked words, our pages begin . . . increasing our margin
> for error by infinity . . .
> impossible to marginalize[11]

Spanish is the starting point, the mother tongue, his (as he says) "safety net" that structures an access, ultimately, to all languages, and to sound itself (personal interview). (He is also working in the European tradition of sound poetry; he cites Veleimir Khlebnikov and Kurt Schwitters, as well as Gerard Manley Hopkins, as influences.) "Son Mi Son" is an interlingual sound piece in which one can hear Spanish-inflected English, Spanish-inflected nonsense vocables, and Spanish, French, and German-sounding nonsense; Torres claims some people have heard Chinese. As he says, "I break borders by changing languages in the middle of a word. What I try to do is break language down, make it a level playing field, then build it back up"[12]:

> Ke - ZARON - ZARON - ZARON
> Quesa - RON - saRON - saRON
> Sa - Ki - RON - KIRON - KIRON
> Keka - KON - CHH - CHH - (ccc)
> [. . .]
> sus cuerPA en mi cuerPO, son mi son
> YA - YE - YO - , YE - YO , YE - YOU

YO , YO , YO

       Mujer desnuda - me

tiene loco con tu culpa, tu cuerpo

[…]

toda mente … -

[…]

completamente mentally -

from toe - to toe - to toe …

HIRIS - ki - ROM k - RUM , hki - RHHUM - meh

KISSY - ROSE - E - ROSE - EROS

so so is so mi sopa de, son mi son

Sis - r know , she - know , she - kno

WHAT - I - LIE , I - LI

WHAT - SHE - LI , SHE - LI , YA - YEYO - YE-

YOU - Que raison - Se RON - D'etre (*raison d'etre*)

De karon, Ka RON - W'etre (*maison tre'te*)

Metre FA , ou Bonne , ou Bonne ,

Ya - se - ci bonne , c'est trexie , si - no - mi - son

me gusta mi sopa de , son mi son, de co - RA – Zon -

    Zon - Zon

SAIT , MARONNE , MAAARRONE ,

    MAAARRRRRRONE!!!

Pestri - W'ETRE , pastry? Croissant – Quiera (*monte*)

ida - noche - a - mano a mano , me toca – me , toca - me -[13]

The videotape of this piece, in contrast to the lavishly colored and high-tech television program in which Piña appears, is grainy, poorly lit, and in black-and-white; Torres, visible primarily from the waist up and dressed simply in a white shirt, dark pants, and heavy-framed glasses, stands spotlit on stage by the microphone and recites into it; utterly unconcerned with visual aesthetics; the videographer moves the camera as little as possible. (Some of the other performers, such as Tracie Morris, were well-nigh invisible on the tape, though their performances had been exhilarating at the actual event.) In this arena of visual minimalism (undertaken, as I have said, not especially for the low-rent look of a certain aesthetic but because the purpose of the tape was strictly documentary), the drama lies entirely in Torres's vocal pyrotechnics and syllabic surprises, the silences, singing, chanting, shouting, and timing of this glossolalic exploration of "*mi corazon*" and the manifestation of its emotions in intimate sexual pleasure. The issue has been raised about whether this subject matter represents a fallback position, a kind of cop-out that relies on sexual stereotypes for its cultural recognizability, namely, that a man—and particularly a man from an ethnic or racial minority—must link his verbal inventiveness with sexual prowess. I would counter that while there is certainly a conflation of sexual and verbal excess and play in the poem, as there is in rap, another tradition in which the convention of proclaiming one's prowess plays a large and formulaic role, there is far more emphasis here on self-dissolving pleasure than on self-regarding prowess; it is not "I'm so great" but "c'est si bon" (*it's so good*). The video of an unassuming-looking man in a white button-down shirt and heavy black glasses (slightly poetic, slightly nerdy) gives the lie to the cliché of the Latin lover, as does the childlike levity of his stream of vocables.

Edwin Torres is the immigrant child (it is remarkable how many American poets grew up bilingual as a result of their immigrant status) whose two languages meld into one. He "hears things people haven't really said," and enjoys it. The crushing overstimulation of the human sensorium Walter Benjamin describes in his analysis of Baudelaire and the emergence, under urban capitalism, of the automaton-like "man of the crowd" is the backdrop against which Torres deploys a hell-bent speed-style that combines images of urban street poverty, tropical flamboyance, and techniques of the Euro avant-garde "sound poem" tradition. In this sense, as a member of one of many immigrant groups in New York, his work shares much with, say, Lenny Bruce's manic polyglot eclecticism and makeshift, survivalist logic, and with a more generalized, multiethnically hyperverbal urban sensibility. "It's an island thing, playing with words, a feeling thing. But it's also New York, such a flux of people and languages and groups," he said to me in 1997. A graphic designer by day (though increasingly drawn into the world of international workshops, festivals, and fellowships), he has designed and self-published three chapbooks: *I Hear Things People Haven't Really Said* (1991), *Lung Poetry* (1994), and *SandHomméNomadNo* (1997), which last title also names a poem about a sandman/nomad as figure for the poet. (Significantly, the "*sand* [English] *homme* [French]" is given an extra syllable and pronounced "sand homáy"—that is a cross between the English-Spanish neologism "sand hombre" and, in current urban, African American–derived vernacular, the neologism "sand homey": "sandman from my own neighborhood.") This do-it-yourself chapbook aesthetic further enhances Torres's stature among experimentalists, who place a high value on efforts at community constitution and creative expression independent of mainstream venues, and who often (with varying degrees of willingness) forgo opportunities for greater distribution and fame through corporate publishing in the interest of controlling their own means of production.

If Torres's ludic extravaganzas could be described as utopian in the idealist-optimistic sense, there are counterexamples aplenty of dystopic "nowheres." Though Judy Lucero's exquisite prison poetry from the 1970s comes to mind as signally bleak, my focus here is on a more recent production. The different/dissident view of life as a bilingual is harrowingly dramatized by Javier Piña's "Bilingual in a Cardboard Box," published in *Word Up!* (Abrams, 1992), an anthology of poetry from Seattle's El Centro de la Raza and then produced in the television series *The United States of Poetry* (1996). This clip appears in the segment entitled "The American Dream" and is offered as a critique and corrective to that cliché (though to some extent the show's exuberant, pluralist optimism subscribes to a questionable patriotism). Besides Piña, the show features powerful critics of the status quo such as Luis Alfaro, Wanda Coleman, and Jim Northrup, and gives nonacademic poetry as well as "alternative" pop culture (in the form of Leonard Cohen and Lou Reed) a fair showing.

Piña himself was twenty-one when he wrote the poem, and had not previously written poetry. Born in San Antonio, Texas, and transplanted to Seattle in his late teens, he spoke only Spanish until the age of four, at which point the power of the school system and other English-only sectors of the public sphere took their toll. While he understands Spanish, speaking it is a struggle; when I asked if he had grown up bilingual, he answered "No."[14] He wrote poems, including "Bilingual," in a workshop at El Centro de la Raza based on the communitarian principles governing Ernesto Cardenal's Solentiname community in Nicaragua. "When Zoe Anglesey [the workshop leader] had us working on bilingual poems, I had to have someone give me the Spanish words I needed but couldn't remember." "Bilingual," however, the exception to this experience of forgetting, came to him in its entirety while he was in the shower. Unlike Torres, Piña does not consider himself a professional poet; indeed, he rarely writes down his ideas, except for the brief period in which he participated in the workshop. At that time he was a maintenance worker in a downtown office building. Of Apache as well as Chicano heritage, as of 1998 he worked in a Native American childcare center.

BILINGUAL IN A CARDBOARD BOX

Soy Mexicano
I'm an American

Puedo cantar canziones del corazón
I am mute

Puedo ver los colores de la puesta del sol
I am blind

Puedo escuchar las voces de los pajaritos cantando
I am deaf

Soy indígena bailando al cielo que llora
I'm forever seated in a chair with wheels

Todos me respetan
I'm labeled by pointing fingers

Tengo mucho dinero
I live in a cardboard box

Estoy riéndome con el mundo alegre
I am sad

Salgo con mis amigos
I am alone

Estoy soñando
and I don't want to wake up![15]

In the video, two Javier Piñas face each other and speak alternating lines; "Spanish" Piña on the left and "English" Piña on the right. (Apparently, there was talk during the course of production of using English subtitles for the Spanish portions, but fortunately this idea fell by the wayside. However, consequently some English-monolingual viewers believed that the lines were semantically equivalent rather than sharply dissonant.) The screen is split into an unambiguous dialectic determined by language, cultural difference, emotional and physical well-being, state of consciousness (dreaming/waking), and social status. When Piña mentions money, half of a U.S. quarter floats across the screen; on another occasion, half a hamburger on half a plate also spins slowly around the screen, as if to indicate that these symbols of hegemonic "American" normalcy can only be semirealized by a divided subject. The poem enacts its divided consciousness: the English words are primarily monosyllabic, while the Spanish words are somewhat more florid but scarcely as hyperverbally flamboyant as Torres's work. That Piña identifies himself as primarily an English speaker makes the contrast between his use of stark, minimalist English and relatively expressive Spanish all the more intriguing. Piña's delivery is soft-spoken and understated, complicating though not disavowing the business (in both senses) of special effects of *The United States of Poetry*. His personal presence is remarkable for its quietness in a series and an aesthetic characterized by loudness, contrasting not only with his immediate environment, the corporate slickness of made-for-TV production, but also with Torres's vocal self-confidence and the performative "mastery of the space" in which he moves.

In Piña's video poem, the borderline is a heavy vertical, separating the two Piñas; the subject is doubled and boxed off from himself, reduced to a passive, disabled American object, on the one hand, and a fantasized Mexican dream-person on the other. It must be pointed out, however, that the Spanish dream is not unrealistic: having friends and money, joy and health are not outlandish aspirations. A synthesis of the Spanish thesis and English antithesis is not within the vocabulary of this poetic event, any more than dreams continue on awakening. I do not mean to suggest that rigid binaries are necessarily part of a border aesthetic. The work of Marisela Norte, Luis Alfaro, Juan Felipe Herrera, and Guillermo Gómez-Peña, among others, would amply refute such an assertion, as would Saldívar's own text. To the contrary, this poem is a protest against binaries rather than a compliant enactment of them. Any resolution to the extreme split articulated in the poem would have to be dialogic, a matter of continual process, rather than a static and teleological "melting pot" assimilationism in which thesis and antithesis fuse and metamorphose in a smooth historical inevitability. Perhaps, if one can speak of a postmodern dialectic, it is one in which there can be no synthesis; solutions have to be more ingenious, more tactical, more provisional and partial. Perhaps there will be no "at home." Perhaps the truest subjectivity of Piña's poem, the locus of the lyric I that is usually so dominant in lyric poetry but so allegorically unlyrical here, is to be found in that noplace of the heavy vertical dividing line. This dividing vertical indicates not a hierarchy (Spanish is "better than" English or English is "more real" than Spanish) but a simultaneity of seemingly incommensurable realities that coexist in one consciousness and the divisive, internal corrosion that results when one language is delegitimated.

And a further thought, which can serve as an

for reasons that will become clear. At the microlevel of analysis to-the-letter permitted by traditional poetic exegesis, the progressivity (oblique, but progressivity nonetheless) of the dialectic can perhaps be displaced by the chiasmatic X of an alternative spelling somewhat akin in intention to the politicized coinage *Nuyorican*. Alfred Arteaga has invoked a "post-pomo" (post-postmodern) Xicano poetics based on hybridity: X for eXchange, MeXico, Xicar (to play).[16] The mystery (X for the unknown solution to an equation) and specificity (X marks the spot) of the X enact a chiasmus, a map of having "changed places." (The classic emancipatory Xiasmus in American literature has been pointed out by Henry Louis Gates, Jr.: Frederick Douglass's famous words, "You have seen how a man was made a slave; you shall see how a slave was made a man."[17]) Genet on his knees in a squalid room in Spain apprehending poetry through anXiety; Piña in the squalor boX of English-only remembering enough Spanish to write a poem that gets on national television; Torres declaiming Spanglish in high-art nonsense on a ratty, archive-only video for a writing center in Minnesota; Robert Duncan abdicating power as the border guard who runs off to join the ranks of the undocumented; Edward Said the Conrad scholar becoming Edward Said the Palestinian nationalist cultural worker—all of these movements are Xings that mark dissonant conjunctions, resonant dissidence. Am I suggesting that if we spelled certain words with X's life would be better for the dispossessed? Of course not. I am, though, making an appeal to the role of the verbal imagination in effecting change.

In spite of their obvious differences in terms of venue and the production of aesthetic value, both Torres's and Piña's poems embrace postmodern techne: Piña's split-screen mirrored self and its appearance in the mass media; Torres's fragmented one-man run-on word festival in the context of grassroots-urban-café life cum avant-garde poetiX. In fact, I would suggest that these two modes, the relatively low-tech, high-art, do-it-yourself "elitism" of the avant-garde and the high-tech, mass culture appeal of the television poem, are not at all at irreconcilable odds. These two works clearly have more in common than either does with mainstream poetry or mainstream representations of Latino/a sensibility and culture. Ongoing tensions and competing agendas—"artistic integrity," "accessibility," the purported "elitism" of the vanguard, the purportedly inescapable compromise with capitalism that marX all of mass culture, and so forth—between them spur further inventiveness and new hybrid ties.[18] One other thing

United States of Poetry and the Torres tape have in common is the agency of Bob Holman, one of the revivers of the Nuyorican Poets' Café, who emceed the reading of the Torres video, co-edited the second Nuyorican anthology (in which Torres's work appears) and coproduced the *United States of Poetry*. (Holman is himself a border-crosser in some ways; though now associated with New York City's electrical high-wire energy, he grew up in a Kentucky mining town where his father was the only Jew.) If postmodernity comprises low-intensity but high-tech armed warfare along the Mexico-U.S. border, in which the arms are pointed one way only and the high technology is used by one side only, postmodern poetiX/poiesis seems to offer some useful possibilities to Chicano/a/Latino/a literary historians and practitioners as utopian cultural praXis. Néstor García Canclini, for example, points toward antecedent "decollecting and deterritorialization . . . in the utopian reflections" of earlier moments in Latin American aesthetics but then differentiates postmodernism by asserting that "artistic practices now lack consistent paradigms" and that "postmodernism is not a style but a tumultuous copresence of all styles."[19] Arteaga and Saldívar are equally engaged with the postmodern and are explicitly enthusiastic about defining Xicano subjectivity in accord with what has emerged as that triumphant not-quite-repudiation-of-but-certainly-an-"oblique" relation to identity that marks a postmodern take on so-called "identity politiX."

Afterwordzz

The first two epigraphs, snippets from Jean Genet's *The Thief's Journal* and Robert Duncan's "Song of the Borderguard," contain seeds for further cultivation in the erogenous contaXzone of the poetic—what Duncan calls the "borderline of sense."[20] Genet is always a good starting point; lest one fall into a condition of American Xceptionalism (even one comprising all the Americas), this French homosXual petty criminal and social outcast who made common cause with the Black Panthers and the Palestinian Liberation Organization can still teach us a thing or two about aesthetic production under Xtreme circumstances, and about the power of language itself as a source of Xperience for members of communities on the edge who struggle hourly for survival through and for creative Xpression. We can also learn a lot about border issues from sXual minorities like Genet and Duncan, not least about the complicated relations of fear, mistrust, and desire that obtain between normative and non-normative citizen-subjects, strategies of affiliations and disaffiliations between different but overlapping oppositional identities (sometimes within the same person), and how each citizen-subject is both not wholly outside of and not wholly one with some real but also not impermeable mainstream.

We are some way from the moment when the INS officials abandon their low-intensity warfare, and we seem to be slipping farther from a society or even a curriculum that reflects the splendors of dissident traditions and the vulnerability of the normative one (in academia there is a sense that trendiness is over, and that it is time to get back to the same old base-suX); a long way from a scene in which, to cite Richard Farina's lyriX of the mid-1960s, the congressmen are taking off their clothes; and we may be at a point, moreover, where we may emphatically not welcome such a display. And, of course, there is always the problematic of desire mixed with power: does the border guard abandon his post, romanticizing the object of his surveillance, without abandoning his power? The 1952 Duncan poem anticipates what is now known as "whiteness" studies, which attempts to demystify the current hegemony, to unmask whiteness as historically and contingently constructed. The homoerotiX of Duncan's poem, in which the borderline is not geographic but discursive—the line between, say, poetic and ordinary language, between the chthonic and the mundane—can nonetheless be allegorized as geocultural. In other words, proXimity can have its effect—one of desire—on the majority culture, and especially on the outposts thereof. A gay San Francisco poet, Duncan refused to live in the Castro neighborhood, which he saw as a gay ghetto, but instead lived in the Mission, a Latino/a neighborhood, where he taught in the poetiX program of New College. In the course of his poetic career he abandoned the guardpost of canonicity, leaving Ezra Pound and T. S. Eliot behind with a resolutely joyful commitment to a spiritual poetiX of homoerotic grandeur. My Euro touchstones here have been Genet and Duncan, forefathers in transgressive sXualities and the languages of rapture. The worX of Edwin TorreX and Xavier Piña, younger bards of illegitimate linguistic desire, have served as multifaXeted diamonds through which to reach toward the refracted light of the poetic. The outer fringes of the soXius unravel to be rewoven with adjacent lives and cultures in the multiple X's of "half-hid warp"—Walt Whitman—that make up the fabric of our Norte America.[21] LeX imagine this already Xtant reality.

9 Loneliness, Lyric, Ethnography

Some Discourses on/of the Divided Self

The Divided Self

Some years ago in a graduate seminar on contemporary American poetry, a particularly gifted student remarked during the course of our discussion on Allen Ginsberg that what was so moving about the Beat poets was their insistence on making the "signifier fit the signified," on fusing them, through violence if necessary—forcing representation to match up perfectly with something putatively anterior to it: "being"—"essence"— one's "true self." Thus the emphasis on nakedness, candor, self-disclosure of an almost compulsive rigor. Through "telling it like it is," in other words, they staked their entire poetic careers on forging—or revealing—a trustworthy unitary subject whose autobiographical pain was immediately graspable through the reading experience whether on the page or on the stage. The "I" in the poem, counter to elaborate academic theories about personae and dramatic irony that abounded at the time, was the I of life, the poet's life. And, this impassioned and eloquent student went on to point out, it couldn't be done: thence the poignancy of the writing—the beauty of the wreckage that the impossibility of getting rid of literary artifice, or the splitting of the self into subject and object of writing, wrought on literature and on their lives. High stakes—impossible stakes—to say the least, as it was founded on a chimera, namely, a single bedrock essence that could, moreover, be articulated—if only one searched and spoke and wrote and declaimed and lived hard enough. Could it have been this very attempt that, as Ginsberg so famously observed, destroyed the best minds of his generation?

I was taken with his proposition at the time and still do not think it was wrong. Speaking to one of the central tensions in the history of modern lyric poetry, the relationship between signifier and referent as allegorized by the lyric I, it could in fact be profitably considered with regard to not only the Beats but many of modernism's participants or modernity's denizens. The crisis would become especially acute for those on the cusp of what we now consider the postmodern: to, right before a generalized acceptance of performativity and multiplicity, take a final ambivalent and anguished stand in favor of a utopian and nostalgic model of unalienated unity. His argument rewrote persuasively the oft-repeated lore that those coming of intellectual and artistic age right after the unprecedented scale of World War II's annihilations were destroyed by the commercialization and sterile suburbanization of USA-style late capitalistic postmodernity; he claimed rather that what caused such anguished and powerful work was the necessarily doomed attempt to deny the inherent, mediated performativity of text and selves in favor of immediate experience. Other scholars, such as gay historian George Chauncey, have corroborated this sense that the sixties culture tried to obliterate self-difference, which had come to be considered a distressing cultural norm; the sixties, for example, marked the era in which the double life of marginalized identity was put aside in favor of, to use idioms then prevalent, "coming out of the closet," "taking off the mask," doing your own thing, being or expressing yourself, embracing your identity—as if you had only one.[1] While Chauncey emphasizes how the unitary identity in "identity politics" was constructed in a political climate that could be seen to violate the well-wrought artifice of double lives that gay men and other minoritized people had crafted, it is easy to see how the Beat ethos (particularly pointed in Beat culture's proximity to gay and black subcultures, which it variously misrecognized, obfuscated, celebrated, and emulated) countered that presumed duplicity, in the service of an aesthetic or a lifestyle in which self-expression precluded any doubling, which latter phenomenon was negatively coded as pretense and subterfuge.

Such protest against duplicity in private life had its counterpart in the public sphere, and much of this elicits a sympathetic nostalgia for the modernist investment in binaries of truth and falsity, frankness, and duplicity. As Robert Von Hallberg has pointed out, part of this insistence on transparency and truth-telling was a critique of the perceived (and actual) mendacity of the state, which critique took its cue from revelations of the falsity of Senator Joseph McCarthy's documentation of communist activities among U.S. citizens and reached its peak in the following two decades, culminating in Daniel Ellsberg's leaking of the Pentagon Papers to the *New York Times*, a media coup that helped to discredit and eventually end U.S. armed intervention in Viet Nam.[2] By contrast, during the postmodern era of Ronald Reagan (whose faith in performativity was such that he confused his performance in movies about World War II with actual service in the war), people came to expect obfuscation and corruption at the highest levels of government, as the cynical phrase "the Teflon president"—an epithet widely used at the time with admiring rather than bitter overtones—attests. Falsification of information, now perceived to be routine (viz. Secretary of State Colin Powell's lack of embarrassment over revelations that the information he presented to the UN Security Council about Iraq's weapons of mass destruction was a forgery), was considered so unethical as to bring down regimes and turn public opinion around.

As the "divided [binaristic] self" of the modernist period, with its separation of inner and outer, good and bad, mask and "real self," public and private, evolved into the fluid and fragmented self of the current postmodern era, it passed through the cataclysm of the 1960s–1980s liberationist era, in which the unitary, "authentic" self was proclaimed as needing emancipation from the false and oppressive roles imposed by an external, hostile, and conformist society. During the 1960s and 1970s, identity, in the singular, was the concept around which social activism organized itself before, primarily, black feminists once again finally reminded us that we are, and live as, more than one or even two selves simultaneously. Dissenting 1960s art, it has often been said, was an anti-artifice art, an art that presumed only the tragic aspect of double consciousness and tried, with some cruelly well-meaning, reductive clumsiness, to fix it.

In the narrower realm of poetry, this amounted, in the eyes of this era's cultural workers, to an emphatic repudiation of what the Agrarians/New Critics/Fugitive poet-critics, frank elitists, had theorized as the autonomous poem purged of any intentional fallacy or surrounding context, the messiness of social, personal, historical, or economic contingency. For the Beats and other dissenting poets of the postwar era, a poetics had to be lived as well as written, in spite of the high cost of such a proposition. In fact, the willingness to incur such a life-exacting cost was an index of true poeticity. However, this insistence on simplification of self to self-sameness was a naive solution; to simply undouble double consciousness as a strategy for cultural expression, not to mention for lived experience, simply didn't work all that smoothly, especially for minoritized individuals. In attacking the elitism of proponents of the decontextualized work, new American poets (Beats and confessionals among them) denied the complexity of the relationship of text to ever-shifting context.

Minoritized subjects such as black and queer people within these dissenting literary communities could not easily or glibly drop the pleasures, the protective maneuverability, or even the historical sorrows associated with the performative, the multiplicity of roles they inhabited. Social outsiders within a society of dissenters, they were neither the complacent bourgeois nor the frostily Eliotic poets who made up the foils against which the New American Poetry constituted its ethos but rather people for whom an unambiguously single "self" was clearly a fallacy, who had not had the historical luxury of living that fallacy, and who had crafted marvelous lives and art out of an ethos of performativity. Finding themselves in a position of adjacency to, rather than fully part of, both mainstream and dissenting cultures that took only the mainstream as their reference point, these minoritized writers' lyric work witnessed and documented both their own psyches and the societies in which they could only partially participate. Over time, some of these poetic projects could not sustain the contradictions of witnessing; the extreme degree of their doubling, as well as the impossibility of self-sameness (undoubling), created unbearable psychic strain. These writers, later in their careers, wandered about in the wreckage rubble of lyric as if it had been an overly ordered, hyperaestheticized cerebral city that had sustained a bombing campaign, their fragments, rants, and expressions of "solitudes crowded with loneliness" testaments to the fragile fiction that modern unified subjectivity had been.[3]

At a certain point after immersion in this 1950s outsider poetry I was struck by its hyperdescriptive, ethnographic content (*Howl*'s enumerations, for instance, can be considered a thick description of the underworld culture Ginsberg romanticized and participated in). I wondered if such work could be considered (auto-)ethnographic (Johannes Fabian provides an important link here by insisting that all ethnography is autobiography, and the poetry of this subculture was noted for its autobiographical content),[4] especially with reference to the poignant "participant observer" role that minoritized subjects are often thrust into when they interact with the mainstream (that is, daily, hourly, and so forth), or, in this case, and even trickier sometimes, an oppositional subculture that claims to provide conditions for an unalienated life but cannot make good on its claims because of its ambiguously complicit relation to the mainstream. I wondered if in fact the breakdown in formal control that characterizes much of this poetry—especially in the later work of Bob Kaufman and John Wieners, who are discussed in greater detail below and who, in the ethnographic distance some of their early work maintained, were related to this strain of being, paradoxically, immersed in a counterculture that claimed to strip pretense away therapeutically but was actually unable to protect its more vulnerable members from the socially punitive consequences of doing so. I wondered if there was any insight into the nature of creative survival and poiesis to be gained from juxtaposing, under the general heading of "discourses of divided consciousness," the subjective processes of ethnographic practices and texts with those of lyric. The subjectivity of the ethnographer and the lyric poet and the way that subject is represented in resultant texts, both defamiliarized from and resonant with its originating (small a) author, seem to have something in common, though the ethnographer has traditionally written a record of external experience under the banner of science, objectivity, and society and the lyric poet has recorded an internal experience under the banner of art, subjectivity, and privacy.

A concept key to this drama of doubling and undoubling is the insight variously formulated by Marx, Freud, Du Bois, and Walter Benjamin, among others: namely, that the subject in modernity is de facto traumatized by alienation and double consciousness. Underlying the self-as-other predicament of the poet and the ethnographer is the traumatized and self-divided modern subject who, through inevitable (rather than self-induced) dissociation, alienation, and double consciousness brought about by social conditions, experiences itself as other. While this is a generalized condition of modernity, it manifests differently for different subjects and under varying conditions. The split subject is at once a pathological effect of specific trauma (in the case of intrafamilial violence or near-death experiences in accidents or wars) or more diffuse historical-collective trauma (in the case, for instance, of historical slavery, wage-labor exploitation, or a history of ethnic or religious persecution) and a normative condition in the modern era. The experience of alienated modernity, as Theodor Adorno argued in "Lyric Poetry and Society" (implying but not stating that this alienation is profoundly traumatic), lies at the core of the modern impetus toward lyric: the social violence of modernity is always implied, even in the most solitary of pastoral verses, which latter function in dialectical counterpoint as compensatory balm to that social violence.[5] Thus, the apparent choice to isolate on the part of the lyric poet or the adventuring ethnographer is not a choice; rather, the already fragmented subject of modern lyric and ethnography creates a narrative of having chosen solitude, to address and yet avoid confronting the traumatic experience and to produce texts that both reveal and conceal, address and circumlocute. These two representations of self-estrangement, ethnographic self-estrangement and lyric subjectivity, though not unilaterally equivalent, are related to the traumatic dissociation of double consciousness ranging from the normativity of the "healthy" modern psyche to the deviance of mental illness. They operate on a continuum of subjective defamiliarization (that benchmark of literary discourse), with strong family resemblances. The modern condition is aptly summed up by Arthur ("il faut être absolument moderne") Rimbaud's "Je est un autre"; Rimbaud, a paradigmatic lyric poet, eventually abandoned the lyric (his masterpiece *Un saison en enfer* constitutes his farewell to it) to emigrate to Ethiopia, where he wrote several essays for French journals of natural history before disappearing entirely from the world of print. Double consciousness, it seems, is the sine qua non of lyric as it is of ethnographic experience and writing; lyric is a dissociative genre; dissociation is an effect of trauma; trauma is a generalizable cultural characteristic of modernity, as is double consciousness. At the normative end of this continuum is the Cartesian subject, whose humanity consists in the talent of self-reflexivity, or the ability to split oneself off from one's body in order to observe, reflect on, judge, and regulate that body's activities; at the other end are schizophrenia and addiction, which we encounter in John Wieners and Bob Kaufman. The dichotomized split of *cogito ergo sum* is now fragmented into multiples; postmodernism is an acceptance of this multiplicity rather than an insistence on its aberrance.

The predicament of whether one could be one or was always multiple, whether one could merge any "I" with a self-regarding "eye," was of course not restricted to poets or ethnographers but characterized the life of the subject in the modern era. Traumatized by the separation of signifier from referent, of "self" from subjective activity, of the individual from the socius, of the worker from empowerment to labor on his or her own behalf, the modern psyche is split. As the subtitle of Paul Gilroy's *The Black Atlantic: Modernity and Double-Consciousness* suggests, an alienated self-consciousness is the cultural norm of modernity. Because it takes trauma as normative, it follows that a forcible undoubling of the double consciousness endemic to modernity would be no less traumatic. A belief in the generalized cultural trauma of modernity is thus at the heart of this chapter, with the significant caveat that this condition is exacerbated for minoritized subjects; lyric poetry and ethnography are two genres typical of the era that well instantiate this claim through their methodological and philosophical reliance on split subjectivity even as they acutely pressure, explore, and expose this problematic.

One further note on the peculiarities of ethnography and lyric in the house of the doubled self, of which these two modalities function as complementary manifestations: ethnography, beyond its foundational divide of self versus other, or home culture versus host culture, is a doubled discourse in an even more fundamental way. It effects an internal split in the putatively singular self of the ethnographer in the "participant observer" mandate, which imposes duplicity and a high degree of anxiety on the ethnographer. In the discussion of ethnography that follows, Bronislaw

Malinowski, to whom the methodology if not the term of participant observation is attributed, provides a case study in the desperation of the performance of self-sameness in the face of overwhelming personal experience of dividedness. One could say that ethnography is founded on the projection of the doubled self onto an external model of "our culture" versus "their culture."

Lyric poetry, with its trademark characteristic use of the first person (the lyric I), likewise claims a sort of self-sufficiency for the speaking subject. But here the splitting happens internally rather than as an outward projection. Through the very nature of discursive introspection, the self has to look at itself as if it were other (which it is). Though the final lines of a poem, especially in contemporary mainstream lyric, tend to gesture toward a reconciliation of the watched self with the commentator self—in other words, an affirmation of self-sameness on the part of the "speaker of the poem," and by extension the author and the monadic epistemological system he or she represents—the genre reveals, through its self-consciousness, the division at the heart of lyric subjectivity. In other words, it is the recuperative unity and not the putatively temporary self-division of the subject that is ultimately suspect. The poetry discussed below exemplifies the crisis that threatens lyric when this is confronted directly.

"Other" Poetry

Jean Genet suggests in *The Thief's Journal* that "there is a close relationship between convicts and flowers."[6] I suggest that there is likewise, under the larger rubric of divided subjectivity, a close relationship between ethnography and lyric poetry, though which is floral and which is criminal is anybody's guess, and changes from moment to moment; perhaps each has a goodly dose of both components. Speculation suggests that lyric poetry and ethnography, having similar genealogies, with roots in the emergence of the modern subject, both perform a kind of self-estrangement within the writer, a doubling of consciousness, effected by but also resulting in loneliness and anxiety. This anxiety serves as the impetus for the mastery of the respective genres—ethnography and lyric literary—and by extension, of the umbrella disciplines—anthropology and literary writing, respectively. As (again) Jean Genet, auto-ethnographer of the underworld of petty criminals and lumpen gender-benders, so aptly puts it, "Then I really felt in exile, and my nervousness was going to make me permeable to what—for want of other words—I shall call poetry."[7] With more sophistication than many of those American dissenting writers who held him in high esteem, Genet locates the poetic as coextensive with exile and (self-)

difference, not as a compensatory move toward reconciliation. Poetry is reliant on the gaps and spaces between the fragments of self and self; it originates there, rather than from a place of wholeness. Genet is writing from a position low on the social order, in which exile is not a matter of choice but one brought about by vagrancy across national borders, of the kind performed by those below the radar of governmental surveillance. The purported condition of ethnographers and self-conscious poets is one of contained self-exile: in the service of eventual expertise, they are willing temporarily to cede certainty and risk the disorientation of immersion in an uncomfortable environment. The classic ethnographer undergoes, during fieldwork, the unmanned, unmoored feeling of cultural confusion and irrelevance. For the poet, self-estrangement comes with an altered, nonquotidian triangulated relationship among self, world, and language; in each case, the dark night of the soul is lived through to find salvation in a reunified, putatively wiser subjectivity on the other side.

Digressive Contextual Core Essential Snore Snore Yes Yes Material

While there have been movements in poetry practice and scholarship that place these in close relation to anthropology, I want to distinguish this inquiry from at least some of them. The ethnopoetics of the 1970s, whose practitioners, primarily translator-anthropologist Dennis Tedlock and poets Jerome Rothenberg and George Quasha, as well as a host of anthologists such as Ulli Beier, wanted to heighten the sensitivity of urban Western English speakers to indigenous people's verbal art, arguing somewhat defensively that it was just as good as the high lyric tradition and deserved aesthetic as well as sociological attention. Although many feel there was some genuine potential for widening the field of poetic activity and scholarship, this movement has been criticized for appropriating indigenous culture in the name of a universalizing modernism that gathers up many different verbal practices under its own (Western avant-garde) standard of poetic language, with little regard for how these verbal events function in their originating cultures. More recently, anthropologists such as Steven Caton, Lila Abu-Lughod, and Smadar Lavie have examined poetry as social practice among Middle Eastern people such as the Bedouin, Northern Yemenites, and Palestinians in the occupied territories; more than the earlier ethnopoetics scholars, anthologists, and poets, they attend to the complexity of the context in which this body of spoken or written work is produced, and to how it functions *within* its particular culture. Subfields within anthropology address folklore, ethnomusicology (with at least some attention to the verbal aspects of music

POETICS FOR A POSTLITERARY AMERICA

making), and the anthropology of creativity. What happens if we look at poetry as ethnography, and conversely at ethnographic practices as poetic? Or at the parallel developments in disciplinary subject formation that shape the putatively responsible ethnographer or the poet as skilled craftsperson, as well as sensitive human(istic) being? How does this distinguish (or not) him or her from the object of study or the objective correlative of lyric content? What is the nature of the continuum along which self and other, poetry and other discourses, subject and object of study, witness and vicitm, citizen and denizen, observer and participant are ranged? And what about the poeticity of fieldnotes? Poet and editor Mark Nowak's journal *XCP: Cross Cultural Poetics* has pioneered such endeavors, especially in issue 3, *Fieldnotes and Journals*; Nowak's own poetry incorporates ethnographic interviews and excerpts from classic ethnographic texts, and in other ways frankly acknowledges a methodological and thematic debt to ethnography.[8] One could consider the careers of anthropologists like Michael Taussig, with his turn toward performance and ekstasis—not into madness and addiction, but certainly away from the norms of ethnographic decorum and into modalities that affirm multiplicity even as they challenge what is permissible within the purviews of anthropology.[9] Edward Sapir, Ruth Benedict, Stanley Diamond, folklorist Susan Stewart, Renato Rosaldo, and Ruth Behar have published poetry; the latter two have explored quite explicitly the affective dimensions of the ethnographic endeavor, with an eye to healing the oxymoronic split of the "participant observer."[10] Some anthropological journals routinely publish poetry; *Anthropology and Humanism* has a poetry editor on its regular roster and publishes several poems in every issue. There are also, to be sure, "rogue anthropologists" who defected from their critical-humanistic distance and were more or less absorbed into the contexts they studied, and their careers and writings could be usefully explored in tandem with those of the poets who have slipped beyond the purviews of the poetic mainstream, but such a project falls outside the boundaries of the current crude template.

One might also usefully ask, why now? The literary turn in anthropology has been a disciplinary fact for several decades, and ethnographic techniques and perspectives have entered literary scholarship through cultural studies, studies of popular and mass-produced literature, and populist-oriented historiographies, starting to inform even the most traditional subfields. What can be gained by revisiting the conjunctions between the poetics of poetry and the poetics and politics of ethnography, as the breakthrough volume *Writing Culture*'s subtitle pithily announced as its purview in 1986?

In exploring the ethnographic preference for novelistic and other literary narrative over the poetic, one finds matters of considerable interest. During the turn to language in the social sciences during the 1980s, anthropology especially availed itself of literary techniques and interpretive theory, seeing in thick description a method for creating ethnographies saturated with meaningful information about the cultures under observation. Clifford Geertz, who imported the term from speech act theory into ethnography, credits Gilbert Ryle with coining it. Ryle contrasts thin description with thick description, claiming for the latter a complex and meaningful communication that encodes subtle differences of meaning depending on context, usage, and cultural insiderhood of the participants in the communication about any given action (his primary example is the schoolboy wink juxtaposed to an involuntary facial tic; in a thin description the two would be indistinguishable, while in a thick description the difference would be meaningfully spelled out and apprehended by the reader or observer). On a literary register, thin description is more paratactical, thick more narrative. No wonder poetry has not been foregrounded in ethnography's turn to the literary; the completed ethnography is intended to familiarize the unfamiliar, to narrate the previously exotic in a manner that renders it transparent to the Western reader. Parataxis would work in the opposite direction, maintaining a mystique around daily practice and cultural institutions that perpetuates their strangeness to the uninitiated—or even creating strangeness anew for those who are in the know (thus the hieratic tone of the Hebrew Bible, the strangeness of much of Gertrude Stein's prose, though she deals with domestic commonplaces, and so forth). When we move back from the finished ethnography to the developmental stages of fieldnotes and diaries, we find that in the lack of hierarchy in the information being accumulated, the affective welter of expression, and the allusive suggestiveness but indeterminacy of much of the material, we are closer to the realm of the poetic, the paratactical. So if thick, organized description—narrative and novelistic—corresponds to the finished mastery of the published/polished ethnography, perhaps thin description—paratactical and poetic, staying on the surface—corresponds more closely to what I find more interesting about ethnographic activity: the poiesis of disorientation, liminality, and a kind of deterritorialized egalitarianism of information that prevails in fieldnotes, journals, and diaries. But: the thickness of thickness, the thinness of thinness; can one ever be too thick or too poor? Thickness and thinness are not quantitative but qualitative terms. Hyperdescription with no organizing hierarchy would still be thin description. Thus the eccentric work of Raymond Roussell or Ronald Firbank, though compulsively, manically descriptive, obsessively nondiscriminatory in its range, has little informational value because there is no subordinating principle at work in the verbal effluvium that constitutes their prose and verse. It disorients through its very verbosity and excess.

The Lyricism of Ethnography

Classic modern ethnography offers itself as a precedent genre in which loneliness and processes of estrangement are established as foundational methodological norms from which great work issues. In his magnum opus, *Argonauts of the Western Pacific* (1922), Bronislaw Malinowski, the acknowledged originator of the method, justified his proposed mode of research, which has become known as the participant observation method of conducting fieldwork, with the following startling rationale: the anthropologist, presumed in Malinowski's text as in all other anthropological texts of the time to be a white man, must banish himself from the company of others like him; the loneliness thus induced will drive him to do his fieldwork.[11] Only the fear of going mad from loneliness, Malinowski reasons, will induce the ethnographer to seek out the company of his (ambiguously inferior) nonwhite subjects. The immersion experience he as a social being undergoes in their culture and which he also, as a scientist, documents thoroughly becomes the basis for his research. Self-estrangement (the split between human being and scientist, the literal distance between the individual and his home culture and the cognitive distance between the individual and his host culture) leads to immersion in a different culture, but rather than wholly heal that estrangement, the ethnographer must maintain it in order to be both a participant and an observer in that culture; he must never forget his allegiance to his work, lest he "go native." The healing, or reconciliation, happens in the other direction: once back in his native culture, the anthropologist's regained subject position as Westerner can subsume the other experience and relegate it to an episodic experiment whose results he now documents and analyzes. The end product, the published ethnography, conceals the messy, disorienting experience of loneliness that midwifed its existence; it is optimally a declaration of mastery of one's discipline, and one's emotions. A subtle gendering and whitening process happens here: the ethnographer remasculinizes and rewhitens himself through the writing that, in a reversal of the original distancing from his own people, now distances him from the host culture and reintegrates him with his own. However, there are traces of fear and abjection to be found in classic ethnography, and this loneliness, which generated the text, remains at its core.

Significantly, Malinowski's exile was not self-willed. His most influential writing and most formative fieldwork in the Melanesian Trobriand
Islands were undertaken when Poland was experiencing the ravages of
World War I and being colonized by the Soviets to the East. Malinowski
was himself interned as an enemy alien in Australia during the war. We
see some of the stakes and experiences that motivated Malinowski's project in *A Diary in the Strict Sense of the Term.* The book, scandalous when it
was first published (posthumously) precisely because of the gap it revealed
between the polished ethnographic work and the messy, abject ethnographic process, is fraught with frequent, anguished passages in which he
is preoccupied with the health and welfare of his mother, the fear of never
seeing her again (this fear did materialize), nostalgic moments of longing
for a Poland he can never revisit, and a more generalized concern for the
fate of his country. The book, an unexpurgated version of which has been
published in Poland and has yet to be translated as of this writing (2010),
was in large part an attempt to explore and regulate through confession
and self-examination the possibilities of relationship—with oneself, with
the beloved, with—to a remarkably lesser extent, given the context—the
famous ethnographic other. Thus it details the struggle to be faithful, both
in the conventional sense of monogamous fidelity and in the related humanistic sense of "to thine own self be true" (never mind that these words
were uttered in a play, and by a character intended to be seen as well-
intentioned but stupid and pompous).

While we can read these traces between the lines and at times explicitly,
we can also appreciate the intention and trajectory toward mastery characteristic of ethnography that is born out of a need to reterritorialize and
integrate one's experiences of alterity, duality, and the shock of modernity.
Even while reviewing his relationship with his recently dead mother and
other lost relationships, even while explicitly articulating the reality of a
modern life lived in fragmented free-fall, toward the end of the *Diary*
Malinowski explicitly asserts his faith in the liberal-humanistic theory of
individual self-sameness, the very one he must suspend or at least call into
question by virtue of the putative belief in cultural relativism that gives
anthropology its intellectual purchase: "My whole ethics is based on the
fundamental instinct of unified personality. From this follows the need to
be the same in different situations (truth in relation to oneself) and the
need, indispensability, of sincerity: the whole value of friendship is based
on the possibility of expressing oneself, of being oneself with absolute
frankness."[12] In fact, the *Diary* itself was, as well as an attempt not to go
mad from loneliness, a deliberate exercise in self-reflection for the purpose of achieving self-sameness (and the eradication of undesirable traits

POETICS FOR A POSTLITERARY AMERICA

and habits, such as "dejection," obsessive novel reading, and womanizing, that obstruct this process) through self-knowledge. Self-knowledge, in other words, is power, in much the same way that intellectual mastery over "his" "savages" or the field of anthropology itself is power. This desire for self-knowledge through self-disclosing narrative resonates sharply with the yearnings of someone like Allen Ginsberg, who attributed the power of his bond with Burroughs and Kerouac to the informal psychoanalytic sessions they conducted in the 1940s and early 1950s in which they took turns lying on the floor and revealing all their secrets in monologues while the other two listened in nonjudgmental silence, much as Malinowski imagined his fiancée, Elsie Masson, as the recipient of his confessional words. (What appears to be different is that Ginsberg, Burroughs, and Kerouac were not attempting to cure themselves of bad habits.)

That one can be entirely "one [and the same] self" at all times is a goal only in an epistemological system that sees multiplicity as counterfeit and downgrades the experience and integrity of those who, in W.E.B. Du Bois's words, "ever experience [their] two-ness."[13] En route to this unambivalent-sounding assertion about his integrity, Malinowski makes it clear that not only does he experience terrific twoness quite often but that even in his most exalted moments, he validates his experience by imagining that he is sharing it with his fiancée; she is an invisible presence suffusing all his fieldwork experiences—especially those in which he appreciates the landscape—with redemptive meaning. This is a kind of self-splitting, an inability to be a unified subject. Moreover, immediately following the declaration of oneness cited above, he adds, "The real problem is: why must you always behave as if God were watching you?"[14] In other words, it is not at all "natural" or easy to be wholly unified and unself-conscious; the sense of being watched by oneself or others, whether that be projected into the figure of God (critically), a loving fiancée (approvingly), or "natives" one does not consider one's equal (unnervingly), seems far more ingrained as his (and perhaps everyone's) default setting. His inner experience is an imagined performance for an omniscient benefit, and derives its meaning therefrom. As in the case of the Beat poets several decades later, the frantic proclamations of self-sameness belie a lived experience of multiplicity, double consciousness, self-in-not-always-comfortable social relationship.

The *Diary* abounds with intense moments of pastoral appreciation approaching transcendent moments of lyric poetry and shares many of its characteristics, linking the practices of ethnography and field diaries to those of lyric poetry. Malinowski has great descriptive gifts; even in translation the passages in which he is transported by the natural beauty

of the tropics approach the dissociative power of the lyrical objective correlative, and are often accompanied by statements about extreme moods,
either "fits of dejection" or triumphant "joy" about internally declaring
intellectual ownership of "my village"; the diary entries in their youth be-
gin in gladness, whereas in the end—and periodically throughout—they
threaten despondency and (the fear of) madness. Auditory hallucinations
and a synesthesia born of both deprivation of the known and a surfeit of
well-being occur: "I had moments of wild longing to hear music and at
times it seemed to me that I was actually hearing [Beethoven's 9th]"[15];
"Marvelous sunset. . . . One could hear and feel that color in the air. . . . I
was not homesick, I didn't think about Poland."[16] Repeatedly, Malinowski
attributes great and overpowering intention and personality to the landscape itself in the best animistic tradition, only to master himself by fantasizing the power and prestige his research will bestow on him in the
scientific West in passages that have been much quoted by Malinowski's
and classical anthropology's critics and revisionists in order to demystify the ethnographer's project and link it unambiguously with colonial
domination. Of course, this critique is correct, but it underestimates not
only the compensatory nature of the ethnographer's grandiosity (which
does not excuse it, but casts it in a dialectical relationship with itself, as
if Hegel's master-slave dynamic were being played out within a single
mind) but also the ways in which his dual (or dueling) psychological state
is an effect not only of individual loneliness but of cultural and historical
trauma.[17] Throughout the *Diary* Malinowski mentions his desire to write
poetry, a few attempts to do so, and occasional feelings of triumph in relation to the process, but it appears that only one poem has survived, and it
predates his breakthrough fieldwork. In January 1912 he wrote "In Wawel
Cathedral," a dark sonnet of death, silver coffins, and martyr's blood that
places the speaker and a companion (a lover? a spirit?) in a cathedral's
"dark nave," feeling the fate of their impending death.[18]

Others from within the discipline Malinowski represents have observed this great interior drama with far more critical acumen than the
foregoing comments demonstrate; the ethnographer's loneliness and
other revelations (particularly the ethnographer's racism) in the *Diary*
have been much written about, and ethnographic fieldwork, its methodology and textualization, have by now moved far beyond mythologized
Malinowskian heroics to such a degree that engaged communication and
intersubjectivity rather than loneliness and participant observation are
considered the constitutive processes of ethnography.[19] But the ways in
which the dynamics of classic ethnography with its global reach intersect
with those of the microdrama of the intensely local lyric I have not been

fully explored. The grandiose-to-abject swings in inner experience such as those described in the *Diary* and implicit in much modern poetry, all the way from "I wandered lonely as a cloud" to you name it, indicate an anxiety over a necessarily unsettled relationship to one's own mind and experience and, by implication, the subject and its social context.

A Note on Wordsworth and Malinowski: Aspects of English romantic poetry—most famously, perhaps, the *Lyrical Ballads* as imaginative appropriations of folk-poetic form motivated by imagined sympathy with their anonymous subjects—are ethnopoetic in orientation. Romanticism witnessed the rise of self-reflection and self-exploration as the highest purpose of poetry; one could say that Romanticism, modernity's first full-fledged artistic sensibility, engendered both self(auto)-cultural and other-cultural discourses. The ultimate object of both discourses is the constitution and development of the poet's/ethnographer's own subjectivity. Thus it was that William Wordsworth could be the champion of "the people's art," of its appropriation for the purposes of high literature, and of the individual psyche tracking its spontaneous overflows of emotion recollected in moments of tranquility: the ethnographic diarist and observer embodied in the lyric poet par excellence. The terms "dejection" and "joy," both of which appear repeatedly in Malinowski's translated *Diary*, are signature elements of the Romantic lexicon.

The Ethnography of Lyric

By transforming the loneliness of fieldwork in a foreign culture into observation-oriented writing, the ethnographer attempts to remasculinize and whiten himself (conquering the feminizing and abject conditions of loneliness and the subject position of the other) through producing text for consumption by his home culture that, though (until recently) downplaying the ethnographer's consciousness, by implication locates that consciousness as searching, perceptive, and, through its very erasure, ultimately omniscient. In lyric, the consciousness itself is foregrounded, attended *to*, as the most interesting element of the text; in ethnography, it is attended *from*, the motor driving the prose, the tastefully backgrounded sine qua non. In modern lyric, especially since the dominance of Eliot's objective correlative, in which the poet sought to route his cognitive and affective process through reflections of these processes in external nature (as if we were not part of nature) or some other mute other (a rainy day = a melancholy mood, shirts flapping on a clothesline = a rapturous angelic though ultimately earthbound feeling), the writer more overtly intends his observations to be traceable to the originary genius of his own mind, and often lets fly an aperçu in the last line that clinches the overlap of perceived object with perceiving subject. But in both cases the author's consciousness exhibits an intact, capable, and (re)unified power exerting itself from the driver's seat after a harrowing apprenticeship in the workshops of internal division. After World War II, this illusion of control was put into crisis; for poets and ethnographers, the temporary excursion and discourse on that excursion conclude implicitly thus: "I'm glad I learned so much about [the Berber, the Lao, the shirts flapping, the rock whose compactness I tried to experience briefly], but mostly I'm glad to be once again human [unlike them] so that I can have the consciousness to make these observations about them and ultimately about myself."

The work of several postwar poets, notably here Bob Kaufman and John Wieners, lays bare the contradiction at the heart of the genre: they convert the solitary, noble fieldworker or poet back into the lonely, dislocated subject. These poets adopted ambivalent participant observer positions to describe the scene they were part of, conveying in somewhat static, stylized terms the West Coast bohemian milieux of coffeehouses, bars, shooting galleries, and urban landscapes in ways that both self-consciously captured the scene for posterity and also distanced them from it through the alienated labor of note-taking and documentation.[20] It is possible to see, in Wieners's and Kaufman's work, the ambivalence, skepticism, and wariness that accompanied their immersion in these alternative communities. Kaufman's and Wieners's nuanced expressions of their relatively complex position on the margins of an already marginal urban and artistic subculture deserve close attention, because these expressions pressure the contradictions of their experience as insiders and outsiders, illuminating the tactics countercultures and oppressed people use in the face of crushing imperatives to knuckle under. In tandem with an emphasis on describing the scenes and celebrating community is a distinct penchant for the trope of loneliness, a penchant these two writers share with their coevals: loneliness was virtually a catchword of 1950s sociology, psychology, and fiction. Loneliness, for Kaufman and Wieners, is not the slightly pleasurable, bittersweet melancholy that afflicts, for example, the pastoral subject of "Lyric Poetry and Society," or even Kerouac's moments of solitude en route across the country, moments that disrupt manic bouts of descriptive effluvia about hitchhiking or driving companions. Rather, loneliness is a mind-altering affliction that actually interferes with this reverie-positive solitude, as is suggested by the tide of Kaufman's first book, *Solitudes Crowded with Loneliness*. Acute loneliness prevents one from experiencing lyric solitude, though it often operates in a dialectical interplay with it (as we see in Malinowski), taking the phenomenological form of short-lived euphoria; in the long run, however, that way madness lies.

Lyric poetry, which had long been one among several types of poetry in European and American literature, became (at the same time as the development of anthropology) the dominant, almost exclusive kind of poetry produced at the upper registers of culture and eventually came to dominate the middle-brow mainstream as poetry tout court. Whether Romantic or modernist, lyric's appeal lay mainly in its ratification of the individual subject observing itself across a range of feelings and thoughts against a backdrop of objective correlatives—symbolically laden landscapes, natural or other objects external to the poet's psyche that nonetheless functioned in concert with the poem's intended import (i.e., an overcast sky suggested the poem's/poet's melancholy, to which direct reference would be clumsy). The apex of lyric achievement, as former laureate Robert Hass stated in a public lecture, is to enact the moment at which a subject becomes aware of her or his own subjectivity–s/he "catches her/himself" in the act of reflection, and in doing so grasps the wider ramifications of her/his meditations on external phenomena.[21] Although a lyric poem's success rests on the effect of closure and holism, this is another kind of participation or observation whereby the poet estranges her- or himself from quotidian, normative, unreflective activity and observes her or his own psyche as if it were a foreign entity. This process must be conducted in solitude; again, as in the ethnographic situation, the abject condition of loneliness is transformed into the powerful condition of the self-isolated genius observing the world: Emily Dickinson's legendary reclusiveness—and her status as denatured female—is possibly the most paradigmatic model here, as is Robert Frost's crusty misanthropy. One could say that the feeling of inferiority is transformed as the poet takes this very feeling as proof of a (presumed superior, more highly developed) interiority.

In the post–World War II era, and especially since the intellectual revolution of the late 1960s, lyric poetry has been attacked for its false presentation of a unified subject, which, these critiques maintain, is an inaccurate representation of human experience post-1945; lyric's attention to precious minutiae as ratifying the poet's powers came to be seen as an act of cerebral imperialism, just as ethnography's roots in world conquest and its reliance on the spurious objectivity of the observer came under heavy criticism and revision, with an eye toward decentering the organizing subjectivity of the writing (Western) ethnographer. The work of the poets I focus on, irredeemably marginal subjects (queer, mentally ill, racially indeterminate, addicted) who could not rehabilitate themselves through writing but wrote anyway, re-exposes, through the tattered and jagged fragmentation of their language, the loneliness at the heart of textual production thematically preoccupied with close observation and "accurate documentation." This work exhibits many of the tendencies of lyric ("beautiful language," for instance, and arresting imagery) but thwarts any sense of closure, completeness, or mastery. The poets' careers are characterized by an initial phase of reaching toward lyrical norms; as their lives progressed (or devolved), their work became increasingly fragmented and undisciplined. Their oeuvre lies somewhere between *écriture brute* (naive writing), conventional lyric, and vanguard experimentation. The trajectory of this writing is, arguably, of a piece with the historical "un"-disciplining of ethnography and poetry.

Most interesting, in terms of the crisis in representation that haunted the humanistic disciplines after the 1960s, the work of certain poets enacts an antecedent and metonymic crisis in poetry as ethnography. While their early work exhibits some characteristics of lyric, it eventually veers sharply away from any possibility of closure or mastery: it tests the limits of the discipline of poetic craft. Moreover, the poets' social dislocations indicate that they inhabit the double consciousness of the minoritized, non-normative subject, and this experience of displacement is the subject matter of their work. One could consider the poets in question—Kaufman, Wieners, others—among those who found that writing *lyrik* after Auschwitz was not only unethical, it was impossible; the disintegration of their psyches in a sense attested to their attempt to find a new, truer way to witness, to embody and inhabit language in (post-)modernity.

Bob Kaufman: "I kept my secrets. I observed those who ... were not Negroes and listened to all their misinterpretation."

Bob Kaufman, as we have seen, reinvented himself in the late 1950s as a San Francisco Beat poet. From being a "family breadwinner" concerned with democratizing labor he became, thanks to the McCarthy-era purges of leftists from labor unions, a member of a subculture in which breadwinning was scorned as conformist and labor was seen as complicit with an oppressive social and political climate, as well as stifling domestic arrangements. Under the Beat sign, family life took on an experimental fluidity, and the "wife and seven-month-old daughter" mentioned in the NMU newspaper's 1946 profile of Kaufman and other strike supporters dropped out of sight and were replaced by another wife and child on the opposite coast.[22] As a poet, Kaufman wrote highly stylized, somewhat dissociated descriptions of his hip milieu, published in *Solitudes Crowded with Loneliness* (1965), a title whose oxymoronicity suggests the challenging situation of double consciousness he negotiated beyond the mere deployment of "loneliness" as a generational buzzword. As a black subject in a social environment that prized black culture but was not necessarily comfortable around black people (that is, he was a black ethnographer in a predominantly white counterculture, many of whose members considered themselves participant observers on the fringes of African American hipster subculture; as in so many ethnographic situations, the gaze goes both ways, though the power does not), he maneuvered skillfully between participant and observer, writing verse that was lyrical without having at its center a stable speaking subject. Though in many of his early poems the speaker is positioned as a participant/observer, he himself was to some degree regarded as an exotic other by his white colleagues in the Beat orbit. His active participation in circulating wild legends about his origins (that he was Haitian; that he was born to an Orthodox Jewish father and a Martiniquan "voodoo queen" mother; that his grandmother, a slave, eloped with the plantation owner's son) provides an interesting instance of the trickster native informant whose multiple and contradictory stories keep the ethnographers guessing. (Another black poet of the era, Stephen Jonas, who similarly traveled in mostly white poetic circles, also maintained several unverifiable and mutually incompatible accounts of his origins. Dramatically instantiating the degree to which, in the 1960s, the "veil" still divided white from black, both Jonas and Kaufman maintained, during their poetic periods, entire lives of which their white poet friends knew nothing and it has proved extremely difficult to research these writers' biographies.)[23] Three of Kaufman's poems illustrate a move from the ethnographic to the shamanistic, as it were, to the unrecuperable habitation of the split itself in the wreckage of history and the wreckage of normative poetic language–habitation of Genet's exilic space, that of true poetry. "Bagel Shop Jazz," "THE POET," and "The Ancient Rain (Bicentennial Poem)" trace an arc from an identifiable participant-observing subject of conventional, descriptive lyric through a frightening amalgam of the *poète maudit* and double consciousness–afflicted subject to, finally, the all-out prophetic and paranoid national jeremiad where language breaks down in apocalyptic terror cum vindication.

In preceding chapters I attended to the tensions "Bagel Shop Jazz" outlines between women, white ethnics, and black hipsters in the Beat counterculture, as well as the excision from this tableau of the highly visible gay scene that formed another dimension of Kaufman's bohemian milieu. The black men are granted an interiority, hiding "terrible secret hurts" behind "cool hipster smiles" as Kaufman acknowledges the loneliness of being misperceived by his white colleagues, who considered him a lovable, wild novelty act, a black man who could extemporize Yeats, Eliot, García Lorca, and Tennessee Williams, all mixed in with street patter and dozens—a team mascot in their ongoing fight with police and squares. He was their noble savage, occasionally flashing clues about his consciousness from "within the veil" of his (at least) doubled social life. I also noted the poem's status as a stylized, Brechtian tableau, almost overly choreographed; this ethnographic depiction of "village life," acknowledged as fleeting (just as many white ethnographers' assumption that indigenous life was on the verge of disappearing gave their work a poignant urgency), is also a bid for social history. (It is noteworthy that though this poem literally eschews the famous lyric I, there is both an implied "we," and what Preston Whaley has called an "ethnographic I" in Kaufman's poetry.)[24] The delicate position Kaufman negotiated as a black man in a white world adds another dimension to the static, emotionally muffled, and thumbnail-sketch quality of the poem; its mildly schizy tinge suggests he is both active within the scene as one of the "Coffee-faced Ivy Leaguers" and observing from a disembodied, hovering position, or watching the pageant unfold from outside the café window (which he once, in a high-spirited moment, kicked in)—the classic victim-witness split. In other words, one could read this apparently innocuous and wistful poem as a symptom of social trauma. And Kaufman did indeed suffer at the hands of his Beat literary confrères as well as the police, enduring racial epithets as well as patronizing affection from the former and physical violence from the latter; he responded with his cool hipster smile, external social inferiority transformed into complex, doubled interiority.[25] Taking into account Freud's outline, in *Beyond the Pleasure Principle*, of the (human) organism's developing a tough skin (consciousness) in response to unpleasant stimulus, provocation, and attack (trauma) from without, one could read the lyric itself as a normative skin, the organ/membrane developed to process and defuse the power of raw shock. Kaufman's lyrics, then, as well as his stance as a hip lyric poet, become the protective layer that his biological epidermis—the history it implied, the ongoing social subordination to which it consigned him despite his best literary and political efforts—could not provide; the understatement of the poem and the cool hipster smile it embodies provide a "veil," an interface mediating inside and outside, behind which he can preserve some autonomous if lonely and alterior selfhood. The poem concludes with an equally veiled reference to the global violence of the atom bomb, neighborhood violence recorded by spray-painted body outlines on city streets, and epic literary violence in its echo of Virgil's commentary on a mural of the Trojan war, *lacrimae rerum sunt* ("Brief, beautiful shadows, etched on walls of night"). Is the poem a protest against the aestheticization of social violence that effected the Beat retreat from politics? Is it an attempt to come to terms with a troubled and doomed counterculture that deserves its downfall? Is it a moment of resistance not only to the invasion of the guilty police but also to its own superficial utopianism?

As Du Bois predicted in his characterization of double consciousness as crippling rather than enabling, the doubled perspective that was Kaufman's survival strategy and that permitted him a foothold in the social order came at too high a price; eventually, in Kaufman's biographical trajectory, lyric failed him. After a period of poetic silence and ambiguously willed anonymity due to disillusionment, addiction, and continued social trauma, he briefly resumed writing; in 1981 a volume of new and previously uncollected work came out thanks to the devoted efforts of Raymond Foye, who followed the ever-more-elusive Kaufman around North Beach, collecting manuscripts and eliciting new material. (In his positioning as the sought-after object, one could say that Kaufman became the "native" to Foye's ethnological pursuit.) The new work was decidedly different in tone and style. Two of those poems, "THE POET" and "The Ancient Rain," reflect how far Kaufman had traveled from the participant observer coolness of the other (see "Two Final Notes") into a hell realm of prophetic isolation and other-worldliness. In the former poem, the heightened sense of doubleness ("I HAVE WALKED IN THIS WORLD / WITH A CLOAK OF DEATH WRAPPED / AROUND ME, I WALKED ALONE, EVERY / KISS WAS A WOUND, EVERY SMILE / A THREAT") no longer pertains to black versus white, interiority versus exteriority, or race as an index of visibility/juxtaposed to invisibility, but to life and death: zombie-like, the poet moves between them, between inertness and vitality, womb and grave. Every sensation, every gesture and relationship, is fraught with terror, duplicity, and misunderstanding. He has himself become a skin, a sensing organ mediating life and death, with no protection from the torture that is human society.[26] This harrowing passage is ambiguously affirmed as a necessary poetic rite of passage ("ONE DAY DEATH REMOVED HIS / CAPE FROM AROUND ME / I UNDERSTOOD WHAT I HAVE LIVED / THROUGH. I HAD NO REGRETS, / WHEN THE CLOAK WAS REMOVED / I WAS IN A PIT OF BONES. / A FISH WITH FROG'S / EYES, / CREATION IS PERFECT"); the poet becomes part Ezekiel, part member of the mass grave of dry bones to be brought back to life, and part observer of the greatest promise of Western civilization, eternal life. But this eternal life is also eternal death, irrevocably marked by the ravages of historical catastrophe.

In "The Ancient Rain," whose long lines enter a different, Whitmanian realm of craft and mastery, the poet prophesies the final reckoning of a racist nation that can't honor its own potential, and that has squandered its promise of freedom. Notably, one of the salient aspects of the apocalypse Kaufman predicts (etymologically, apocalypse is "uncovering," as in the final removal of the veil, a final undoubling) is that "All the symbols shall return to the realm of the symbolic and the reality become the meaning again. In the meantime, the masks of life continue to cover the landscape." That is, part of the end of life as we know it is the collapsing of the dual realms of referent and sign, a dualism on which our social life is structured, liberal humanist disavowals notwithstanding. Kaufman's poetry appears to have lost whatever conventionally "critical humanist" edge had characterized the earlier work (its note of satirical commentary), which property Bruce Albert asserts as anthropology's value as a discipline.[27]

Du Bois's efforts at ethnography did not drive him mad or do him in, but their failure, in his eyes, to effect real change in the lives of blacks in the United States drove him away, first from the genre, and then from the United States itself, which was both his home culture and his host culture (thus the ironies of double consciousness). Written as an appeal to the universal humanism he believed resided in individual enlightened white psyches if not white society, *The Souls of Black Folk* sets forth in oratorically masterful ("poetic") prose brimming over with rhetorical doubling, formidably irrefutable historical detail, and experimentally hybrid chapters and genres the critical apparatus of double consciousness, now a cornerstone of contemporary race theory. Du Bois's hope of explaining, as auto-ethnographer, the rich interiority of "them that live within the Veil" was not fulfilled, and eventually, after many more engaged experiments in black social and political uplift, disgusted with the intractability of the U.S. political self-interest that continued to fuel oppressive policies, he emigrated to Ghana, where he continued his lifelong and long-lived activism.[28] It is in the failure of the attempt at ethnography as activism (the fault lying in the reception rather than the creation or production) and the corollary disillusionment with the humanity of the humanists that I see similarity with the poets under consideration here, as well as—primarily—in Du Bois's thorough exploration of the possibilities and limitations of double consciousness.

John Wieners: "I am one of them."

John Wieners's (1934–2002) trajectory was similar to Kaufman's, if his sensibility was different. While Kaufman was a street poet, often condescended to as a populist by other San Francisco Bay Area poets, Wieners, though of working-class origin, came to San Francisco via Boston College and Black Mountain College, his avant-garde credentials intact. In his early "A Poem for Tea Heads," which is probably also his best-known poem, a drug user, the protagonistic but dissociated lyric I, documents the underworld of drugs and gay sex as if he were observing himself from the outside; it is clear that trauma underwrites his engaged disengagement, his lively but distant voice:

A POEM FOR TEA HEADS

I sit in Lees. At 11:40 PM with
Jimmy the pusher. He teaches me
Ju Ju.
    Hot on the table before us
shrimp foo yong, rice and mushroom
chow yuke.
    Up the street under the wheels
of a strange car is his stash. The ritual.
We make it. And have made it.
For months now together after midnight.
Soon I know the fuzz will interrupt will arrest Jimmy and
I shall be placed on probation.
    The poem
does not lie to us. We lie under its
law, alive in the glamour of this hour
able to enter into the sacred places
of his dark people, who carry secrets
glassed in their eyes and hide words
    under the roofs of their mouth.
            6.16.58

An addict who became schizophrenic in his later years, Wieners thematized loneliness throughout his career, sometimes in yearning lyrics, sometimes in freeform schizobabble that also somehow had "poetic" political and social content. In this poem, even though he is describing putatively pleasurable sensory stimulants—food, drugs, the intimate company of an attractive man who is initiating him in vernacular magic—there is a ritualized, automaton-like quality to his description of their activities. Clearly recounted for the benefit of an outsider-onlooker not familiar with the world of drugs or of homoerotic miscegenation, the moment is not one of intimacy between the lyric I and "Jimmy," but, if anything, with the idea of the poem mediating a fundamentally alienated encounter; there's a "what am I doing here" quality to the writing, underscored by the mystery and magical exoticism Wieners imputes to his partner in drugs and sex: though he is certainly sensitive to the differential social power in their relations (the man of color will be treated more harshly than the white man for the same illegality), this seems to heighten his glamour for the poet-ethnographer.

In his isolation, writing kept Wieners company. In Wieners's ethnographic view, Jimmy is not isolated; he has "dark people" who are initiates in juju, and the secret "words [hidden] under the roof of [his] mouth" (echoing Kaufman's "secret terrible hurts") indicates his participation in a putatively nonalienated orality, in contrast to Wieners's decentered and, as became evident, increasingly deterritorialized literacy. In prose passages of his journal *707 Scott Street*, written in the late 1950s but not published until forty years later, Wieners likewise describes San Francisco as an urban scene of great desolation despite its frantic activity and "glamour," emphasizing also his own deterioration in prose that feels slo-mo, stunned, paralyzed by incredulity: "the city is a fabled labyrinth, and sustenance there is subterranean. Life on the surface regiment, ordered mechanized the people move as robots, displaying neither love nor fear." It continues: "At night when there is only one eye and the police prowl as roaches thru every layer. Searching like poets every face, gait, manner of dress. Under the streetlights only the eccentric stands out garbed in the costume of his game." The poet wonders, "How long? Two years at it and I am worn out. My teeth half gone at 25. A racking cough all night. Little food and sour stomach in the morning unless drugs, not to deaden one, but open doors for the fantasy world. Sur-real is the only way to endure the real we find heaped up in our cities."[29]

Thus, as if ethnographic precision or the notion of being sought out by cops could cure loneliness, for sustenance Wieners gives allegorical meaning to his struggles to survive, to score, to find companionship. The loneliness here is observed sociologically and contained in the strangely static tableau of the scene, as if the decay of his own body took on some compensatory meaning when placed in a larger historical context, or as if his isolation were mitigated rather than exacerbated by the possibility that isolation is a psychic state of the era; at least he didn't have to take personally its ravages on his person. Wieners's journal is at once a writer's journal that records a sorcerer's apprentice–style submission to the discipline of magic, a set of ethnographic fieldnotes, a foreshadowing of future madness (when the split becomes untenable), and an attempt at survival through distancing himself (through writing, observation, and articulation) from the traumas of postmodernity, drug abuse, poverty, and homoerotic passion in a repressive era. One further observation can be made about this fragment and "Bagel Shop Jazz," with regard to the positioning of the writer and reader in respect to the content. Although both passages are written in the present tense, there's a sense of memorialization, as if the scenes being described were already over and in need of commemoration. Johannes Fabian has aptly described the relationship of ethnographic time to "the other" in terms of domination and objectification: the host culture being described as more primitive than the ethnographer's home culture is fixed as if static through the conventions of the genre; the present of descriptive ethnographic prose is an eternal present, unchanging, and hence implicitly a means of reifying both the ethnographer's past experience in the field and the ongoing past-in-the-present of the objects of study.[30] In Kaufman's and Wieners's work, that of the minoritized poet-ethnographer, there's a related future anterior sense haunting the use of the present: this is what we will have lived through—if we survive. ("Bagel Shop Jazz" is, in fact, entirely composed of sentence fragments; the only full sentence—"the guilty police arrive"—marks the aggressive intrusion of real-world time into a suspended utopia made up of shards of real-world detritus.) The distancing function of ethnographic time here serves as a buffer for the traumatized subject, a temporal displacement similar to spatial dissociation: not only is the sufferer having an "out-of-body" experience matched by his being "out of his mind" on drugs, alcohol, or loneliness but by imagining the scenario in a timeless bubble, it becomes more of a pageant and less of a wounding, terrorizing experience.

Romantic objectification is yet another expression of this phenomenon of self as both subject and object, this splitting of subject from subject, or watching of the subject by the observed object. Reminiscent of Malinowski's fantasy of being constantly both watched by God and accompanied by his fiancée, many are the scenarios in Wieners's journal of unnamed sexual partners either anticipated or missed immediately after their departure; as Michel Foucault has written, sex itself is not interesting; it's the moment when the lover disappears in the cab and one can light up a cigarette and fantasize the foregoing night that it becomes significant. Then one can write about it, endowing the freshly departed or never-actually-came lover with all the properties one could wish for. Jadedness is the other side of this yearning. Either way, note the ethnographic reaching for and escaping from intimacy by withdrawal into a world of note-taking about the intimate encounter:

> And in the night lovers come
> where there was no light before.
> They bring their animal groans.
> They creak the bed and cause
> the dog to bark. At the moon.
> I will endure this solitude.
> I will rise to a new day.

> There is a princess in the tower.
> And steps like inside the Statue
> of Liberty lead up to her.
> Wooden, with grass and sunlight upon them
> I could climb the stairs or stay
> here in the poem[31]

In yet another expression of dissociation, Wieners is both the princess trapped in a tower and the princess who *is* a hollowed-out tower (again, echoes of Kaufman, who also writes of the poet's experience of his subjectivity as subject to, and rattling around inside, his body); he is, moreover, also the seeker who can climb up into her, as well as the writer—the writer both inside and outside the poem—who has to choose between the poem and active contact with others. Sex itself is seen as ethnographic, an a priori split between observing and participating, a retreat into the scientism of observation and recording; a professional, socially sanctioned version of the tormented dissociation that has marked so much of Wieners's and Kaufman's relationship to the physical world. As Jeff Derksen writes, tongue-in-cheek, "So would you like to, uh, ethnography."[32]

Elsewhere in Wieners' work there is no mitigating presence of the romantic other whatsoever, but a stark declaration of aloneness. This bleaker encounter with disappointment could be valorized as less exploitive (there is no fantasized or projected-upon other to be deified or vilified) and less inclined to palliative sociological rationalizing, but it is almost unbearably painful to read. "To Sleep Alone," for example, is primarily a catalogue of activities rendered in the infinitive, suggesting that the loneliness is without conceivable cessation—that is, infinite:

> To sleep alone   to play alone
> To wake alone   to work alone

| to walk alone | to grow alone |
| to wash alone | to mourn alone |

| to write alone | to climb alone |
| to see alone | to fall alone |

| to think alone | to dress alone |
| to die alone | to strip alone[33] |

Paradoxically, the overwhelming repetition of the word "alone" doesn't seem to empty it out semantically. Rather, the many verbs' variety is eviscerated by the inevitability of the word "alone" at the end of each line to negate, with Poe-esque finality, any particularity or pleasure in everyday human activities.

Wieners's writing is clearly "minority discourse" with its "high degree of deterritorialization."[34] The subject is "beside" or "outside" himself, as the ethnographer's imperative requires.[35] Also, stylistic or aesthetic concepts such as multiperspectival, disoriented, or high degree of self-consciousness, which implicitly acknowledge a divided subject, bring these descriptions of psychic states to bear on "outside" or vanguard styles of writing. Robin Blaser's essay on Jack Spicer's poetics, "The Practice of Outside," and Nathaniel Mackey's title *Discrepant Engagement: Dissonance, Cross-Culturality and Experimentalism* are signal texts that elaborate this resonance between outsiderhood, cultural borders, and alternative artistic production. The psychic alienation described by Wieners is both peculiar to his sensibility and typical of the split between public and private spheres that many minoritized folks negotiated without paying the high price of their sanity—but this is not to say that they didn't suffer. John Wieners lived through both epochal transitions, from "divided self" to the mandate to be "authentically gay," and from that era of liberation activism to the current permission to be multiple without apology. While his survival testified to the resilience of creative imagination, the conditions of that survival testified to the extreme psychic hardships these changes have entailed.

On his return to Boston in the 1960s, Wieners's mental illness progressed, and his work became less disciplinedly lyrical, instead dramatizing internal scripts in which he adopted the personae of glamourous female figures such as Bette Davis or the Virgin Mary. However, at times it continued to be auto-ethnographic, as in the harrowing "Children of the Working Class," written "from incarceration, Taunton State Hospital, 1972":

gaunt, ugly, deformed

broken from the womb, and horribly shriven
at the labor of their forefathers, . . .

their sordid brains don't work right,
pinched men emaciated, piling up railroad ties and highway ditches
blanched women, swollen and crudely numb
ered before the dark of dawn

scuttling by candlelight, one not to touch, that is, a signal panic
thick peasants after *the* attitude . . .

there are worse, whom you may never see, non-crucial around the
spoke, these you do, seldom
locked in Taunton State Hospital and other peon work farms
drudge from morning until night, abandoned within destitute crevices odd
    clothes
intent on performing some particular tasks long has been far removed
there is no hope, they locked-in key's; housed of course

and there fed, poorly
off sooted, plastic dishes, soiled grimy silver knives and forks,
stamped Department of Mental Health spoons
but the unshrinkable duties of any society
produces its ill-kempt, ignorant and sore idiosyncrasies.

There has never been a man yet, whom no matter how wise
can explain how a god, so beautiful he can create
the graces of formal gardens, the exquisite twilight sunsets
in splendor of elegant toolsmiths, still can yield the horror of

dwarfs, who cannot stand up straight with crushed skulls,
diseases on their legs and feet unshaven faces and women,
worn humped backs, deformed necks, hare lips, obese arms
distended rumps, there is not a flame shoots out could extinguish the torch of any liberty's state infection

1907, My Mother was born, I am witness t-
o the exasperation of gallant human beings at g-
od, priestly fathers and Her Highness, Holy Mother the Church

persons who felt they were never given a chance, had n-
o luck and were flayed at suffering.

They produced children with phobias, manias and depression,
they cared little for their own metier, and kept watch upon
others, some chance to get ahead

Yes life was hard for them, much more hard than for any blo
ated millionaire, who still lives on
their hard-earned monies. I feel I shall
have to be punished for writing this,
that the omniscient god is the rich one,
cared little for looks, less for Art,
still kept weekly films close for the
free dishes and scandal hot. Some how
though got cheated in health and upon
hearth. I am one of them. I am witness
not to Whitman's vision, but instead the
poorhouses, the mad city asylums and relief worklines. Yes, I am witness not to
God's goodness, but his better or less scorn.

The First of May, the Commonwealth of State Massachusetts,
1972[36]

That Wieners continued documenting his mutable sense of reality as
well as his class outrage, witnessing and being witnessed by a God who
regards the poor with indifferent, uninvested contempt, indicates a need
for the process of documentation itself (as well as the proliferation of
interacting voices) as a counter to the loneliness on which he has blamed
his schizophrenia. However, the poem also reveals, both in its content
and in its broken syntax and orthography, the extent to which the critical distance of formal writing has become untenable; his "powers of observation" no longer confer power on him but merely allow him, as one
"under observation" in the blind panopticon of the state psychiatric hospital, to experience with full cognition the humiliation of being watched;
"returning the gaze" is not a satisfying reversal of power but an exercise
in further despair. Possibly, what he sees there of himself and others is
so painful and self-indicting that, again like Malinowksi, he projects his
observations onto an all-powerful but here uncaring gaze. His feeling of
impending punishment is not only metaphysical guilt but also the fear of

actual recrimination if his descriptions of the hospital inmates are made public, like the scandal that followed the showing of Frederick Wiseman's *Titicut Follies*, an exposé of a hospital for the criminally insane (also in Massachusetts), in public cinemas around the same time. One could, but unconvincingly, appeal to the heroics of writing under incarceration: the legend of Genet writing *Our Lady of the Flowers* on the brown paper prisoners were supposed to make into bags, having the entire manuscript confiscated and destroyed, and having to reconstruct it, is rousing but not pertinent here. While the term "critical distance" (as well as "liberal humanism"), with the emphasis on "distance," is inappropriate, Wieners is both critic and analyst, as is Kaufman in his final jeremiads.

Two Final Notes: (A) Word on Community, and (B) Follow-up

A. In spite of the overwhelming despair and unrecuperability of Kaufman's and Wieners's psychic states, physical frailty, and material poverty toward the end of their lives, they were much loved and cared for by their respective poetic communities, which were, perhaps not quite as dramatically, likewise struggling for psychic and material survival. One cannot say that they ended up like Malinowski or Du Bois, world renowned and certain of having made widely acknowledged contributions to human knowledge; their works and lives are only marginally recuperable into any liberal humanist discourse of greatness or achievement; there exists, after all, a salient model for the poet as secular prophet; the Romantic tendency, however mediated and qualified, away from obvious artifice and toward at least the appearance of spontaneity; the personal-degradation-combined-with-consummate-artifice, as in the cases of Baudelaire or Verlaine; and the model of heroic struggle of creative individuals with obstacles both internal and external. Both these poets share something with these paradigms, though ultimately they are not contained by any of them. But, for all their falling off the map of the conventional literary career trajectory, during the last decades of their lives they were surrounded by younger poets as well as surviving friends from earlier generations who collected and published their messy and scattered manuscripts, fed and housed them, dropped in daily to see if everything was okay, took them to hospitals and to readings. A dynamic of devotion played itself out, one of survival at the edges of possibility that indexes a different—though perhaps not all that different, like convicts and flowers—kind of community from that of the illustrious, beloved mentor in the academic community (Malinowski) or the auratic, legendary public intellectual in self-imposed exile (Du Bois). Where these final musings are taking me in a comparison of lyric and ethnography under the lonely sign of the divided self, I'm not sure. Perhaps you can help.

B. So, what happened to the student whose initial proposition opened this essay, the proposition that the Beats were attempting the impossible by forging a ("re")unity between sign and referent? Marc Penka went on to write a brilliant if contorted dissertation on Hawthorne, and, after his defense, disappeared into the Southwestern desert, where he often camped out solo. A year after anyone at school had seen him, we learned that he had died of a heroin overdose in the desert among the wildflowers and succulents in which he had found past solace. This essay, which I imagine burnt, curling into fragile and sculptural ash in the shape of roses, is offered as a wreath laid on an imaginary grave, a garland of criminally complicit flowers, a cenotaph for a fallen warrior of the sign.

10 Poetries, Micropoetries, Micropoetics

Elegy on the Outskirts

I liked absurd paintings, pictures over doorways, stage sets, carnival backdrops, billboards, colored prints, old-fashioned literature, Church Latin, erotic books badly spelled, the kind of novels our grandmothers read, fairy tales, little children's books, old operas, silly refrains, naive rhythms.

—ARTHUR RIMBAUD, "ALCHEMY OF THE WORD," *POÉSIES*

Micropoetries: Ephemera, doggerel, fragments, "weird English" (props to Evelyn Ch'ien), graffiti, community and individual survival—*écriture brute*, folk letters, textile patterns evocative of "writing"; naive lettrism (as well as *belletrisme* and *lettrisme brute*); wise oraliture, gnomic thought-bytes and lyrical bullets, clairaudient visitations with a hermeneutic spin—traces of (in) decipherability, banality morphed into something more—the marriage of esotericism and exotericism, banality and exoticism. Embedded in contextual specificity (sociohistorical, etc.) but deracinated—the historic exile, the monadic nomad, the centrifugal community that lets fly its auratic verbal detritus. These are poetries that fly beneath the radar of accepted poetic practice, which foregrounds objects over processes. . . . Elsewhere I've cited my debt to Mark Slobin's term *micromusics* . . . and to W.E.B. Du Bois's "Of the Sorrow Songs," wherein he tells of his grandfather's grandmother bringing a song with her, which traveled not only spatially across the Middle Passage but also temporally down the generations to have been sung to him when he was a small child. He prints the music, transliterating syllables he doesn't understand, and from that archaeological fragment constructs a theory of cultural transmission.

And thus was born a Cultural Studies: the presence of fire in resonant landscapes—resonant for the ones with big ears.[1]

Revisitation

"Micropoetries" functions analogously to "poetries" as the term "micro-cultures"—out-of-the-way subcultures—does to "cultures." Contemplating this inviting term "poetries" begs the question, what do micropoetries do, and what are they, now that the scholarly terrain is more receptive to the literary study of nonliterary poetry? Because times have changed. The current swell of scholarly research inhabiting the matrix of poetry, poetics, and cultural studies is almost inspiring. Despite its arrival some twenty to thirty years after the heyday of Birmingham School–style cultural studies, this gesture toward a systematic academic approach to poetry-and-cultural-studies has just begun, though of course there is a prehistory as well as this contemporary flowering. Has a moment been reached? The MLA's Poetry Division is headed in a positive direction (poetry and war, poetry and the global/local, poetries), and while MLA's 2006 presidential address invoked the rubric of "cultural studies" as a foil for the promotion of poetry scholarship, a special session at the same conference, "Poetics and Cultural Studies: Engaging the Debate," drew a worthy audience (MLA 2006 was generally a banner conference for poetry, thanks to the efforts of Marjorie Perloff). It took my coeditor Ira Livingston and me almost seven years to secure a publisher for our *Poetry and Cultural Studies: A Reader*; the conflicting readers' reports it left in its wake en route to contractuality (contractual actuality) embody precisely the agonistic terms in which a meeting of "poetry and cultural studies" is still experienced in contemporary poetry scholarship. Everyone who learned about the volume or read some part of it agreed that "something like this is needed," timely and urgent; no one agreed on what it should be. One reader said not enough women or folks of color; another said, in effect, not enough dead white men (in other words, "traditional" poetry or selections that dealt with pre–World War II material). One reader hated about half the poetry we wanted to include; the other reader hated the other half of the poetry, and neither was shy about flaunting personal taste as a bellwether ("forgive my lack of enthusiasm for *X*'s poetry" was offered without analytic qualifiers) rather than asking what cultural work each selection performed. (We ended up axing all of the poetry.) It was "the debate" in nuce, though many individual works of scholarship might suggest that we have moved on.

"Micropoetry" is not a rubric generally embraced by those who write it; it is not generally published as such. Poets and poetry scholars (with the perverse exception of people like me), still longing for the big time, eschew the double marginalization they experience from being categorized as micro; studies of graffiti artists by sociologists or ethnographers turning to work on the local or to (sub)cultural poetics tend for the most part to shy away from claims about poetry. Moreover, many find the term "micropoetries" too inexact to be useful: is it "found poetry" tout court? Well, no, though that might be a subset thereof. Is it synonymous with doggerel, as someone asked incredulously after I delivered a paper on the subject at a 1998 MLA special session, "Poetics Out of Bounds"? No, though I have delivered such papers in the persona of Mademoiselle Doggerelle (now *I wanna be your dog*).[2] The term (micropoetries, not Mlle. D) is deliberately loose and capacious, intended to encompass a range of paraliterary shards of expressive culture that, like Du Bois's lullaby fragment, can become the basis for cultural analysis, or, as the opening chapters of Henry Louis Gates's now canonical *The Signifying Monkey* posit, an anonymous urban ballad as a springboard for a theory of reception and production of African American "high" literature. Intensely context-specific, micropoetries require substantial elaborations from their analysts in order to convey their full significance; in this, the attempt to overcome the "you had to be there" quality inherent in micropoetic power, the critic becomes a thick describer, an over-amped lit-crit Tom Wolfe, crazily trying to summon the ambience in which the micropoetic moment achieved the epiphanic. One might say that "poetries" is the academic rehabilitation, the "making-useful," the "coming-of-age," of micropoetries, a term that may have to remain furtive and idiosyncratic to retain its contrarian, frictional purchase on literary studies. (For example, mainstream publishers in the early 1970s rushed to publish anthologies of prison poetry, but to my knowledge its first mention in MLA calls for papers was for a 2006 panel. In general, the American Studies Association convention, representing an explicitly interdisciplinary field, has a better representation of panels on populist poetries, in connection with ethnic studies or under other interdisciplinary auspices). To be sure, if one Googles "poetries," one finds a range reaching into the high ether of the avant-garde and the broad ripples of middlebrow taste in production and consumption, as well as solidly capital-P poetry, indicating that the term need not be restricted to the noncanonical or the paraliterary.

If, then, "poetries" simply recapitulates "micropoetries" in a mainstreaming moment, is the minoritizing prefix worth preserving? "Poetries" accomplishes or promises (at least) two things not anticipated by "micropoetries": it implicitly includes standard literary poetry, which "micropoetries" explicitly excludes, and it indicates that a wider understanding of poetry and the social, as well as an especially intellectual curiosity about it, has become institutionally acceptable, indeed has become a potential source of cultural capital for the scholar who undertakes such study. What then could be useful about hanging on to the cranky prefix? Is it symptomatic perhaps of a superannuated and stubborn clinging to margins that are no longer marginal? Do micropoetries inhabit a subset—a demimonde—of poetries in ways that contribute usefully to a generically broader understanding of poetry? Does the term evince a desire to find ever more edgy edges, ever more nervous systems (in Michael Taussig's terminology), ever more tracy traces? Is it the local to poetries' global, acting in productively inseparable concert with it, even as an irritant? Micropoetries are traces of the poetic within the everyday, unworked-over—raw material left raw instead of being cooked into artistically self-conscious collage, pastiche, retelling, or other incorporative literary genre. Micropoetries are conversely also the banal that raises its spectrally perverse dread-head in the field of the "poetic": the clunker, the cringe-worthy line, the obstinate appearance of the groaner in a field of niceness; a micropoetry analysis might be a way of redeeming the banal by grasping its sociohistorical and affective hauntings. It becomes a way, furthermore, to honor the Kristevan thetic rupture of normative, seamless discourse, whether that discourse is a blandly acceptable poetic one disturbed by "wrongness" or topdownwardly organized urban landscapes marked with some arresting graffiti or bricolaged outdoor home decorating. But the term micropoetics also points to, conversely, the appearance of what would otherwise be doggerel in contexts that render it dignified, moving, appropriate: the child's poem read at her father's funeral, for instance. "Daddy, daddy, why'd you leave / and left me sitting here to grieve?" at a Cape Verdean funeral in Falmouth, Massachusetts, after the young father of three died in an early morning car accident in which the standard euphemism, "driver lost control of the vehicle," tells part of the story.

The term micropoetries may be too self-marginalizing to be useful to scholars at large. Does it marginalize what doesn't warrant or desire marginalization, despite its clear distance from either academic or middle-brow mainstream? Micro to whom, by what measurement? Marginal to what ever-moving, ever-morphing center? One thoughtful undergraduate, who wanted to write about his autistic sister's writing for his "micropoetries" assignment, was troubled by the micro-izing effect of the term, even as he understood that her writing would not be considered seriously as such by the mainstream, nor did he want to treat it as symptomatic or epiphenomenal to her illness or, for that matter, to see her illness as a stigma. "Poetries," by contrast, elegantly and tactfully addresses this embarrassment by erasing signs of hierarchy and exclusion.

As in Mark Slobin's elaboration of his own coinage "micromusics," micropoetries do not have an exclusionary and isolationist relation to commercial, academic, or official verse culture; they continue to inform and replenish such culture, whether through resistance or commodification, much as poetry as "antidiscourse" (Karlheinz Stierle's contention) lives side by side with and in continual polylogue with institutionalized, "prosaic" discourse. To the contrary: in their original conception, micropoetries fully involved analyses of mass-cultural and commercial artifacts (poetry on beer caps, tea bag packaging, coattail-riding nomenclature like "Baudelaire Beauty Products," greeting cards and billboards as well as hip-hop and street jive, whose commodification as well as ongoing potential for ever-renewable, productive friction has been well documented). But one can fruitfully explore the fluid relations of the not-quite-assimilable

—that is, a limbo mediating the generally acknowledged world of "art," on the one hand, and on the other, the kitschy underworld Rimbaud enumerates in the epigraph: "billboards . . . erotic books badly spelled . . . silly refrains, naive rhythms"—comprising 'zines, liminal literary productions such as the spoken-word world, or the new media work of outsider/pioneer/insiders like rural anarchist mIEKAL aND, whose preoccupation with the continuum between plant life and cyberspace life-forms informs the projects of his visionary community Dreamtime Village, in West Lima, Wisconsin, including the press Xexoxial Editions and digital/film/video production group Driftless Media; Australian feminist artist mez (Mary Anne Breeze), whose invented language Mezangelle dis/articulates the mutilations and multi-ululations of Internet language reinvented as bleeding code; and Brooklyn-based factotum Alan Sondheim, who coined the now standard descriptor "codework" for an electronic poetry aesthetic that foregrounds the language, usually hidden, of computer programming itself, yet remains marginal to the burgeoning world of "new media creative writing"

—with mainstreaming mechanisms such as MFA programs, academic conferences and publications such as this one. This is what the rubric "poetries" adds to the mutating landscape of poetry studies. By leveling that landscape, it forces a revaluation, perhaps a more subtle recalibration ("recalibration"), of the power relations so starkly announced in the antecedent term.

Elegiac Visitation

However, micropoetries continue to bubble up furtively both as object of study and ephemeral phenomena. As suggested earlier, many of these instances are elegiac, though that word feels inappropriately leisurely and retrospective ("contemplative," my midlevel dictionary has it), while the emotions that fuel an expression of loss are often extreme and desperate rather than wistful and pensive. Peter Sacks has written of the origin of the mourner's elegy in a matrix of funeral rituals (stemming, even earlier, from rituals surrounding the cycle of vegetation deities' deaths and re-births), including processions, wind instrument performance ("the flute song of grief"), and human song in an attempt to make absence present.[3] The elegiac poem itself, like Apollo's wreath, is a made object intended to represent and magnify the departed; the object, again like the laurel wreath, accrues meaning of its own beyond that of memento; it becomes a vehicle for creativity. For many people who do not identify as professional poets, poetry functions as an emotional as well as linguistic technology that is particularly apposite for moments when affect exceeds linguistic expression; poetry is a valuable resource because of its overdetermined and compressed nature. Here is a poem written by Susan Lannen, who does not self-identify as a poet, about her daughter, Ariel Alyssum, who died at age twenty-five in the summer of 2005. Since Ariel's death, Susan has been unable to leave poetry alone, and her words about it, when I asked her what role words have played in her mourning process, confirm its usefulness for her: "I don't know about words, but for poetry, it's the new love in my life since Ariel's death. I think there's something about poetry that says it without wearing you out by saying too much; especially for a grieving person to be given words that are really dense and full is really helpful. . . . It's like medicine, concentrated."[4] Months after Ariel's death, the *Phoenix*, Boston's alternative weekly newspaper, ran an online article on memorial sites on MySpace, where friends and e-quaintances continue to write to someone's account even after that person's death or disappear-ance as a way of staying in touch, mourning, memorializing, processing. The article focused in large part on Ariel, whose MySpace name was/is äRRiel and whose account featured her vivid writing on her experiences as a runaway, a street kid, a homeless person. You can experience it at www.myspace.com/aRRiel, http://arrielgurl.livejournal.com, or her site *Cardboard Box*, at www.geocities.com/little_sister_shotgun:

ARIEL:ARRIEL
A Reflection on a Virtual Memorial
by Susan Lannen

Death: ordinary shadows absorbed
reflections screened out, darker now.

Her name though not in any phonebook nor etched in stone,
Is simultaneously entombed and resurrected in cyberspace, and
can be occasionally found scrawled on the cover of a book of
matches
that could still set a fire,
now quietly resting, however,
next to a number that won't reach her anymore.

Having consumed the Nothing and been consumed by it
She is Nowhere.

Not on the morning shuttle
No longer riding St. Christopher
Not dancing
Nor pouring her heart out/in ink.
And brothers, father, mother, family & friends ache and & make
do.

Yet from beyond and through
Her continuance, still aRRiving
descending: lighting
Everywhere and always
riding, dancing
pouring

Nowhere and now here.

Even in this poem by someone with no training, formal or informal, one
finds a grasp of the significance of the smallest elements of standard poetic
language: language play that embodies a philosophical stance toward its
subject matter ("continuance," "nowhere and now here" invoking the Bud-
dhism that has made sense of life under emotional duress); internal rhyme
("ache and make do"); thematic invocation of a series of overlapping/
juxtaposed cenotaphic surfaces—monument, tombstone, computer screen,
printed page, matchbook cover—on which a life is written and unwritten;
the inscription of affect in orthography ("äRRiel"/"aRRiving"). There is
much skill in this expression of suffering.[5]
    Ariel took the cybername äRRiel for her strong presence on MySpace
where she helped set up safety mechanisms for its participants. She rode
a chopper bicycle with SCUL (Subversive Choppers Urban Legion) under the name Pigpen, designed and executed drawings for 'zines, wrote

her own superhero comic book (*Dirty Gurl Chronicles*, whose cover shows its heroine, a street kid who found the superpower-conveying garment while Dumpster-diving, asking, "Does this leotard make me look fat?"), and marketed her punk fashion patches over the Web. When Susie told me about SCUL's Pigpen Memorial Ride through Somerville and Cambridge, I told her I wanted to write about it but had to find the right moment. This is it. That is, beyond the presence of the conventionally "poetic" in elegiac, funereal, or memorial contexts—that is, the highly charged, formal verbal artifacts intended as lyric—the rituals surrounding such events are themselves highly charged with a haptic or kin/synaesthetic energy, a poetics that requires some descriptive effort, including thumbnail sketches of "colorful characters," uses of subculturally specific jargon, and so forth.

The SCUL Pigpen Memorial Ride, a parade on wheels, was one such mourner's procession (akin to the New Orleans funeral march phenomenon). It constituted a varied group of bicycle bricolage geniuses, including Skunk, the founder of SCUL (www.scul.org/SCUL/Pilot/Pil_Skunk.html), who, according to Annie Kessler, a friend of Ariel's family,

> came equipped (he was a work of art himself!) . . . with a handmade leather belt made from cast-off found materials; the belt contained a hand-sewn leather pocket/purse-like thing in front that opened to show a full line of bike repair materials in it to help in case anyone's bike broke down. Also he had on him some outlandish gear, he wears dresses and handmade boots fashioned out of large pieces of rubber, with brass screws all around to keep the boot-shape in place. He came with boxes of bike-bells so we could all make our bells work in unison at appropriate times on the ride, to memorialize Ariel. He mounted bells on each bike as each person arrived.[6]

Susie, the bereaved, "rode on the back of a two-seater, an old old bike, with Skunk . . . who had a cooler; while we were riding he'd pass people drinks from the cooler. It was a big old cooler with ice in it! We rang the bells consistently while we went through Harvard Square [where Ariel spent a lot of time in the 'subway pit,' as do many homeless kids]."[7]

Tightgirl, a six-foot-tall, highrise-platform-shoes-and-skimpily, bare-midriffed   black-bikini-w/-orange-pompom-tassels-with-lacy-black-evening-jacket-wearing tattooed and heavy black booted Unitarian Universalist minister, a chaplain at St. Elizabeth's Hospital with long blond hair in ponytails that stuck straight up ("you gotta dress up when you're celebrating someone's life"), attracted a lot of attention during the ride; it was impossible to look away from. And others (see "The Pilot Standings" under "Personnel" at www.scul.org/SCUL/SCUL.html for the full cast of characters with nicknames, pictures, and verbal profiles). Everyone wore colored cloth armbands saying "Pigpen is my Co-Pilot" and also tied them around bikes, waists, necks, heads as banners, flags, sashes, sweatbands, riding disassembled and reassembled bicycles festooned with cheerleader-tinsel streaming out of handlebars, bicycle equivalents of bumper stickers, paste-on stars, and so forth. The chopper phenomenon and SCUL look are here described by Kessler, whose participation in the wheeled parade was her first SCUL ride:

> The bikes were of a big variety of unusual concoctions that people had put together themselves: handmade bikes made from parts of other bikes, and parts of other nonbike things as well: one bike had a piece where the handlegrips.... Well, underneath the whole frame of the bike shifted to the right or left like a hinge; you'd be holding your hands off to the right or left but your seat would still be going forward; really dangerous and really fun. Unusual bikes, with seats 10–12 feet up in the air, pedaling by other means; tandems, three-wheelers, low-riding concoctions with low seats, . . . interesting vehicles. The people on them (thirty-six in all) [were] kind of shocking physically because of their hair, their dress, their tattoos, their piercings, [there was] a lot of shock value in the look . . . I'd been to the memorial service and I knew how open and loving they were; a lot of people would have been scared of them though, the Goth look , the chains and all black. . . . There were teachers, fathers, carpenters, married people . . . all ages, not just Ariel's age; lots of professional people. A good slice of Americana. . . . Later for dinner we gathered at a very cool restaurant in Cambridge and of course there we talked about Ariel. It was a one-of-a-kind experience, the experience of a lifetime; I'd do it again this year if I could, if they're doing it again. I've never experienced anything like it before.[8]

She also described the extremely well-organized ride, the maps that were handed out, the idiosyncratic terms for taking a left or right turn, for warning about oncoming traffic, and the rhythm of the way this information was called from one bike to another back through the cortège, the iteration-and-difference of the verbal relay, the way she felt protected by the group and Pigpen's strong presence; people were wearing Pigpen's designs, riding her bikes, and wearing her name on their bodies. These objects and their continued utility constitute forms of elegiac creativity intended to invoke her presence, as does a quilt that was made for her by her SCUL friends.

The prose that has continued to well up and manifest in the aftermath of Ariel's passing, the messy punk designs, Ariel's own writing still available on *LiveJournal*:

> (I walked through Harvard Square in a daze almost, only trying to get to the bus stop, but there was so much between that bus stop and me. I saw the ghosts of payphones, now only oddly shaped holes in the brick sidewalk. I sat on those benches so many times, often crying. Sometimes I wonder how many tears are in the wood of those benches, the desperate tears of junkies. Like me),[9]

and that of her cyberfriends who still write to her there, are elements of a poetic microclimate flourishing in the highly commodified environment of MySpace, which has become a conglomerate ploy to capitalize on youth's need to be connected, that furious yearning drive outward that finds fulfillment in a combination of vulnerable self-disclosure and anonymity, proximity and distance, solipsistic fantasy and tentative reaching out. Susan's poem, the chopper parade, äRRiel's Web site and its continued life through her punked-out, lively friendship network and the continued availability of her "gorgeously rough-hewn, deftly narrated, and frank first-person prose,"[10] are all facets of a microculture that is highly poetic.

Now what does that mean, "poetic"? Here the vivid language resides not only, though most important, in Ariel's surviving language-presence but in the ritual languages of SCUL: the name each member takes on (Skunk, TightGirl, Pigpen; Ariel's parents, Larry Dobie and Susan Lannen, were affectionately addressed by SCUL members as "Mr. Pen" and "Ma Pen" respectively), the names members gave their bikes (Ariel's two bikes were St. Christopher, a heavy blue craft with yellow stars and blue tinsel streamers; and Man's Ruin, a lighter bike), and their idiosyncratic vocabulary form a linguistic constellation charged simultaneously with efficiency and awkwardness, the compactness and defamiliarization so intrinsic to mainstream poetic values. Their vision, counterculturally activist, is highly self-conscious and enjoined with a sense of play. The "philosophy and creed" announced on SCUL's Web site (subtitled "The Counterculture to Americas Love for the Automobile"), for example, typos and all, assert the values of form over function, the aesthetically motivated defamiliarizing of that form in the interest of missions rhetorically (only partly tongue in cheek) associated with the military but obviously aligned with the poetic, the bricolaged, the aestheticizing/functionalizing of found materials. Under the heading "SCUL lingo," the fanciful space-movie/military jargon of this constantly evolving dictionary spells out a

POETICS FOR A POSTLITERARY AMERICA

functional sociolect reflecting the political aspirations and low-tech values of the group; a "CBU: Carbon based unit. A person, usually someone not in SCUL"; "Clip: One dozen donuts"; "Fuel: coffee"; "H.A.R.V.: High Altitude Reconnaissance Vehicle. A Tallbike"; and so on.

Another elegiac set of events saturated in the poetic was the aftermath of the passing of Lyx Ish, aka Liz Was, aka Elizabeth Perl Nasaw, cofounder of Xexoxial Editions and Dreamtime Village, writer, musician, herbalist, yoga teacher, and den mother to the upper Midwest avant-garde. A parade through the small town of LaFarge, Wisconsin, similar to the bike ride for Ariel, as well as a number of objects (a pair of boots, handmade musical instruments, a gourd on a bedsheet) supersaturated with Lyx's presence, is described in a special "Elegies" section of online journal *BigBridge*. In the same special section, mIEKAL aND, who had been Was/Ish's partner for seventeen years, posted a koanic visual poem he had written for her after she lost her powers of speech but before she died:

HELLO BELOW THE SERIF OF INDESTRUCTIBILITY

Even what to hold on to?
A boggle of speakers.
Come alive when
thinker is no longer speaking.
Can I come aboard? [11]

, a haunting question mark hovering behind the words. Later I cross-stitched this poem and surrounded it with representations of animals that had symbolic significance (turtles were Lyx's guardian animals, and doves are spiritual messengers in the Judaic tradition; moreover, symmetric and doubled animals also abound in funerary folk art as guardians of the gates to the next world). aND had it framed; it now hangs in the dining room of the "Post Office," his home at Dreamtime Village, so it has become a household object in the former home of the deceased, marking her place, as well as a visual poem that augments the online network of visual poetries and their producers.[12] A site of collaborative poems at a wiki, *Writing Dubuffet's Titles*, was also dedicated to Elizabeth Was (and to visual poetry pioneer Bern Porter),[13] as is a memorial site (www.gourdgoddess .net) and a tribute on Dreamtime's home page.[14] In this case, many of the contributors, participants, and artists already conceived of themselves as poets, unlike Susan and others, who have been catalyzed into the poetic through the trauma of sudden loss. However, one still witnesses the degree to which the death of loved ones galvanizes a drive to create that seems bound up in the primal drives Freud initially hypothesized. Could it be that, rather than simply instances of sublimation, these creations spring out of some nexus, some meeting place, some dialectical jouissance of, or agonistic showdown between, (the) pleasure (principle) and whatever goes beyond it? And the elements of movement through familiar and meaning-saturated space (the processions), a shared community meal, and conversation about the beloved absence, are instinctive ways of creating social order around the torn fabric of everyday life in the rituals surrounding death, even in these alternative subcultural enclaves. An approach to elegy that would blend literary theory with ethnographic attention to specificity would be a useful though vast project, toward which the foregoing are merely breathless notes.

11 Electronic Poetics Assay

Diaspora, Silliness, and–?Gender?

UNTIL I RECEIVED an e-mail from Loss Pequeño Glazier asking me if I had anything to say about gender and e-poetry for a *Cybertext Yearbook* issue on "ergodic" ("difficult," "writerly") poetry, I'd resisted entering the world of electronic poetry criticism despite a seemingly good fit between me and the subject.[1] Over the previous six years I'd gotten involved, through collaborating with poet and publisher mIEKAL aND, with the world of electronic, Web-based, mostly hypertext poetry. I'd been to conferences and festivals, and our work (notably *Literature Nation, Eros/ion*, "Erosive Media/Rose E-missive," and "Semetrix") had been shown, mostly through aND's entrepreneurial spirit and Web renown, in exhibits around the world.[2] So one might reasonably assume I had some interest in theorizing on the subject, which is also a subfield within the hot field currently known as new media studies. The reason for my resistance must be less obvious to all but me. My engagement has been not as a theorist or even a fully immersed practitioner at the level of the medium—aND is the techno-wizard and design genius—but more as a sort of participant observer fellow-traveler, a platonic groupie, an anthropologist semiwistful but not quite willing to "go native," a permanent apprentice—at this point I'm thinking GENDERGENDER as an obvious if subtextual category to characterize this list of characterizations. And in fact, our relationship has been quite gendered in traditional ways; he was the tech guru who can learn any system in no time, while I did the fluffy, lyrically fragmented writing (though he writes too, his style is decidedly less baroque and more "experimental" than mine) and the pretty photography that he then defamiliarizes with groovy programs and an equally groovy confidence in his know-how. This writing has been a source of energy, enjoyment, and expansion, and I have not held it to any critical standards or taken any initiative in seeking publication opportunities, as aND has posted our work on his Web site, www.joglars.org, and responded to opportunities to publish our work in book form.

I saw no social urgency in analyzing digital poetics, no acute need for my advocacy in the field, as there is for the kind of micropoetries, populist verse, marginalization, or extreme eccentricity the pathos of which generally commands my attention and labors. Advocacy for ergodic digital poetry as opposed to argotic poetry would be a mere plea for recognition for a usually overlooked subfield within poetics rather than an intervention related to larger issues of social justice, or even the many theoretical offshoots from the post-1968 era that have come into play around those issues: postcolonialism, gender and sexuality theory, ethnoracial studies. In fact, it may be worth questioning what the investment or collective interest is, embedded in the term *ergodic*, in maintaining a distinctly modernist division between an "avant-garde" or "writerly" text/aesthetic and the plethora of other possibilities that take advantage of this new, quintessentially postmodern medium. The e-poets I know in the experimental world—that is, those who write the sort of work that carries over from the print (or visual art, or musical) avant-garde to the digital medium—seem by and large to be a happy lot. In fact, much of the work, such as Jim Andrews's "Nio," with its swinging a capella sound track, or Komninos Zervos's several works with their cartoonish, childlike playfulness, conveys a sense of freedom and even joy, perhaps a sort of rejoicing at being (virtually) freed from the body, like the exuberance of participants at gravity-defying thrill rides at carnival midways. Even works that don't exhibit the same kind of exuberant happiness—I'm thinking here of, for example, Brian Kim Stefans's beautifully unruffled "The Dreamlife of Letters," John Cayley's pastoral riffs on Wang Wei, or Reiner Strasse's many globally conscious projects—have a kind of serenity born of aesthetic certainty, a self-contained sequential orderliness that elicits admiration for a closed object, although there is plenty of movement inside the objects. Not the kind of messiness that signals lack, longing, or desperation and toward which I feel critically drawn.

Perhaps I found the messiness and anxiety lacking because when I arrived in the e-poetry world I was already pretty well jacked in to a situation of institutional privilege and security myself (well, let's not exaggerate: a tenured position at a second-rung land grant research university), with little serious sense of material struggle with which to empathize with the tattered fringes of the scene. Perhaps it was because, other than with aND's deliberately tenuous and dramatically alternative lifestyle at Dreamtime Village, my only firsthand contact with e-poets was at the E-Poetry 2001 Conference/Festival, a warmly expansive international symposium dominated by loving kindness and goodwill to all, with an explicit caveat against "quoting Adorno," a prohibition, I took it, against cultural pessimism as well as against the cultural cachet acquired by dropping the pessimist's name. The internationalism of the conference was an opportunity for utopian celebration of mutual recognition, a chance to join in on "Hey, baby, they're singing our song" or "We are the (unacknowledged legislators of the) world," rather than an opportunity to identify and track differences born of different material and political circumstances, an analytic perspective that had been part of my intellectual training and generational hard-wiring. Where's the materialist angle? Simply celebrating the much vaunted access enabled by the Web—the opportunities for instant publication, the short-circuiting of the protracted "vetting" system of print publication—didn't seem sufficient, intellectually or politically, to compel my thinkerly energies, especially since so many others had made similar points years ago, and with more eloquence and conviction than I could muster. Also, quite simply, I have been reluctant to contaminate my little ludic space, my ergodic garden, with the professional concerns of meeting rigorous analytic or critical standards. But contamination is the point; thinking aloud about the circumstances of my own production, for example, as well as that of the writers whose work I like to study, becomes a form of materiality here.

Why hadn't I seen it before? Considerations of performativity, diaspora, fragmentation, identity, and access, all issues that preoccupy me, are central to Internet poetics. The messy, broken aesthetic, the lyric-gone-awry that Nathaniel Mackey calls an aesthetic of "discrepant engagement" in critical essays that examine "dissonance, cross-culturality and experimental writing," is not alien to web art, and is not inherently uncongenial to the medium that many experience as sterile and hypermediated.[3] In fact, much work on the web derives its power precisely from explicitly working the boundaries of what we consider organic/inorganic, from the Australian artist Mez (Mary Ann Breeze)'s use of "code" (or protocol) punctuation to convey linguistic/affective/bodily brokenness to mIEKAL aND's explicit concern with networking between the worlds of "permaculture" and "hypermedia" (neologisms that help to convey the utopian ambition of integrating the botanical and the wired, the premodern and the postmodern). That Mez's work is knotted, self-interruptive, and challenging while aND's is multisensory and expansive (see, for example, *Seed Sign for Philadelpho Mendes* and *Floraspirae*) suggests that there are innumerable ways to foreground, analyze, and embody in Webwork the issues of nature/technology, body/machine, organicity/inorganicity, life/death.

In what follows, however, I approach these issues obliquely, from an angle not usually found in considerations of either engagé critique or cyberpoetry: that of the inanity and foolishness to be found in throwaway texts. Why fill up precious pages with analyses of the spontaneous, intentionally ephemeral poetic detritus that follows when I could spend my scholarship on socially conscious Web projects? Because messy, hit-and-run proliferative work creates a texture, a discursive thickness, a culture, out of and against which any e-canon (or, in Talan Memmott's more apt phrase, "provisional short list") emerges and derives its significance.[4] Attending to the subcultural textures, the white noise or the ongoing processes (processes of both development and devolution of language and meaning) of a literary locus—"poetic activity" rather than "poetry" per se—reveals its values, its sociality, its—to use a phrase from a bygone political and cultural era—relevance to everyday life. So, in addressing e-poetic culture, I'm decisively not trying to establish an alternative canon but rather attending to writing processes, and to writing that embodies a "space-taking" or "world-making" postliterary vision.

The Dialectical Historian as Refugee/The Internet Poet as Diasporic Historian

The much quoted "Theses on the Philosophy of History," generally accepted as Walter Benjamin's final piece of writing, outlines a method and an ethos for the dialectical historian that is simultaneously a description of the state of mind of, and hortatory address to, small wonder, the refugee (that is, it is prescriptive and descriptive). In 1939 or 1940, writing as a moving target (his German citizenship anulled by the Third Reich, he had been living on the run in France; the piece was written between an internment and his death by suicide in a Spanish coastal town after escaping across the Pyrenees), he urges that "Nothing that has ever happened should be regarded as lost for history" and, even as he himself entertained strong suicidal urges, describes the underdog, exilic survivor's traits as "courage, humor, cunning, and fortitude," that peculiar collective resiliency that supercedes questions of individual survival. Furthermore, his invocation of the "memory that flashes up in a moment of danger" as the paradigmatic object and method of study for the aspiring materialist historian corresponds also to the paradigmatic cognitive experience of the refugee living in a constant "state of emergency."[5] The alertness, the charge of adrenaline flashing up in a moment of danger, the fragmentary nature of the essay itself as a series of aphorisms and s.o.s.es: all indicate the desperate conditions under which intellectual survival and creative expression are undertaken.

As diasporics have embedded or encrypted in their collective counter-memory the experience of displacement, flight, exile, violent deracination through kidnapping and slavery or other traumatic origins of their global scatterings, artifacts of diasporic expressive culture evince these character-istics of twisted resilience, refracted optimism, frenetic displays of disci-plinary virtuosity—especially those verbal arts that also enact the "art of being off-center,"[6] among them the techniques and styles called avant-garde, which represent the most compelling case for the Shklovskian de-familiarization that putatively characterizes all literary language. While a claim cannot be made that formal properties of textual fragmentation and dispersion are particularly diasporic, or that diasporic writers are more drawn toward these expressive techniques than to others, it seems to me that there is a felicitous fit, as it were, or misfit, between a diasporic sensi-bility and the avant-garde effect.

If we can make this transition from the acute case of the refugee to the more generalized and less urgent condition of diaspora, we can hy-pothesize a diaspora poetics that reproduces itself not solely thematically, though it certainly can and often does address questions of collective trauma at the level of content. Equally compellingly, however, and ar-guably intellectually more interesting, diaspora poetics reproduces itself through formal and mediating characteristics: through gesturing at ex-haustiveness or excess, as if trying to account for everything that has ever happened in history, thought, or text; through an aesthetic of scattered-ness, incoherence, and disorientation in the immediate text, though a dis-cernible coherence can be apprehended in the whole; through a medium that itself enacts a kind of randomness, anonymity, and even glut or surfeit that seems to function side by side with an insufficiency: through print literature, or whispered oral transmission, through radio and television, and most recently through the net, the World Wi(l)d(e) Web, the lat-ter an image of loose global connectivity not far removed from that of diaspora itself. It would be useless to suggest that excess, exhaustiveness, and a surface incoherence characterize all diasporic writing; on the con-trary, much of it—Celan, Jabès—is characterized by a compact austerity. Nonetheless, the mandate to name all social phenomena has its diasporic footsoldiers—its cultural workers—who deal obsessively in salvage work, and there is, as well as a sense that the "usable past" is heavily mediated by present needs, urgency in the diaspora subject's investment in encyclope-dic salvaging (based in part on an intuition that the apparently "useless" may end up being the very key to insight). Through reference to cyberpoet Alan Sondheim's work, I recognize the fractured Internet aesthetic as a site of diasporic excess, and that, conversely, the excess and depressive mania we associate with the Internet inhabits a diasporic aesthetic: polyglot, haunted, rapidfire, wrecked.

It may seem unlikely to pair Benjamin, with his strongly (though not dogmatically) dialectical, Marxist-critical orientation, and Sondheim, whose work is more properly in an aesthetic avant-garde tradition and who sees himself as a practicing artist, if one theoretically informed and engaged, rather than a critic. But it is precisely the task of diasporic vanguard thinkers and writers, or, if that risks excessively privileging the diasporic, of interdisciplinarity itself, to pair the unlikely, to see across counterintuitive dissonances, to discern apparitional analogies. In doing so, such scholarship and art practice address what falls between the cracks of methodological/disciplinary/national/identitarian categories and the partial subjects they inevitably call into being. Carrie Noland asks perceptively, "Does it matter that Sondheim isn't threatened with extinction? Or does the threat appear in a mutated form?"[7] While one could not contradict the simple observation that both Benjamin and Sondheim are diaspora subjects, and further, that they both belong to the same diasporic group (European and/or European-descended Jewry), this does not render their situations equivalent. As Brent Edwards pointed out in his useful resuscitation, via Yosef Yerushalmi's influential work *Zakhor*, of the distinction between the Greek *diaspora* (dispersal) and the Hebrew *galut* (exile), there is no automatic meaning of immediate suffering that accrues to the word diaspora; it lacks the moral weight and the implication of suffering that necessarily accompanies the sense of exile, oppression, guilt/responsibility of galut. While not precluding these, "diaspora" is a neutral term with respect to cause, effect, and historical outcome.[8] While it is obvious that the situation of Benjamin's last few years was one of extreme displacement compared to Sondheim's safety in the United States, it should be kept in mind that most modern German Jews of Benjamin's generation had felt an equivalent safety in Europe until the rapid ascendancy of the Third Reich. This irony has indeed left a historical residue in Jewish American consciousness that is well articulated by Noland's "[d]oes the threat appear in a mutated form?"[9] In other words, current safety, always contingent, is no guarantee of permanent safety. Though a thorough examination of ethnic paranoia would not be appropriate, and conclusions about the ultimate validity of these anxieties must be set aside as somewhat beside the point here, one can assume from the work, as well as from the ubiquity of similar sentiments expressed by middle-class Jewish Americans who have not otherwise, at least to all appearances, personally suffered the economic, social, or cultural effects of institutionalized racism/anti-Semitism that Sondheim experiences himself to be working

POETICS FOR A POSTLITERARY AMERICA

under a constant threat to his being, however hypothetical it might appear to others.[10] Both Benjamin and Sondheim share a belief, born of this sense of impending catastrophe, that every phenomenon in the world is of interest, an ethical commitment to debris (spam), recursion (looping), and anonymous/mass/vernacular cultural ephemera rather than to culturally or historically acknowledged grand moments, or the monuments and reified great poems that codify such moments. Does this move to study Benjamin alongside Sondheim debase Benjamin's memory or that of other unsuccessful refugees, and does it turn the immeasurable loss of diasporic experience into an effect of style? Does it privilege diaspora as a dehistoricized stance or a depoliticized aesthetic available to anybody whose work is nonlinear, excessive, fragmented, redundant? No. Rather, we study an instance of diasporic genre, significant, understudied, and informing other texts such as the "Theses" and *The Arcades Project*, which in turn offer some nonformalist context for understanding the "Sondheim effect." Juxtaposing two differently historically and disciplinarily situated writers, who nonetheless share a diasporic sensibility of h(a)untedness, creative restlessness, and eclecticism and a shared modern history, can lead one to propose the possibility of a "diaspora poetics": conjectural articulations between aesthetic, sociopolitical positionings—or something more tentative, processual, undisciplined: a diaspora *poiesis*.

Diaspora

The aesthetic of "wrongness," which preoccupies this volume, emerges even in as high-tech and sophisticated a medium as Web poetry. All of the many, sometimes contradictory characteristics enumerated previously (no one could possibly, for instance, term Mackey's work doggerel, and he might argue that the latter category of verse acquires its lowly status precisely through its clumsy attempts at rightness) are particularly apposite in discussions of Alan Sondheim's work. Sondheim, who comes from the (post-punk/Fluxus) avant-garde art and music world of 1970s New York City, takes issues of process to heart so deeply that each performance is a spontaneous, one-of-a-kind event: he displays videos and photographs, and plays sound tracks accompanied by his live, real-time typing response along the bottom of the computer screen.[11] Often there are four things to look at simultaneously—more than one of them is moving—as well as a compelling sound component that drives the piece rhythmically. Mastery and dissolution are both on overwhelming display, a frenetic dispersion of letters, words, images, sounds. The performance is both abject (much of the work involves ludicrous and/or disturbing nudity in a kind of self-parodic exhibitionism, syntagmatic fragmentation, or other indices of failed communication; much of the thematics of the text-in-process is Kristevan, psychoanalytic, confessional, preoccupied with polymorphous perversity) and perfect (the performances always seem to hang together aesthetically as well as narratively or theoretically—whichever mode is appropriate to the given piece and, in spite of the sensory overload, they always last exactly as long as they're supposed to for any given venue). These live performances are hypnotic; unstoppable semio-sacred garbage pours across the screen or pulsates in several overlapping frames, like tarot cards come to exhilarating but terrifying life in a dance that predicts the sublimity of failure, the excess of absence, the abundance of loss. Sondheim's embrace of all infohuman detritus and debris mandates a sense of unfinishedness; though it is not celebratory in theme, its endless generativity and scattering suggests some kind of diaspora machine, swirling out material with a hangdog-humorous, Beckettian persistence in the face of the impossible.[12] Sondheim dwells in impossibility equivalent to Dickinson's eerie possibility.

My first exposure to Sondheim's work was through the Poetics Listserv, to which the poet Charles Bernstein introduced me in 1995. The list, despite the limitations endemic to that form, opened a world to me of experimental, "avant-garde" poets, poetry, and poetics. Sondheim, an obsessive writer, posted work to the list several times daily. I found the verbo-emotional flotsam and jetsam of his effluvia captivating in their twisted simplicity; a theoretical and emotional acuteness clearly underlay even the most accessible or (deliberately) clumsy text. On July 7, 2002, for instance, this typical though relatively simple piece came over the screen as I was laboring with this assay:

From: Alan Sondheim <sondheim@panix.com>
Subject: # my leaky sieve ##
To: POETICS@LISTSERV.ACSU.BUFFALO.EDU

my leaky sieve

drwx--s--x	lrwxrwxrwx	drwxr-xr-x	drwx--S---	-rw-------	-rw-------
-rwxrwxrwx	-rw-------	rw-------	drwx------	-rw-r--r--	-rw-------
-rw-------	-rw-------	-rw-rw-r--	-rw-------	-rwxrwxrwx	-rwx--x--x
-rw-------	-rw-------	-rw-------	-rw-------	-rw-------	-rwxrwxrwx
drwx--x--x	-rwx------	-rw-------	-rw-------	-rw-------	-rw-------
-rw-------	-rw-------	drwx--s--x	-rw-------	-rw-------	-rw-------
-rw-------	-rw-------	-rw-------	-rw-------	-rw-------	drwx--s--x

POETICS FOR A POSTLITERARY AMERICA

```
-rw-------   -rw-------   -rw-------   -rw-------   -rw-------   -rw-------
-rw-------   -rw-r--r--   -rw-------   drwx--s--x   -rw-------   -rw-r--r--
-rw-------   -rw-r--r--   -rw-------   -rwx------   -rw-------   -rw-rw-rw-
-rwxrwxrwx   -rw-------   -rw-------   -rw-------   -rw-------   -rw-------
-rw-------   -rw-------   drwx--s--x   -rw-r--r--   -rw-------   drwx--s--x
drwx--s--x   -rwxrwxrwx   -rw-------   drwx------   drwx--s--x   drwx--s--x
drwx--s--x   -rw-------   drwx------   -rw-------   -rw----r--   -rw-rw-r--
-rw-rw-r--   -rw-------   -rwxr-xr-x   drwxr-xr-x   -rw-------   -rw-------
-rw-r--r--   -rw-rw-r--   -rw-------   # my leaky sieve ##
```

i never stole anything i once ran away from a dying animal i once
had sex with a minor i once thought i was going crazy i once
tried to kill myself with iodine i once was a coward i once killed
a mouse i once insulted someone i never raped anyone i once insulted
anyone i once touched someone i once abandoned someone i once
slapped anyone i never hit anyone i once was a coward i never killed
anyone i once ran over a cat i never hit a deer i once killed a
raccoon i never stole anything i once was rude i once was fired i
once failed a course i once was shameful i once had an accident i
once wasn't driving i once abandoned someone i once was responsible
i once was beaten i once had jaundice i once was ill
1068171603111112111111111111111211111112111111121
11111111211111111111111111112117211232212111111211111

my leaky sieve

Recognizable through repetition-with-the-occasional-slipup are both
excess and minimalism, accessibility and impenetrability. A sharply restricted vocabulary and series of simple declarative sentences pull the piece
in one direction, while lack of punctuation (old tricks in the modernist
poetry world), weird lapses in normative idiomatic use, and above all the
unintelligible-to-print-literates frame of letters, dashes, and numbers create a headlong rush in the opposite direction. The combination of formulaic confession ("i once"), defensiveness ("i never"), repetition, serious and
comic elements, terror and tongue in cheek, hyperverbalist and nonidi-
omatic phrases ("I once slapped anyone") and the words' emergence from
and then total breakdown into letters, dashes, and numbers—all point
to a survivalist mode of expressive culture traceable to the more outré
permutations of diasporic language style (think Lenny Bruce, Gertrude
Stein, the Marx Brothers, Franz Kafka, Franketienne, Nathaniel Mackey,
Bob Dylan's early surrealism, or even James Brown's vocables).[13] It is now
axiomatic that diaspora, no longer designating the condition of one or

two stigmatized and displaced groups (Jews, Armenians), now typifies the postmodern condition; though far from normative in the world of representation, which still favors the "traditional family" and the monoracial, -lingual, and -cultural stasis the phrase euphemizes, diaspora has become the experiential and/or demographic norm rather than the exception, in spite of violent nationalist backlash. So the genre of e-poetry, both because of its diffuse medium and because of poetry's designated role as laboratory where the microeffects of subjectivity in discourse can be experimented on and with through the manipulation of language, could provide a key to contemporary diasporic consciousness.[14]

What more can be said about the gibberish at the outset of Sondheim's poem, letter clusters separated by Dickinsonian dashes? Are these instances of the semiotic, written language's most basic units (letters and punctuation) stammering and conglomerating, separating and sizzling? In fact, though one can read the piece successfully this way, further discussion of "# my leaky sieve ##" on the poetics list revealed that these were meaningful within the context of computer programming. Jerrold Shiroma explains to a skeptic that

> basically, any perl script on the web must have certain permissions assigned to it by the owner of the script (i.e., the webmaster, programmer, site admin, etc.) . . . each script has different permissions granted to the user, group, & world . . . with these permissions being "read" (the "r" in the above text . . . allowing the permission to access the script), "write" (the "w" . . . granting the permission to write, or alter, the script), & "execute" (the "x" granting the permission to run the script) . . . where alan mentions that there are too many "777"s means that there are too many instances where the permission to write to the script are granted to everyone.[15]

In addition, the numbers represent numerical values given to each permission script (detailed information is available at http://www.linuxlookup .comlhtml/guides/chmod-chown.html#2.2). So Sondheim is using computer code, commands usually suppressed in the final text, in this case known as "permissions," as an explicit part of his piece. And the piece is about "permission"—what is permitted and what is not, what one is permitted to say and what should remain unsaid, control over knowledge, information, and speech.[16]

In short, the piece is legible and garbled (what is opaque to some is transparent to others), accessible and "coded," manic and controlled, a compound of natural language and computer code, a confession and a disavowal, a gesture of intimacy and distance, of shame and self-assertion.

While this could be said about many non-e-poetry texts (I suggested some of them; I could add Kathy Acker's *Blood and Guts in High School* and Eve Kosofsky Sedgwick's more confessional essays), this example from Alan Sondheim's sprawling oeuvre specifically uses Web technology; the incorporation of command language into the poem creates a hybrid language that gestures at intelligibility, framing the intelligible but thematically disturbing natural-language text. Expressions in this medium are saturated with affect. One can bond with anything, after all, and part of the pathos of Sondheim's work is that its tenor, its means of production, its form and its content—that is, its general vibe—embodies this desperate openness to which nothing (post)human is alien.

Sondheim has been posting several of these fragments a day for many years, dispersed and published in this ad hoc way to a community of poets and electronic media artists on several different listservs, some of whose members sometimes beg for respite and campaign against his "intellectual diarrhea," only to elicit exhortations from the rest of us to continue, continue, keep on going on though you can't go on.[17] The response to "# my leaky sieve ##" and other poems, the usual I hate Sondheim/I love Sondheim debates on Poetics List, took a curious turn. Though some of the attacks were imaginative and entertaining (for example, John Tranter's anagrammatic "Insane old ham. [Denials? Oh man!]"), one pro-Sondheimite exhorted poets to be each other's "best friends," and challenged the membership of the list, some of whom had accused Sondheim of being a bandwidth hog who monopolized the list as a form of self-publication, to post their own poems. One by one, poets whose work we had never seen started to share their work; some lurkers came out of hiding, and well-known poets joined in with new work. Thus, Sondheim's commitment to sharing his work, rather than drowning others ("Help!" was the subject line for the anti-Sondheimers' pleas), catalyzed a new phase in community formation. On a list usually more devoted to theory/poetics than praxis/poetry, the border between the two, the permeability of which had been the topic of an unusually thoughtful and high-quality discussion a week or so earlier, became a hybrid space in practice as well as theory.

Sondheim's boundarilessness disturbs people, even in avant-garde circles where he would seem most welcome. He has been accused of net-imperialism, of inflicting himself on us with no sense of propriety. His work has the vibe of the refugee knocking on the door, refusing to go away; its insistence is a pain in the ass. At a conference presentation on Sondheim I was asked how he differed from the (considered retrograde) confessional poets of the 1950s to 1970s, insisting on himSelf in his embarrassingly intimate self-disclosures and thus in secret league with the bourgeois ego expressed in the convention of the "lyric I." On the contrary; these confessions are flavored with Kafka rather than Sexton, with Bruno Schultz rather than Robert Lowell, in their exaggerated, allegorical theatricality. There is a performativity here that, though narcissistically inflected, is only incidentally autobiographical; the "I" is tenuous. More germane is the ritualistic river of undifferentiated phenomena, much of it trivia, that is spun as having the greatest import and thus acquiring that import. Nothing that has ever happened should be lost to history, and the history of individual consciousness is the purview of the poet as dialectical historian.

This paradoxical pairing—exhaustiveness and fragmentation, excess and incompleteness, continuity and brokenness as twin characteristics of a diaspora aesthetic—makes intuitive sense when we invoke the names of writers whose work exhibit these traits: Allen Ginsberg, Edmond Jabès, Georges Perec, David Grossman, Gertrude Stein, Hannah Weiner, Rachel Blau DuPlessis, Louis Zukofsky, Kamau Brathwaite, Will Alexander, Nathaniel Mackey, one could go on. . . . (The latter is interestingly bifurcated: Mackey's prose is exhaustive, his poetry fragmented, but both are characterized by their formal appearance as parts of unending series.) An effect of improvisation might be invoked here, understood as metonymic for a larger survivalist logic that uses whatever resources lie to hand for immediate deployment. Daniel and Jonathan Boyarin have written of the "powers of diaspora" in an attempt to depathologize the diasporic subject and situation, to reverse the terms that see diasporic cultural strategies as compensatory or victim-oriented.

How can these paired paradigms of exhaustiveness and fragmentation be articulated as empowering: what do they enable?[18] Fragmentation can be somewhat glibly ascribed to a literalization/textualization of diaspora: a scattering, a diffusion, great spaces between units of "meaning," partial and discontinuous utterance, difficult linearity or nonlinearity, and so on, a mimetic, imitative or reflective aesthetic in which the formal properties of a work enact a diasporic mapping. However, there are other possibilities. Fragmentation, for example, implies dismantling, disassembling for easier portability, evoking the familiar Jewish trope of the book as portable homeland.[19] Could we then postulate the powerbook or laptop as a portable homeland, though slightly more obtrusive than Jabès's tiny book, the Torah, carried clandestinely in the crook of the exile's elbow? The powerbook as laptop implies a smuggling of the so-called family jewels as contraband across borders for the purpose of reproduction— spasmodic, jerky, stuttering, *spora*dic, the reproduction that scatters itself under duress, virtual ejaculation in the age of mechanical globalization.

POETICS FOR A POSTLITERARY AMERICA

Language, a portable material, occupies little space, and can be further fragmented to facilitate survival. Broken-up scraps of material, or utterance, or memory, micromusics and micropoetries slip sideways into a transatlantic consciousness.

What about exhaustiveness or discursive excess? The same examples come to mind: Stein's *The Making of Americans*; the elaborate semiotic riffs in Nathaniel Mackey's fictional series, *From a Broken Bottle Traces of Perfume Still Emanate*, in which the characters' intensely realized musings on cultural signs preempt the reader's achieving an unmediated, self-congratulatory exegetical epiphany; or Benjamin's *Arcades Project*, Sisyphean by nature, which manages to be both fragmentary and exhaustive: exhaustiveness and excess here imply unfinishability. (If it would have been enough for God to do even one of the things he is thanked for in the litany of Passover miracles, what humans do or could do is never enough for themselves or each other.) The term "exhaustive" has positive if pedantic connotations: attempted thoroughness, hyperconscientious completeness, having left no stone unturned. It also has negative ones: exhaustion, glut, saturation, overinsistence. If the controlled flow of Nathaniel Mackey's fictional semioticians demonstrates thoroughness, Alan Sondheim's avatars (Internet personae), mostly sexually abject females with names like Jennifer, Julu, Nikuko ("meat-girl" in Japanese), and Susan Graham, inhabit an uncomfortable contact zone just this side of unbearable in their rawness and insistence on appearing on our screens unbidden, pushing the limits of how much sexual masochism and how much just plain verbiage we can handle—a compulsively Sadean transgression into the cool blue-gray screens on our desks (at least he doesn't use the names Justine and Julie, though he gestures at them through the J-names above). Sondheim's work overflows with these disposable beings-in-language, adding in turn to the mass of raw material that gets cycled into Google poetry and spam poetry, those latest phenomena contributing to the wayword, swirling auratic dust-cloud, the sporeflux of Planet Media. In fact, the title of Sondheim's book *The Wayward* embodies metonymically the uncontrollable wordiness that is also willfulness and impetus, a sendup of religious discourse (I am the Wayward vs. I am the Way), an emphasis on the word AS the way, on waywardness AS an ethic, and on the concept that one finds one's way by spending words; the real can't be known before its utterance. It would be excessively corny to point out that AS, the poet's initials, comprise an English word that, be it in the form of adverb, conjunction, pronoun (!), or preposition, always necessitates relation and process—but if one can't wax excessively corny in an essay such as this, then where? And if not now, when?

This discursivity, this exegetical overkill, knows that its excesses stem from diaspora's limitlessness, loss, and absence. Yet it is not merely compensatory, a simple address or redress of a space emptied by loss. But if exhaustive discursivity is not compensatory, or at least not *merely* so, how then is it to be understood? Perhaps through recourse to salvaging, collecting, the Benjaminian or Ginsbergian hoarding/spending of scraps and detritus of history, of literary language, the conviction that not only is nothing uninteresting, nothing is only itself, but rather a trace of some much larger narrative worthy of uncovering or intuiting. Even left unexcavated the trace itself is sufficient sometimes; the fragment is itself holy. Think of Ginsberg's profane blazons at the end of "Howl" and "Kaddish": "holy the asshole," etc., and "O Mother what have I left out." To leave something out is to consign it to memory-death, to fail in one's task as a dialectical historian cum refugee; at the same time the monstrosity of Mother or holiness lies in the unreassemblability of the severed parts. Again, consider this an ethical commitment to debris. Sondheim's exhibitionism/confessionalism can look like a lazy or narcissistic refusal to edit, but is rather a form of record-keeping or even humility, in that we (and he) are in no position now to know what piece of this mess will be useful in the future, so we have to document it all, save it all, spend it all by getting it into public discourse, show it all, expose, publish, self-publish it all. Consider also that it was precisely the "personal," confessional, or emotional elements—"sentimental" and "Romantic" were the pejoratives used—in Benjamin's writing Adorno termed "undialectical" when he saw a first draft of the now iconic Baudelaire essay; Benjamin's refusal or inability to separate the intimate and interior from the rigorously theoretical led to many of his key pieces being rejected for publication, to be heavily edited before publication, or to ambivalent reception once published. Beyond what his colleagues regarded as fuzziness or residual (and regrettable) mysticism in his work, however, and in spite of his embrace of randomness and the brilliance of his before-the-fact counterintuitive (and after-the-fact "isn't-it-obvious?") associations (the gestures of striking a match, of gambling, of jabbing at the page with the pen in a near-automatonlike trance, of dueling, and of bowing compulsively in a crowded street all gathered on a continuum of resonances in an essay on lyric poetry and the nineteenth-century city are, by any account, an astonishing roster of sliding, not-quite-equivalent homologies), Benjamin is committed to a kind of intentionality, as his complex relationship to the dialectic evinces. Even as his life was increasingly embattled and at the mercy of historical movements far beyond his control, his intellectual productivity, while intimately related to this upheaval, cleaved to the task of rigorous explication of social phenomena; that is, he conducted his dialectical experiments in order to achieve a truer, more supple, more emancipatory and responsive dialectic.

Sondheim, on the other hand, through the Internet and "codework" (his coinage, which has become coin-of-the realm standard vocabulary for Web art that employs as content the language of coding; that is, the commands that usually underlie invisibly the overt message or picture one receives on the screen), courts and achieves not only the effect of randomness but often randomness itself, due to the commands he gives the computer and then lets it spit out whatever it's looping (see "After Auschwitz," for example). While there is, of course, a degree of intention in this aesthetic, and while its use does not compose the sum total of Sondheim's compositions, the medium and its effects, as well as the authors' overt theoretical motivations, interrupt any seamless matching-up of Benjamin's and Sondheim's oeuvres.[20] This juxtaposition of Benjamin and Sondheim, of diaspora and avant-garde, "overlap and intersection, not equivalence and identity," produces a tension of recognition and dissonance.[21] As Barrett Watten observes,

> Benjamin never really surrenders intention, even as he is lost in the quotable archives. He chooses his texts, while Sondheim chooses techniques that generate texts. At times, it is the automatic dimension of this product that is important; but this immediately interprets the subjective/needy side of the writing. So we have the man/machine interface that turns out to be a needy child, looking for a very human, fleshy connection.[22]

Nonetheless, there is a sense that both writers are at the mercy, not only of historical forces that inevitably shape their respective work (Benjamin's immediate circumstances clearly more dire than Sondheim's), but also of the very material (language, thought, phenomena) that constitutes both their content and their media. As servants of the word, bearers of the book, diasporic poets are at the mercy of language (as much) as historical exigency. And on the Internet especially—a medium made for excess, anonymity and the unpolished wreckage of human verbal, capital, cultural circulation—language is indeed experienced as a virus from outer space, an eleventh plague on all our houses, or a visitation from an unfamiliar signifier in the form of an embattled, ethnically overdetermined, nerdy technogeek poet.

"lovely irma input" (December 23, 2004), riffing obliquely on Freud's Irma dream with its excessive orality, exemplifies an exhaustiveness that attends to every bit of linguistic minutia, every bit of precious alphabetic detritus generated by humans: nothing that has ever been thought or said must be lost. It is a list of words that, except for the first four, which focus on the "js" configuration, feature "rm." Though spatially/visually they form solid blocks of unremittingly unpunctuated and syntactically isolated verbs, nouns and adjectives, temporally/aurally these words create a gloriously rich, concatenating, oceanic swell, which at moments has semantic resonance for diasporic concerns: "informants intermarriage intermarried intermarry intermarrying intermediate intermingled judeogerman"; "unconfirmed undetermined"; "germanyiddi an form an form germanyiddi." Sliding alphabetically along its inexorable chain of signifiers, the piece moves without going anywhere. Its punctuating chorus, "lovely irma input/ for pete's sake" (or "for cryin out loud"), interjects a bit of contrapuntal irritation, evincing Sondheim's awareness that his work tests the limits of readers' patience; the hyper-*goyishe* yahoo voice interrupts the molten flow of vatic nonsense to provide a formal frame. About "lovely irma input"'s compositional process, Sondheim writes, "'rm' was a sorting factor; I think the sorting was done with a mathematical function, but at this point I'm not really sure. But definitely every word; they're from the 'ethnologue' list atftp://ftp.cerias.purdue.edu/pub/dict which is a series of word lists useful for hacking, passwords, etc. I've been fascinated by it for a long time."[23]

Hacking and passwording are, of course, highly charged metonymic concerns related to larger issues of access, border crossing under high-surveillance conditions, or entry into esoteric textual practices. Hackers are the opposite of hacks: experts of anarchic geekery who belie systems' claims to infallibility through break-ins, rather than mediocre creators pitiably intent on preserving their own status as individual writers. Like infiltration, subversion, smuggling, poaching, and other subterfugic crossings, hacking can be spun as a threat from above (invasion by stealth, subtle vanguards of imperialist takeovers) or below (the well-rehearsed "immigrant story," desperate tales told triumphantly by later generations), just as Sondheim's desperate self-publishings on listservs have been read as both arrogant impositions and abject outsider's implorings. Courage, humor, cunning, and fortitude anyone? These residual characteristics saturate Sondheim's manic, unboundaried corpus. In "lovely irma input"'s reliance on strange words (after all, he does not use "term," "formalism," "performance," "informal," or any of the more banal "rm" words I've used here), shibboleths and word-magic, Sondheim's diaspora places a high value on the metaphysical consequences of manipulating language down to interpretive strategies involving letter-magic (Kabbalah) as a gateway to spiritual and intellectual enlightenment. As in Adeena Karasick's work, this Kabbalistic preoccupation with textual exegesis and layering of metacommentary is both ludic

POETICS FOR A POSTLITERARY AMERICA

and scholarly (not to mention theological). The abject performance of the feverishly devoted exegete or textual magician—the inhabitant of an un-funhouse (Kafka's Kastle™?) of reified midrashic material—resonates with the *Arcades Project*, internally exiled for years (almost literally under prison-house-arrest of/in language) in the Bibliothèque Nationale. Learning is on compulsive and compulsory display, but at the same time, thinking/writing semiotic production is not done solely for the human other, the interlocutor whom some might argue is a stand-in for the ultimate interlocutor. In a deft reading by Norman Finkelstein, poet Allen Grossman's work argues that unlike non-Jewish poets, Jewish poets speak directly to God and no other; thus the stakes are that much higher. This exclusive and awed address, with its exaggeratedly asymmetric power relation, can account for the "autism-in-public" aura that accrues around such monologistic outpourings; they are witnessed but not shared by readers or hearers; they are intended to be overheard, but the poet is not responsible to any audience but Absence. The writing/exegesis is a life pulse, a *sine qua non*, of diasporic subjectivity, and a fulfillment of the mandate (an eleventh commandment?) to leave not a scrap of history unattended to, uncollected, unremembered, unaccounted for, or, if loss is inevitable, unmourned. This is a ticket to survival, or if not survival, freedom.

Looking at these "bleeding texts" (the phrase is Mez's) against the backdrop of collective history, e-poetry could be considered diasporized language at its most ethereal, mobile, and rootless. It is "rootless cosmopolitanism"—Stalin's term for Jewishness–dis/embodied. Much of the most interesting e-poetry features mutating, swarming, or dancing ("winking," one critic puts it) letters (see Stefans's "Dreamlife of Letters" and mIEKAL aND's "After Emmett: A Typofantastic Voyage"), morphing fonts and language made both visible and sonic beyond what we usually think of as orality and literary, "verbivocovisual" in ways beyond what Joyce imagined. While e-poetry is not the apogee of deracinated poiesis, it makes up an increasingly significant category of the postliterary. It's a taste of outer space, that diaspora-to-be, as Sun Ra and William Burroughs have indicated—"natural" home to the queer, distorted and dissonant, the parasites (in the creative sense of the word) of the planet; the misfits, the whackos . . . as well as the next frontier for the weapons industry and the military.

Silliness

The silliness of these Sondheim bits and other e-poetry texts deserves further exploration, because silliness's proximity to (through hysteria and hyperrealism—gee, hasn't that last word gone out of style?)—and wisdom about—horror can instruct us about surviving postmodernity with grace. Silliness lacks the ominous edge of hysteria but is nonetheless a relatedly "ungrounded" experience, a relatively pleasant symptom of anxiety, tension, disturbance. Silly means, among other things, to be rendered empty-headed from a blow; this kind of semi-euphoric response to trauma has repeatedly been associated with postmodernity and a postmodern aesthetic. While blank, postmodern emptiness is not identical to silly light-headedness, there is sufficient overlap and continuity in the experience of dissociation that these permutations can illuminate rather than cancel each other out. The over-the-top hysteria of, for example, Kathy Acker's routines in *Blood and Guts in High School* is both comical in its adolescent excess and horrific in its subject matter (treating, among other things, ambiguously metaphoric father-daughter incest, sexual slavery, cervical cancer contracted through sexual abuse, etc.). The reader can process this material as an instance of the hyperreal, a cartoonishly funny exaggeration that dramatizes the degree to which female sexuality is oppressed, repressed, and mangled in U.S. society.[24]

Without overstating the relationship between catastrophe and silliness, one can posit the close connection of trauma, play, and experimental writing.[25] The Oulipo (Workshop for Potential Literature) and other writers, particularly Georges Perec and Raymond Federman, obsessively created writing exercises using constraints or substitutions, often with hilarious results, finding structures to contain and represent a surplus of shock, sorrow, and loss from World War II. While not as directly or primally traumatic in its genealogy, postwar U.S. poetry has been seen (as has much of global postwar culture) as a reaction to the shocks of the atom bomb and the concentration camps, combined with the hyperaggressive domestic anticommunist purges of the 1950s (which successfully, if temporarily, depoliticized literary culture) and ethnoracial oppression. The more "experimental" of those poetries—Beat, Black Mountain, the black arts movement and other emancipation-oriented movements, women's poetry, the New York School—embodied responses to these upheavals in fiercely "trivial" (New York School), fragmented (Black Mountain), ragingly confessional and countercultural (Beat), and, later, overtly politicized vernacular (ethnoracial, women's, etc. liberation movements) poetries, all of which foregrounded the values of spontaneity, collaboration, and anti-academicism.

A small listserv called Flarf, devoted to the aesthetic of goofiness and comprising younger poets mostly in New York City but also in California, started in the summer of 2001, but reached new heights of activity and intensity in the wake of 9/11. (Would it ruin it to add to this description that the members of Flarf are also serious poets who publish work that fits the category of the avant-garde or progressive?) While Sondheim's ongoing project clearly works the border between humor and terror, Flarf, though considerably more firmly committed to silliness, also thrives in a performatively posttraumatic space of resilience and ingenuity. After a brief hiatus directly following the September 11 attack on the World Trade Center, Gary Sullivan, generally known as Flarf's originator, who was also posting long and harrowing accounts to another list about his day working in Manhattan and walking home through human dust with thousands of others, posted this parody on Anne Waldman's 1973 poem of universal womanhood, "Fast-Speaking Woman":

FAST-POSTING FLARFY

I am a scared and pissed off Flarfy!
I am a post-traumatic stress Flarfy!
I am a gritting my teeth in my sleep Flarfy!
I am a waving several flags at once Flarfy!
I am a trying to remember the words to God Bless America Flarfy!
I am an unable to sing the national anthem Flarfy!
I am a retaliating in ever-widening circles Flarfy!
I am a gas-mask and antibiotics buying Flarfy!
I am a suddenly blurting out hateful things in public without realizing it
    Flarfy!

In terms of its reliance on Web or electronic media, Flarf draws most heavily on the language of search engines, as well as the content of successful or failed searches, setup options ("Signature Include a set quantity of X at the end of every message. You can include your contact information, favorite OOHHHHHHH YEAH BAY-BEE! or anything you want in your FELINE TELEPHONY. Lick on Options and then on Signature to find out more"), spam ("THIS IS NOT A GET-RICH-QUICK SCHEME! Remember—you can sleep with Ostrichs made of remote controlled sailboats to get to the top if this doesn't pan out! . . . If you remember that time in the car, on the way home from seeing the doctor, and getting so incredibly angry, yelling at your mother and telling her that you hated her then YOUR FINANCIAL PAST DOES NOT HAVE TO BE YOUR FINANCIAL FUTURE!"), teen chat-rooms ("Maybe you should go to the crocodile forum here. My grammar is fine maybe you should work on getting a life. Maybe you should have said elimination diet didn't work for you. Screw you and screw him") and other mass-cultural Web annoyances. While Sondheim foregrounds the suppressed matter of programming as content, Flarf focuses on the in-your-face everyday garbage we have to wade through in this supposedly sped-up and disembodied communicative medium. It uses the detritus of hypermediated culture as material for specifically but ridiculously literary genres: primarily plays and poems, though sometimes also in mass-cultural forms like mock news articles ("The SBPTX Flarf Index dropped three percent today, as real-life grim wackiness continued to outpace Google-derived transitional objects for flavoricious fluffy-luv"). Sometimes, too, a serious cause for alarm is signaled by a comically worded subject line: the subject heading "fuuuuuuck" gave us a Web site for an article head-lined, "New Tests Confirm Acrylamide in American Foods: Snack Chips, French Fries Show Highest Levels of Known Carcinogen." Here are the first two stanzas of K. Silem Mohammad's 2002 poem "Sestina":

> Your search—"I hate blow jobs"—did not match any documents.
> Your search—"I hate Stonehenge"—did not match any documents.
> Your search—"I hate monitor lizards"—did not match any documents.
> Your search—"I hate Tender Vittles"—did not match any documents.
> Your search—"I hate Boethius"—did not match any documents.
> Your search—"I hate vasectomies"—did not match any documents.
>
> Your search—"I hate US imperialism"—did not match any documents.
> Your search—"I hate al-Qaeda"—did not match any documents.
> Your search—"I hate Jacques Derrida"—did not match any documents.
> Your search—"I hate Bessie Smith"—did not match any documents.
> Your search—"I hate tuna melts"—did not match any documents.
> Your search—"I hate lymph glands"—did not match any documents.

'Nuff said? The effect here combines male adolescent—that most performative of all life stages—humor (smart, juvenile, scatological, misanthropic but politically progressive to the degree that it's political at all—think Simpsons) with poetic talent. Thus Flarf's delightful and ridiculous ephemera are dominated, though not entirely, by manic forty-somethingish men who clearly delight in assuming younger personae for the purpose of posting. In a verbal competition distantly related to the street-sparring insult game of the dozens (more juvenile, less mother-oriented, and more scatological, indulging in greater displays of formal literary erudition), the Flarfies egg each other on, riffing off each others' newly achieved heights of silliness, sometimes complimenting a particularly successful flarf with the single-word post, "Dude." Gary Sullivan's responding post to the above follows:

WHAT I BELIEVE

Searched the web for "I believe in deodorant". Results 1.
Searched the web for "I believe in George W. Bush". Results 2.
Searched the web for "I believe in population control". Results 4.
Searched the web for "I believe in dinosaurs". Results 6.
Searched the web for "I believe in social darwinism". Results about 7.
Searched the web for "I believe in marxism". Results about 11.
[...]
Searched the web for "I believe in evolution". Results about 844.
Searched the web for "I believe in love at first sight". Results about 888.
Searched the web for "I believe in America". Results about 1,070.
Searched the web for "I believe in ghosts". Results 1,160.
Searched the web for "I believe in everything". Results about 1,200.
Searched the web for "I believe in santa claus". Results about 1,270.
Searched the web for "I believe in nothing". Results about 1,420.
Searched the web for "I believe in love". Results about 18,300.
Searched the web for "I believe in God". Results 38,100.

In the world of Flarf, silliness is raised to the level of an aesthetic, and at the same time it is obviously a form of abjection, a dramatic departure from the self-contained dignity of either the "real man" or "real poetry," but recuperable through its display of superior intelligence. This manifestation of self-indulgent, masculine hysteria, inviting, participatory, and collective, serves as a salutary counterexperience to the masculine hysteria of militarism. At the same time, it must be distinguished from feminine hysteria, which is covert and isolated; it is much more difficult for a woman to perform hysteria or silliness in public, as the social opprobrium is far more severe. With certain exceptions (Lucille Ball), female silliness isn't funny. Typical themes for improvisation on Flarf are squids, chimps, "words that are always funny" (snood, wimple, chimp, panties, spork), top ten imaginary hits or bestselling books, sex with Britney Spears, poetry and poetics. To handle the amount of material coming in, some members of the list have created special silly addresses: joe flarf writes from flarfy@ hotmail.com, Flarfety Flarf Flarf from toomuchflarf@hotmail.com; a third, Sir Flarfalot, posts from flarfalot@hotmail.com (explaining, "I like to flarfalot"). There is a sense of in-group, collaborative competition; guys racing to find and post the URL to the weirdest site on the Web.[26] Though individual posts are single-authored, the point is not the individual posts or—God forbid—Authorship but the thick texture of inanity that accrues to provide a gloriously anarchic parallel narrative to the working day. As Charles Bernstein has pointed out, "[the comedic] collapses into a more destabilizing field of pathos, the ludicrous, shtick, sarcasm; a multidimensional textual field that is congenitally unable to maintain an evenness of surface tension or a flatness of affect." The "manic pace of life" and the "mechanized routine" of (post)modernity become the "manic routine"— in the sense of "wild shtick"—of the comic, and the polar tyrannies of flat affect and catastrophic disaster are mediated by hilarity; fragmentation of contemporary life is e-mediated here by collaboration. In this sense hilarity is always a shared process—one needs, optimally, an engaged and participatory audience that is equally active as creative force. With some exceptions, comedy is better non-solo, as the concept of the "troupe" or the "team" conveys; Groucho just wasn't as funny when he went out on his own. Even the solo comic—Lenny Bruce, let's say—relies on a kind of in-joke-ness, or cult following, for his/her power; the essence of the "hip comic" is specialness, some degree—though not absolute—of esotericism. Again, the group experiments of Oulipo, the Surrealists and Dadaists, and of New York City's St. Mark's Church Poetry Project Workshops, come to mind as arenas in which poets keep their work en procés, not necessarily intended for publication. Flarf considered some forms of collective publication—the stupidest possible: a print collection idea was proposed and then abandoned, only to be taken up again years later, and an early Flarf reading at a Brooklyn café reportedly erupted into a food fight, a kind of schoolboy spoof on, for instance, a Bukowskian bucket-of-blood, barroom-brawl-style poetics.

?GENDERGENDER?

Initially, two female Flarfies posted work (I exclude myself because my flarf is so bad, I'm mostly a fellow traveler on the list), though not as often as men, and in fewer numbers. Only Katie Degentesh posted regularly (and until she changed her nom de flarf from Flarfety Flarf Flarf to Flarfette Jones, her gender was not clear to me); her flarf was especially aggressive in its bawdy humor, including the magnificent "The Sausage: an Essay," its companion pieces "The Banana: an Essay" and "The Popsicle: an Essay," and a somewhat menacing piece rendered from the results of Google searches for "kiss my . . ." + "scissors," which earned the praise, "Now *that's* flarf," from a male colleague. These pieces are especially focused and tough, with no sentimentality discernible, unlike, say, Sullivan's death-of-a-favorite-pet jag right before September 11, 2002. Flarfette Jones's pieces, sexually themed though they be, did not engage "women's" issues, or even gender issues more broadly (unless one could characterize a phallic or occasional castration theme as such) but did participate in the general adolescent bawdiness of Flarf, though with the occasional extra edge of anger (scissors, for example). Social critique was downplayed in favor of dark humor.

The other original female flarfie did not participate in the sustained manic abandon of her male counterparts. Nada Gordon posted a series of "v imp" sonnets ("very important," in e-talk, also suggesting a vampish imp, an impish vamp, a virtual sprite . . .). When I asked her permission to include one in my discussion of Flarf, she immediately qualified her consent. Though posted to the Flarf list, the series was, according to Gordon, intended for conventional print publication and was generated in a notebook rather than online—indeed, she doesn't consider them "flarf per se," though they are to some degree "silly," by which she intends reference to another etymological ancestor—"happy." She wrote,

> Not that these are happy poems; it's just that they strain for a kind of levity in a context that clamors for anxiety at every turn. . . . Which is not to say flarf poems don't have anxiety at their core—they are simply less transparent, more effective defense mechanisms than are these "very important" sonnets. The sonnets are "very important" because they aren't, of course. And because they are, in the vicious private way that poetry is important in the social organization of the contemporary USA whose official dictum is that poets are either irrelevant buffoons or spewers of irrelevant pablum. The sonnets *are* parodic, at times, but—unlike pure flarf, which takes as its satiric object all of creation—mostly of *literature*, in a characteristic wrestling bout with literary "problems" (as if there were nothing more truly urgent to address in these gloomy times).

The difference she pointed to, the stakes of her endeavor, are immediately obvious when one reads the sonnets. Silliness there is self-parodic; a woman committed to struggling with literary problems has to sillify them in a disarmingly, if mildly, self-disparaging way. To be too serious about being a smart woman leads to the same social opprobrium as to be too silly or hysterical; but Gordon is too serious (or is it, in John Cayley's felicitous coinage, "sillious"?) about literature as an activity to sacrifice anything by dissembling either her seriousness or her playfulness. In fact, the series thematizes, among other things, the specifically gendered nature of her literary struggles. Each sonnet has a v imp title: "Vaudeville Improvisation," "Vaguely Impudent," and so forth. V imp sonnet 1 is:

Wild fauns create chaos
in the romantic-repressive moss!
Where pulses! found in seething birds!
loose their girlishness onto paratactic rock!
Kakemono! O Kantacky! What color is (c)lover?!
Roll me over in the burdock and the Indian buckwheat!
Roll me over in the plantain and the chickweed!
Your melting flesh is too-too solid,
your enigma putative as tungsten rose!
Hey, whoa! There's the cat that ate my gnostic suit!
I hold these truths (!) to be self-evident,
though some restrictions apply!
Look out, here comes the me(te)rmaid:
keep your hands on your chant!

Though it shares characteristics with both Sondheim's work and other Flarf, this series is far less concerned with using the e-medium for anything but distribution among friends. Over the course of Flarf's development, several other women, notably Mel Nichols ("illuminated meat") and Sharon Mesmer (no nom de flarf) have written flarf masterpieces (especially Mesmer's "Annoying Diabetic Bitch"), the listserv/collective has added and lost both men and women, many books of flarf have been published, and flarf has become an internationally recognized if ridiculously improbable avant-garde movement with violent detractors, helplessly giggling fans, and its share of controversy. And while gender has taken a thematic back seat, so to speak, to diaspora and silliness here, the gloriousness of bad poetry in the hands of skilled poets brings a new dimension to the postliterary.[27]

Conclassay

I have attempted to demonstrate continuity between classic vanguard poetic movements and the emergence of e-poetry, or "digital poetics." One might ask about the wisdom of using a postmodern medium to reproduce a fundamentally modernist category. One might productively ask about new poetries from other margins. What are poets doing in regions less known to myopic U. S. Americans: to paraphrase Frank O'Hara, what *are* the poets in Ghana doing these days? Or on the Standing Rock Lakota Reservation, for that matter? Korean anarchist artist Young Hae Chang creates Web pieces for "Heavy Industries" in English, Korean, and French. One piece which may not be considered ergodic but nonetheless uses Web technology (and for which the author cites the first few of Pound's Cantos as direct influence)[28] to promote a jazz/post-Beat aesthetic is her "DAKOTA" (www.yhchang.com/DAKOTA.html), which moves from a spoken-word style, angry-young-man, road-trip poem into a diatribe against the limits placed on racialized American subjects. Using only a percussive sound track (an Art Blakey solo) and black-on-white words to unfold its narrative, the text functions as a series of slaps in the face as the words and phrases hit the screen successively and make way abruptly for the next; it's a bombardment that grows in intensity as the piece progresses. Although it conforms to a teleological narrative structure, its presentation in word and phrase fragments creates a surprisingly nonlinear effect—each word is a new blow, an entirely visceral, whole-body attack that has the effect of altering time (just like the experience of getting beaten up by police might or getting kicked by a rival gang)—although time is also kept regular through Blakey's aggressive drumming. Here regularity itself becomes a springboard for entry into an altered state, just as the relentless predictability of police state, hate crime, or intragroup gang violence against people of color becomes a medium for entry into a state of double consciousness, or indeed, in a postmodern world, of multiple consciousness. Chang's work is taken seriously in the digital (ergodic) poetry world (see Thom Swiss's "Distance, Homelessness, Anonymity, and Insignificance: An Interview with Young Hae Chang Heavy Industries"), as is exciting work from Brazil (again, a country with a powerful modernist experimental tradition) and Indonesia.

E-poetry proliferates, growing in aleatory, nondirectional ways. This form of aesthetic experience continues to permeate our everyday lives, corrupting it irretrievably and making us all distant, homeless, silly, anonymous, and insignificant in the most helpful way: as part of the fragile World Wide Web of sentient and nonsentient being.

Notes

1. Walter Benjamin, "On Some Motifs in Baudelaire," *Illuminations*, trans. Harry Zohn (New York: Schocken, 1967).

2. Jack Spicer, *The Collected Books of Jack Spicer* (Santa Barbara:
Black Sparrow, 1975) 61.

3. Barrett Watten, *The Grand Piano, Part 3: San Francisco, 1975–1980:
An Experiment in Collective Autobiography*, ed. Steve Benson et al.
(Detroit, MI: Mode A, 2007) 85.

4. Stephen Vincent, "Re: Outsider Art," posted 10 Mar. 2007 to
<poetics@poetics@listserv.buffalo.edu>.

5. Gilles Deleuze and Félix Guattari, *Kafka: Toward a Minor Literature*, trans. Dana Polan (Minneapolis: University of Minnesota
Press, 1986).

6. Joseph Lease, telephone conversation with the author, 10 Feb.
2008.

1. The Jewish Entertainer as Cultural Lightning Rod

1. For several works on the cultural meaning of Jewish language
use, see Sander Gilman, *The Jew's Body* (New York: Routledge, 1991),
esp. chap. 1, "The Jewish Voice," and *Jewish Self-Hatred: Anti-
Semitism and the Hidden Language of the Jews* (Baltimore: Johns
Hopkins University Press, 1986); Benjamin Harshav, *The Meaning of
Yiddish* (Berkeley and Los Angeles: University of California Press,
1990); Max Weinreich, *The History of the Yiddish Language* (Chicago:
University of Chicago Press, 1980); Maria Damon, "Talking Yiddish
at the Boundaries," *Cultural Studies* 5.1 (1991): 14–29, and "Gertrude
Stein's Doggerel 'Yiddish': Women, Dogs and Jews," in *The Dark
End of the Street: Margins in American Vanguard Poetry* (Minneapolis:
University of Minnesota Press, 1993) 202–35.

2. Lenny Bruce, *How to Talk Dirty and Influence People* (Chicago:
Playboy Press, 1972), 6.

3. For a useful summary of censorship cases involving artists and
entertainers in twentieth-century United States, see Edward de

Grazia, *Girls Lean Back Everywhere: The Law of Obscenity and the Assault on Genius* (New York: Random House, 1992).

4. Michael Fischer, "Ethnicity and the Post-Modern Arts of Memory," in *Writing Culture*, ed. George Marcus and Michael Fischer (Berkeley and Los Angeles: University of California Press, 1986) 194–233; James Clifford, *The Predicament of Culture* (Cambridge, MA: Harvard University Press, 1988); Houston A. Baker, *Blues, Ideology, and Afro-American Literature* (Chicago: University of Chicago Press, 1987); Renato Rosaldo, *Culture: and Truth: The Remaking of Social Analysis* (Boston: Beacon Press, 1988), 190–93; Riv-Ellen Prell, "Why Jewish Princesses Don't Sweat: Desire and Consumption in Postwar American Jewish Life," in *People of the Body* ed. Howard Eilberg-Schwartz (New York: SUNY Press, 1992) 329–60; for an instance of hero-worship, see Frank Kofsky, *Lenny Bruce: The Comedian as Social Critic and Secular Moralist* (New York: Monad Press, 1974). Serious work on Bruce includes Ioan Davies, "Lenny Bruce: Hyperrealism and the Death of Jewish Tragic Humor," *Social Text* 22 (Spring 1989): 92–114, and an abbreviated but interesting discussion of Bruce in social context in Andrew Ross, *No Respect: Intellectuals and Popular Culture* (New York: Routledge, 1989) 89–92.

5. Honey Bruce, *Honey: The Life and Loves of Lenny's Shady Lady* (Chicago: Playboy Press, 1974); Lenny Bruce's letter to Judge Horn, trial transcript, 1962, 2.

6. On Bruce's use of Yiddish to mark a boundary of inclusion/exclusion, see my "Talking Yiddish at the Boundaries."

7. Henry Louis Gates Jr., "Writing 'Race' and the Difference It Makes," *"Race," Writing and Difference*, ed. Henry Louis Gates Jr., (Oxford: Oxford University Press, 1985) 1–19.

8. David Antin, letter to the author, 15 Nov. 1990, responding to an essay I'd written in which I argued that Antin's simultaneous assertion of and self-distancing from Jewishness indicated his "ethnic anxiety."

9. The poignant ambiguity of titles, nobility, and class status among Jews is nowhere better illustrated than in Proust's *Remembrance of Things Past*, which could be profitably reconstrued as *Remembrance of Folks Passing*.

10. Bruce, *How to Talk Dirty*.

11. W.E.B. Du Bois, *The Souls of Black Folk* (New York: Signet Classics, 1969) 45; Fischer, "Ethnicity" 196.

12. And clinical schizophrenia.

13. Kimberle Crenshaw, "Demarginalizing the Intersection of Race and Sex: A Black Feminist Critique of Antidiscrimination Doctrine, Feminist Theory and Antiracist Politics," *The University of Chicago Legal Forum* (Summer 1989): 139–67.

14. Lenny Bruce, *The Essential Lenny Bruce* (New York: Ballantine, 1967) 65.

15. Bruce, *The Essential Lenny Bruce* 36.

16. Bruce, *The Essential Lenny Bruce* 41–42.

17. See, for example, two back-to-back articles that advocate "experience-near" anthropology and generalized theory, respectively, each implying that

the approach favored by the other is more imperialistic: Unni Wikan, "Toward an Experience-Near Anthropology," *Cultural Anthropology* 6:3 (August 1991): 285–305, and Nicholas Thomas, "Against Ethnography," *Cultural Anthropology* 6.3 (August 1991): 306–22.

18. Author's notes, July 1989.

19. Damon, "Talking Yiddish at the Boundaries" 21–22.

20. Author's notes, July 1989; see also Ralph Ellison, *Invisible Man* (New York: Vintage, 1980), 13.

21. Trial transcript 134.

22. Bruce is explicit about the relationship between dependence and performance anxiety, or, conversely, mastery as the right to command performances. See, for example, his "Look at Me" routine, in *The Essential Lenny Bruce* 110–11, in which he quite plainly ascribes the performer's desperation to Oedipal power relations, just as elsewhere he ascribes the Jewish performer's desperation to the Egyptian captivity ("How Jews Got into Show Business," ibid., 50).

23. Trial transcript 276–77.

24. Lenny Bruce, "A Pretty Bizarre Show," *What I Got Arrested For* (Fantasy Records, 1966).

25. John D'Emilio, *Sexual Politics, Sexual Communities: The Making of a Homosexual Minority in the United States 1940–1980* (Chicago: University of Chicago Press, 1983), esp. 176–95.

26. As a result of his many obscenity and drug trials and convictions, Bruce was eventually unable to get a cabaret card and was driven out of work; on the day he died from a drug overdose, he had received a foreclosure notice on his home.

27. Author's notes, July 1989.

28. Susan Griffin, author's notes, August 1990. Daniel Boyarin brought my attention to a relevant joke: A Jew is sleeping in the upper bunk of a train; a Hungarian officer sleeps below him. Every five minutes, the Jew sighs, "Oy am I thirsty." Finally the officer can't stand it any more and brings him a glass of water. After five minutes of blessed silence, the voice rings out, "Oy was I thirsty."

29. Bruce, trial transcript 141.

30. Bruce, trial transcript 50, 62.

31. Bruce, "Blah, Blah, Blah," *What I Got Arrested For.*

32. Bruce, trial transcript 190–91.

33. Author's notes, July 1989.

34. Bruce, trial transcript 188–89.

35. Author's notes, July 1989.

36. Bruce, trial transcript 305.

37. Bruce, trial transcript 307.

38. Bruce, trial transcript 313.

39. Bruce, trial transcript 314.

40. Bob Kaufman, *Abomunist Manifesto*, in *Solitudes Crowded with Loneliness* (New York: New Directions, 1965) 80. Many African American hipsters of the

jazz milieu, including Kaufman, Philly Jo Jones, and Eric Miller (a bassist who played the "colored friend" in "How to Relax Your Colored Friends at Parties") appreciated Bruce's artistry. Kaufman glosses Bruce's fortunes pithily in his poem "[The Traveling Circus]": "There are too many unfunny things happening to the comedians." *The Ancient Rain: Poems: 1956–1978* (New York: New Directions, 1981) 25.

2. Jazz-Jews, Jive, and Gender

1. Lenny Bruce, *The (Almost) Unpublished Lenny Bruce: From the Private Collection of Kitty Bruce* (Philadelphia: Running Press, 1984) 63.

2. Rogin focuses on Al Jolson, who was the frequent butt of Bruce's and Mezzrow's irritated disavowal.

3. Work by, among others, Ella Shohat and Ammiel Alcalay has done much to break down monolithic and essentialist conflations of "Jew" with "European" or "Euro American." However, my personal investment as well as the biographies of the persons under consideration specify European America as my context.

4. A line delivered by a colleague at his memorial service: "'I love to measure,' Al would say almost guiltily."

5. See David Biale's study of eroticism in Jewish (male) history, in which he discusses the late nineteenth-century Jewish literary phenomenon of novels featuring tortured intellectual Jewish men who become involved with devouring, castrating-type Gentile women (*Eros and the Jews: From Biblical Israel to Contemporary America* [Berkeley and Los Angeles: University of California Press, 1992] 173–75).

6. "Words as if all worlds were there." Robert Creeley, *The Collected Poems of Robert Creeley, 1945–75* (Berkeley and Los Angeles: University of California Press, 1982) 221.

7. Dizzy [John Birks] Gillespie (with Al Fraser), *To Be or Not to Bop: Memoirs of Dizzy Gillespie* (New York: Da Capo, 1979) 281.

8. Mezz Mezzrow and Bernard Wolfe, *Really the Blues*, 1946 (New York: Citadel, 1990) 52.

9. Miles Davis and Quincy Troupe, *Miles: The Autobiography* (New York: Simon and Schuster, 1989) 414–15.

10. Ben Sidran, *Black Talk*, 1971 (New York: Da Capo, 1981) xi.

11. Nat Shapiro and Nat Hentoff, *Hear Me Talkin' to Ya* (New York: Dover, 1955) 227.

12. Louis Armstrong, *Satchmo: My Life in New Orleans* (New York: Da Capo, 1954) 205.

13. Michael Rogin, "Blackface, White Noise: The Jewish Jazz Singer Finds His Voice," *Critical Inquiry* 18.3 (Spring 1992): 417–53.

14. For two equally incoherent examples of the confusion over collective designations of Jews, see E. San Juan, "The Culture of Ethnicity and the Fetish

of Pluralism," *Cultural Critique* 18 (Spring 1991): 215–29, and Michael Lerner, "Jews Are Not White," *Village Voice* 18 May 1993, Special section: "White Like Who?": 33–34.

15. See Mark Slobin, *Tenement Music* (Urbana: University of Illinois Press, 1982). My grandmother used to tell of a man appearing at her home when she was a young girl and announcing to her mother, "Liebe, don't you remember me? I was Itche Moishe and I played at your wedding in Smargón. Now I'm Irving Morris and I'm with the Boston Opera. Here are some tickets to Aïda." There are many works of literature that attest to the importance of music in secular Jewish life, its portability and peripatetic nature, and hence its significance in mediating the shift from Old World to New. For a postmodern "talk-poem" version of such a tale (in which a violin that passes from hand to hand through generations appears as a recurrent trope), see David Antin, "Dialogue," *tuning* (New York: New Directions, 1984) 219–68.

16. Henry Louis Gates, Jr., *The Signifying Monkey: A Theory of African-American Literary Criticism* (New York: Oxford University Press, 1988). Since Mezz Mezzrow was so explicit and theoretical about his love of "jive," Gates quotes him fairly extensively in his descriptions and definitions of "signifying" intended to educate a non-African American readership (69–70).

17. Freud's *Jokes and Their Relation to the Unconscious* (New York: Norton, 1960) is sometimes, but not sufficiently or regularly, recognized as a kind of ethnic manifesto; Benjamin Harshav, *The Meaning of Yiddish* (Berkeley and Los Angeles: University of California Press, 1990), and Max Weinreich, *The History of the Yiddish Language* (Chicago: University of Chicago Press, 1980). Weinreich points out an astonishing phenomenon that speaks directly to a love of wordplay he characterizes as specifically Ashkenazi: in several places in Germany and Eastern Europe, Jews celebrated holidays by eating food whose names in Yiddish were puns for the name of the prayer or holiday in Hebrew. The day featuring a prayer beginning *kol mevaser* (the Voice of the Messenger), for example, was observed by eating cabbage soup, *kohl mit vasser*! Only in Yiddish, he says, would language be so literally a binding agent between cultures, and cross-cultural puns be so literally actualized in material practice (4–5). Right away a similar African diaspora example comes to mind: the accommodation of the identities of Christian saints to West African deities based on details of appearance etc. Not linguistic puns, but visual puns operated in this cultural cross-referencing.

18. Jack Kugelmass, *The Miracle of Intervale Avenue* (New York: Schocken, 1986) 81.

19. Mezzrow and Wolfe, *Really the Blues* 53–54.

20. See Riv-Ellen Prell, *Fighting to Become Americans: Assimilation and the Trouble between Jewish Women and Jewish Men* (Boston: Beacon Press, 2000).

21. Mezzrow and Wolfe, *Really the Blues* 316.

22. Ronnie Spector (with Vince Waldron), *Be My Baby* (New York: Harper-Collins, 1990) 171–72.

23. Spector, *Be My Baby* 57–59.

24. Spector, *Be My Baby* 97.

25. Mezzrow and Wolfe, *Really the Blues* 49.

26. Lenny Bruce, *How to Talk Dirty and Influence People* (Chicago: Playboy Press, 1972) 6.

27. Lenny Bruce, "A White White Woman and a Black Black Woman," *What I Got Arrested For* (Fantasy Records, 1971).

28. The opening, and powerful, example of Toni Morrison's major thesis in *Playing in the Dark: Whiteness and the Literary Imagination* (Cambridge, MA: Harvard University Press, 1991) is a passage in which Marie Cardenal's attendance at a Louis Armstrong performance catalyzes an ultimately healing, but excruciating and harrowing, breakdown. Morrison speculates usefully on whether a performance of a European piece of music by a European musician would have conveyed the same (de)familiarizing shock.

29. Duke [Edward Kennedy] Ellington, *Music Is My Mistress* (New York: Da Capo, 1973) 36.

30. Ellington, *Music Is My Mistress* 89.

31. Gillespie, *To Be or Not to Bop* 405–7. Gillespie suggests that Granz was trying to set the musicians against one another: "[Jazz at the Philharmonic] wasn't much musically because Norman Granz got his nuts off by sending two or three trumpet players out there to battle each other's brains out on the stage. And he'd just sit back and laugh. . . . Norman had a weird sense of competition. He thought that the battle would not only be on the stage, but that the guys would have a funny feeling toward one another afterward." Here's Granz on the same subject: "The whole basis for the [Jazz at the Philharmonic] was initially to fight discrimination to break down segregation and discrimination, present good jazz and make bread for myself and for the musicians as well. I felt that it made no kind of sense to treat a musician with any kind of respect and dignity onstage and then make him go around to the back door when he's off-stage. So wherever we went, we stayed in the best hotels. [A great musician is] supposed to be treated as a great artist on and off the stage."

32. James Brown (with Dave Marsh), *James Brown, the Godfather of Soul* (New York: Thunder's Mouth Press, 1990) 94.

33. Bill Crow, *Jazz Anecdotes* (New York: Oxford University Press, 1990) 137.

34. Allen Ginsberg, "Caw Caw," *Holy Soul Jelly Roll* (Rhino Records, 1994), liner notes.

35. Gillespie, *To Be or Not to Bop* 183.

36. Billie Holiday (with William Dufty), *Lady Sings the Blues* (London: Barrie and Jenkins, 1973) 170.

37. Bruce, *How to Talk Dirty* 35, 46.

38. Frank Kofsky, *Lenny Bruce: The Comedian as Social Critic and Secular Moralist* (New York: Monad Press, 1974) 87–99. Kofsky analyzes (too schematically) Bruce's comedianship in terms of three Jewish religious roles—the rabbi, the

maggid, and the *tzadik*—and then discusses Bruce's aesthetic and ideological debt to jazz musicians in how he structured his monologues.

39. Mezzrow and Wolfe, *Really the Blues* 226.

40. Mezzrow and Wolfe, *Really the Blues* 300–1.

41. Mezzrow and Wolfe, *Really the Blues* 331.

3. Triangulated Desire and Tactical Silences in the Beat Hipscape

1. See "Victors of Catastrophe: Beat Occlusions," *Beat Culture and the New America, 1950–1965*, ed. Lisa Phillips (New York: Whitney Museum of American Art, 1995) 141–49; "Jazz-Jews, Jive and Gender: Ethnic Anxiety and the Politics of Jazz Argot," in this volume and *Jews and Other Differences: The New Jewish Cultural Studies*, ed. Daniel Boyarin and Jonathan Boyarin (Minneapolis: University of Minnesota Press, 1996) 150–75; "Other Beats," *Hambone* 13 (Spring 1997): 177–85; "The Jewish Entertainer as Cultural Lightning Rod: The Case of Lenny Bruce," in this volume and *Postmodern Culture* 7.2 (January 1997); "Callow But Not Shallow: John Wieners, *707 Scott Street*," *XCP: Cross Cultural Poetics* 3 (1998): 137–47.

2. See David Roediger, *The Wages of Whiteness* (New York: Routledge, 1993), for a historian's view of how the social commodity of "whiteness" (itself a social construction rather than a biological category) had to be earned by incoming members of the labor force from Ireland as well as from Eastern and Southern Europe. By the 1950s, these Jews and Italians were safely "white," but there were also, for example, quotas limiting Jewish admission to universities, and other forms of institutionalized prejudice. Moreover, the imaginative literature of the time continued to explore the anxieties experienced by these subjects. See in particular Brossard's roman à clef, *Who Walk in Darkness* (New York: Grove Press, 1952), in which an Italian American woman is romantically torn between a "passed Negro" (based on Anatole Broyard) and the narrator, a white man named, suggestively, Blake.

3. John D'Emilio, *Sexual Politics, Sexual Communities: The Making of a Homosexual Subculture, 1940–1980* (Chicago: University of Chicago Press, 1986).

4. D'Emilio, *Sexual Politics*, Kevin Killian and Lew Ellingham, *Poet, Be Like God: Jack Spicer and the San Francisco Renaissance* (Middletown, CT: Wesleyan University Press, 1998).

5. Hettie Jones, *How I Became Hettie Jones* (New York: Penguin, 1991).

6. Amiri Baraka, *The Autobiography of Amiri Baraka/LeRoi Jones* (New York: Morrow, 1984).

7. Richard Cándida Smith, *Utopia and Dissent: Art, Poetry, and Politics in California* (Berkeley and Los Angeles: University of California Press, 1995).

8. For an extended discussion of gay writing and Platonic thought, especially with regard to the North Beach 1950s and 1960s, see the first few sections of my "Dirty Jokes and Angels: Jack Spicer and Robert Duncan Writing the Gay

Community," *The Dark End of the Street: Margins in American Vanguard Poetry* (Minneapolis: University of Minnesota Press, 1993) 142–55.

9. Bob Kaufman, *Solitudes Crowded with Loneliness* (New York: New Directions, 1965) 14.

10. Robert Duncan, "The Homosexual in Society," *Politics* (August 1944): 290–311.

11. Robert Duncan, "An African Elegy," *The Years as Catches* (Berkeley, CA: Oyez, 1966) 34.

12. John Wieners, *707 Scott Street* (Los Angeles: Sun and Moon, 1997) 53–54.

13. Jack Spicer, *The Collected Books of Jack Spicer*, ed. Robin Blaser (Santa Barbara: Black Sparrow Press, 1975) 344.

14. Spicer, *Collected Books* 341.

15. Spicer, *Collected Books* 348.

16. Russell FitzGerald, *The Diary of Russell FitzGerald*, unpublished manuscript. n.d. 19.

17. Kaufman, *Solitudes Crowded with Loneliness* 6.

18. FitzGerald, *Diary* 49.

19. FitzGerald, *Diary* 66.

20. FitzGerald, *Diary* 66.

21. FitzGerald, *Diary* 67.

22. Ben Vereen, "I'll Make Me a World: A Twentieth-Century History of African Americans in the Arts," PBS interview, 1 Feb. 1999.

23. Robin Blaser, "The Practice of Outside," *The Collected Books of Jack Spicer* (Santa Barbara: Black Sparrow Press, 1975) 325.

24. Blaser, *The Practice of Outside* 375.

4. Displaysias

1. Gertrude Stein, *The Making of Americans*, 1925 (New York: Harcourt Brace, 1966) 21.

2. Nancy A. Harrowitz and Barbara Hyams, eds., *Jews and Gender: Responses to Otto Weininger* (Philadelphia: Temple University Press, 1995) 5.

3. Otto Weininger, *Sex and Character* (London: Heinemann, 1906) 311.

4. Weininger, *Sex and Character* 327–28.

5. Weininger, *Sex and Character* 312.

6. Weininger, *Sex and Character* 343ff.

7. Sander L. Gilman, *The Jew's Body* (New York: Routledge, 1991) 133.

8. Gilman, *Jew's Body* 138.

9. Gertrude Stein, *Painted Lace and Other Pieces: 1914–1937* (New Haven, CT: Yale University Press, 1955).

10. Gertrude Stein, *Q.E.D.*, in *Fernhurst, Q.E.D. and Other Early Writings* (New York: Liveright, 1971) 57.

11. Weininger, *Sex and Character* 321–22.

12. Stein, *Making of Americans* 84.

13. Weininger, *Sex and Character* 313.

14. Weininger, *Sex and Character* 315.

15. Stein, *Painted Lace* 94.

16. Stein, *Painted Lace* 209.

17. Stein, *Painted Lace* 202.

18. Stein, *Painted Lace* 203.

19. Stein, *Painted Lace* 215.

20. Stein, *Painted Lace* 207.

21. Stein, *Painted Lace* 151.

5. Imp/penetrable Archive

1. The "storm from paradise," the pile of wreckage, and the angel of history are all drawn from Walter Benjamin's oft-cited images in "Theses on the Philosophy of History," *Illuminations*, trans. Harry Zohn (New York: Schocken, 1969) 253–64.

2. Adeena Karasick, "The Wall," *Dyssemia Sleaze* (Vancouver, BC: Talonbooks, 2000) 40–60.

3. Walter Benjamin, *Gesammelte Schriften*, vol. 2 (Frankfurt: Suhrkamp, 1977) 243, qtd. in Momme Brodersen, *Walter Benjamin: A Biography*, trans. Malcolm R. Green and Ingrida Ligers (London: Verso, 1996) 118.

4. Adeena Karasick, *The House That Hijack Built* (Vancouver, BC: Talonbooks, 2004) 95.

5. Adeena Karasick, *Dyssemia Sleaze* 60.

6. Karasick, *Dyssemia Sleaze* 43.

7. Adeena Karasick, interview by Nada Gordon, <http://home.jps.net/~nada/karasick.htm>.

8. Karasick, *Dyssemia Sleaze* 5.

6. Kinetic Exultations

1. Stephen Jonas, "Boston, Mar. 2, 1961" (letter to Cid Corman), *that: short sets of writing*, 23 (July 1993): 1.

2. Bob Kaufman, "Perhaps," *Solitudes Crowded with Loneliness* (New York: New Directions, 1965) 54.

3. Ed Morales, "The Last Hispanic," *Aloud: Voices from the Nuyorican Poets' Café*, ed. Miguel Algarín and Bob Holman (New York: Holt, 1992) 99.

4. Guy Debord, "Rapport sur la construction des situations et les conditions de l'organisation et de l'action de la tendance situationiste internationale," qtd. in Greil Marcus, *Lipstick Traces: A Secret History of the Twentieth Century* (Cambridge, MA: Harvard University Press, 1989) 182.

5. Stanley Aronowitz, "Is a Democracy Possible? The Decline of the Public in the American Debate," *The Phantom Public Sphere*, ed. Bruce Robbins (Minneapolis: University of Minnesota Press, 1993) 75–92.

6. Rachel Buff, *Immigration and the Political Economy of Home: West Indian Brooklyn and American Indian Minneapolis* (Berkeley and Los Angeles: University of California Press, 2001).

7. Giorgio Agamben, *The Coming Community* (Minneapolis: University of Minnesota Press, 1994).

8. Dante Alighieri, *De Vulgari Eloquentia*, ed. and trans. Steven Botterill (Cambridge: Cambridge University Press, 1996).

9. Jack Spicer, *The Collected Books of Jack Spicer*, ed. Robin Blaser (Santa Rosa, CA: Black Sparrow Press, 1975).

10. "Problèmes préliminaires a la construction d'une situation," *Internationale situationniste* 1 (June 1958), 12; qtd. in Greil Marcus, *Lipstick Traces: A Secret History of the Twentieth Century* (Cambridge, MA: Harvard University Press, 1989) 181.

11. Mary Caroline Richards, *Centering in Pottery, Poetry, and the Person* (Middletown, CT: Wesleyan University Press, 1989) 59.

12. John Beverley, *Against Literature* (Minneapolis: University of Minnesota Press) 1993.

13. Henry Louis Gates, Jr., *The Signifying Monkey: A Theory of African-American Literary Criticism* (New York: Oxford University Press, 1990).

14. Henry Louis Gates, Jr., "Sudden Def," *New Yorker* 19 June 1995: 41.

15. Steven Caton, *"Peaks of Yemen I Summon": Poetry as Social Practice in a North Yemeni Tribe* (Berkeley and Los Angeles: University of California Press, 1990); Lila Abu-Lughod, *Veiled Sentiments: Honor and Poetry in a Bedouin Society* (Berkeley and Los Angeles: University of California Press, 1986); Barrett Watten, *The Constructivist Moment: From Material Text to Cultural Poetics* (Middletown, CT: Wesleyan University Press, 2003); Charles Bernstein, *A Poetics* (Cambridge MA: Harvard University Press, 1992), and *My Way* (Chicago: University of Chicago Press, 1999).

16. Jorie Graham, interview, *A View from the Loft* (Minneapolis: The Loft, 1994) 8.

17. See especially Paul Beatty, *Big Bank Take Little Bank* (New York: Nuyorican Poets' Café Press, 1990).

18. Kurt Gegenhuber, conversation with the author, 18 Feb. 1989.

19. Tricia Rose, *Black Noise: Rap Music and Black Culture in Contemporary America* (Middletown, CT: Wesleyan University Press, 1994).

20. Chris Felver, *West Coast: Beat and Beyond* video, 1982. George Lipsitz, "Listening to Learn and Learning to Listen: Popular Culture, Cultural Theory, and American Studies," *American Quarterly* 42.4 (December 1990): 615–36.

21. Adam Harden, slam, Nuyorican Live Touring Visit to the Twin Cities, 18 Nov. 1993.

22. Walter Benjamin, "The Work of Art in the Age of Mechanical Reproduction," *Illuminations*, trans. Harry Zohn (New York: Schocken, 1967) 217–53.

23. Adam Harden, Tracie Morris, and Paul Beatty, conversations with the author, November 1993.

24. Duke [Edward Kennedy] Ellington, "Categories," *Music Is My Mistress* (New York: Da Capo, 1973) 38.

25. Adam Harden and Diane Glancy, conversations with the author, November 1993.

26. TW, slam, Nuyorican Live Touring Visit to the Twin Cities, November 1993. I have had numerous arguments with friends and colleagues about the literary merits of this poem, which fascinates me. What fascinates me is both my attachment to it and to other "bad poetry," which I want at some point to theorize more thoroughly beyond an insistence that "you had to be there," and my friends' and colleagues' rabid adversity to it. It makes me believe that I am not wrong to locate, still, a strong faith in "merit" in the poetry community, even the community of scholars in distinction to that of writers.

27. Tim Brennan, "Off the Gangsta Tip: A Rap Appreciation, or Forgetting About Los Angeles," *Critical Inquiry* 20.4 (Summer 1994): 663–93.

28. Mark Slobin, *Subcultural Sounds: Micromusics of the West*. Middletown, CT: Wesleyan University Press, 1993.

29. W.E.B. Du Bois, "Of the Sorrow Songs," *The Souls of Black Folk* (New York: Signet Classics, 1969) 264–76, esp. 268ff.

30. George Lipsitz, "Popular Culture: This Ain't No Sideshow," *Time Passages: Collective Memory and American Popular Culture* (Minneapolis: University of Minnesota Press, 1992) 3–20.

31. Bob Perelman, "Write the Power," *American Literary History* 6.2 (1994): 306–24.

32. Nancy Fraser, "Rethinking the Public Sphere: A Contribution to the Critique of Actually Existing Democracy," *The Phantom Public Sphere*, ed. Bruce Robbins. (Minneapolis: University of Minnesota Press, 1993) 1–32.

7. When the Nuyoricans Came to Town

1. Miguel Algarín and Miguel Piñero, eds., *Nuyorican Poetry: An Anthology of Puerto Rican Words and Feelings* (New York: Morrow, 1975).

2. Algarín and Piñero, *Nuyorican Poetry* 15.

3. Miguel Algarín and Bob Holman, eds. *Aloud! Voices from the Nuyorican Poets Café* (New York: Holt, 1994).

4. For an extended poetic polemic on this theme, see Antonio Benitez-Rojo, *The Repeating Island: The Caribbean and the Postmodern Perspective* (Durham, NC: Duke University Press, 1996).

5. See, for example, "Literary Model: The Loft Grows Up, Reaches Out," *Minneapolis Star-Tribune* 10 Oct. 1996: A26.

6. For example, see Mark Nowak, "Open Book, Case Closed: The Democratic Paradox of Minnesota's New Literary Center," *Workers of the Word, Unite and Fight!* (Los Angeles: Palm Press, 2005).

7. Charles Bernstein, *A Poetics* (Cambridge, MA: Harvard University Press, 1992).

8. Joanna O'Connell, letter to the author, November 4, 1996.

9. Diego Vasquez, interview, *SHOUT!* November 1996.

10. Bob Holman, e-mail to the author.

11. Bob Holman, letter to the author, 20 Nov. 1996.

12. Steven Caton, *"Peaks of Yemen I Summon": Poetry as Social Practice in a Northern Yemini Tribe* (Berkeley and Los Angeles: University of California Press, 1990).

13. Mary Louise Pratt, *Imperial Eyes: Travel Writing and Transculturation* (New York: Routledge, 1992) 4.

14. Howard Becker, *Art Worlds* (Berkeley and Los Angeles: University of California Press, 1982) 1.

15. Bob Gale, interview by Michael Brown, "A Man, A Plan, A Slam," *SHOUT! Your Guide to the Spoken Word Universe*, March 1996.

16. Edwin Torres, "Ugilante" and "Indian Hand Poem," *I Hear Things People Haven't Really Said: A Collection of Poetry by Edwin Torres* (New York, 1991) n. pag.

17. The phrase is Lisa Gail Collins's, from her essay "Anguished Pleasures: Black Female Sexual Politics and Poetics," *Colors: Opinion & the Arts in Communities of Color* 4.5 (September–October 1995): 26–30.

18. Tracie Morris, "Ten Men," "The Spot," "Project Princess," *Chap-t-her Won: Some Poems by Tracie Morris* (Brooklyn, NY: TM Ink, 1992) 15–17, 40–41, 13.

8. Avant-garde or Border Guard

1. Jonathan Monroe, *A Poverty of Objects: The Prose Poem and the Politics of Genre* (Ithaca, NY: Cornell University Press, 1987) 16, and "Poetry, the University, and the Culture of Distraction" *Diacritics* 26.3–4 (1996): 3–30, 4.

2. Karlheinz Stierle, "Identité du discours et transgression lyrique," *trans.* Jean-Paul Cohn, *Poétique* 32 (November 1977): 422–41. 431. Author's translation.

3. Bernice Zamora, *Restless Serpents* (Menlo Park, CA: Diseños Literarios, 1994) 74.

4. José Saldívar, *Border Matters: Remapping American Cultural Studies* (Berkeley and Los Angeles: University of California Press, 1997).

5. Ed Cohen, conversation with the author, 14 Oct. 1997.

6. Juan Flores and George Yudice, "Living Borders/Buscando America: Languages of Latino Self-formation," *Social Text* 24 (1990): 57–84.

7. Saldívar, *Border Matters* 185–97.

8. Mary Louise Pratt, *Imperial Eyes: Travel Writing and Transculturation* (New York: Routledge, 1992) 4.

9. A reference to hookworm. In the second quarter of this century, owing in part to the United States' active underdevelopment of Puerto Rico, the incidence of hookworm among (mostly rural, but not exclusively) Puerto Rican children was close to 40 percent because of the scarcity of shoes (hookworm is contracted from the ground through the feet). Though the stereotype of the

slow and barefoot Puerto Rican has survived, knowledge of this bit of medical and economic history can rectify some of the assumptions that accompany it.

10. Edwin Torres, *I Hear Things People Haven't Really Said: A Collection of Poetry by Edwin Torres* (New York: Edwin Torres, 1991) n. pag.

11. Edwin Torres, "Seeds Sown Long Ago: Are You the Layer?" *XCP: Cross Cultural Poetics* 1.1 (1997): 89–91.

12. Edwin Torres, interview by the author, 14 Oct. 1997.

13. Edwin Torres, *SandHomméNomadNo* (New York: Edwin Torres, 1997) n. pag. Ellipses, orthography, and emphasis as in original.

14. This information and comments about and by Javier Piña were supplied by Piña in conversation with the author, 3 Feb. 1998.

15. Javier Piña, "Bilingual in a Cardboard Box," *The United States of Poetry*, ed. Joshua Blum et al. (New York: Abrams, 1996) 92–93.

16. Alfred Arteaga, *Chicano Poetics: Heterotexts and Hybridities* (New York: Cambridge University Press, 1997) 154–55. The X does not originate with Arteaga; Ana Castillo, for one, has also proposed it as an alternative, politicized spelling. But Arteaga discusses it in the context of poetry and poetics, so his insights are particularly useful here.

17. Qtd. in Henry Louis Gates, Jr., *The Signifying Monkey: A Theory of African-American Literary Criticism* (New York: Oxford University Press, 1988) 172.

18. Regarding vanguard elitism, see Nathaniel Mackey's fictional jazz violinist Aunt Nancy (Anansi)'s response when her band is called to task for playing "elitist"—that is, avant-garde—music outside a shopping mall in Santa Cruz teeming with rich hippies: "The wretched of the earth . . . can hardly be accused of elitism" (Nathaniel Mackey, *Bedouin Hornbook*, 1986 [Los Angeles: Sun and Moon, 1997] 78).

19. Arteaga, *Chicano Poetics* 242–44.

20. Robert Duncan, "The Song of the Borderguard," *Selected Poems*, ed. Robert Bertholf (New York: New Directions, 1993) 22–23.

21. Walt Whitman, "Democratic Vistas," *Whitman: Poetry and Prose*, ed. Justin Kaplan (New York: Library of America, 1982) 982.

9. Loneliness, Lyric, Ethnography

1. George Chauncey, "The Strange Career of the Closet," lecture, University of Minnesota, May 1998.

2. Robert Von Hallberg, conversation with the author, 13 Mar. 2003.

3. *Solitudes Crowded with Loneliness* (New York: New Directions, 1965), Bob Kaufman's first book of poems, is discussed below. Loneliness was a major sociological and philosophical preoccupation of this era, epitomized by titles like David Riesman's sociological treatise *The Lonely Crowd* and Alan Sillitoe's work of fiction, *The Loneliness of the Long Distance Runner*. In the forcibly depoliticized 1950s, the political and economic dimensions of Marx's alienation had become psychologized and affectively rendered, so that the term became

resonant with "dissatisfaction" or "anomie" rather than "exploitation" or "exchange value."

4. Johannes Fabian, *Anthropology with an Attitude* (Stanford, CA: Stanford University Press, 2001), esp. "Ethnographic Objectivity" 12–13 and "Ethnology and History" 75.

5. Theodor Adorno, "Lyric Poetry and Society," *Telos* 20 (1974): 56–71.

6. Jean Genet, *The Thief's Journal*, trans. Bernard Frechtman (New York: Grove Press, 1964).

7. Genet, *Thief's Journal* 53.

8. See *XCP 3: Fieldnotes and Journals* (1998), and Mark Nowak, *Revenants* (Minneapolis: Coffee House Press, 2000).

9. See, for example, Michael Taussig, *The Magic of the State* (New York: Routledge, 1996).

10. Renato Rosaldo, *Culture and Truth: The Remaking of Social Analysis* (Boston: Beacon Press, 1989); Ruth Behar, *The Vulnerable Observer: Anthropology That Breaks Your Heart* (Boston: Beacon Press, 1996.)

11. Malinowski does not appear to have actually used the phrase "participant observation" himself, though in the course of the discipline's development it has become attributed to him as the standard method and terminology. While George W. Stocking, Jr., has convincingly demonstrated that other ethnographers were de facto involved in this kind of fieldwork strategy, Malinowski has been mythologized as first turning it into a de rigueur methodology. Stocking, "The Ethnographer's Magic: Fieldwork in British Anthropology from Tylor to Malinowski," *Observers Observed: Essays on Ethnographic Fieldwork*, ed. George W. Stocking, Jr. (Madison: University of Wisconsin Press, 1983) 70–120.

12. Bronislaw Malinowski, *A Diary in the Strict Sense of the Term*, trans. Norbert Guterman (Stanford, CA: Stanford University Press, 1989) 296.

13. W.E.B. Du Bois, *The Souls of Black Folk* (New York: Signet Classics, 1969).

14. Malinowski, *Diary* 297.

15. Malinowski, *Diary* 63–64.

16. Malinowski, *Diary* 67.

17. For just two instances of the degree to which the language of dualism beyond the classic dualism of Westerner and other permeates meditations on the nature of anthropology and participant observation, see Richard Handler's discussion of anthropology experienced by anthropologists as an uneasy and dynamic synthesis of or struggle between science and art, and Herbert Gans's discussion of the extreme anxiety produced by the necessarily duplicitous role of the participant-observing social scientist. Handler, "The Dainty Man and the Hungry Man: Literature and Anthropology in the Work of Edward Sapir," in *Observers Observed: Essays on Ethnographic Fieldwork*, ed. George W. Stocking, Jr. (Madison: University of Wisconsin Press, 1983) 208–31; Gans, "The Participant Observer as Human Being: Observations on the Personal Aspects of Fieldwork," in *Field Research: A Sourcebook and Field Manual*, ed. Robert G. Burgess (London: George Allen and Unwin, 1982) 53–61.

18. Malinowski, "W katedrze na Wawelu" ("In Wawel Cathedral"), trans. Frank L. Vigoda (Yale University Library Special Collections, New Haven), manuscript.

19. See, for example, Bruce Albert, "'Ethnographic Situation' and Ethnic Movements: Notes on Post-Malinowskian Fieldwork," *Critique of Anthropology* 17.1 (1997): 53–65; Fabian, "Ethnographic Objectivity"; and Stocking, "The Participant Observant as Human Being."

20. While I am not concerned with intervening in the emerging subfield of Beat scholarship, looking at Beat writing as an ethnographic endeavor problematizes the assumption that all writing and culture swept up under the Beat rubric cleaved to a naive concept of "spontaneity" and undocumentable ephemerality. The Beats were partially attempting, in delineating the boundaries of their dissenting enclave within consensus-culture 1950s, to outline a counternationalism; these artistic "scapes" both described and prescribed (with the scribe as outsider and insider) the roles of the denizens of Beat, as well as the territory itself. This writing is ambivalently autoethnographical as well as being, in many cases (such as Kerouac's romans à clef and Ginsberg's "Howl," which functions as a Who's Who of the inhabitants of his hip nation), an outright bid for literary posterity. As self-proclaimed deviant subjects, Beat writers hewed powerfully to an ethos of survival through community, though they strove to distinguish that community's folkways and culture from those of the communities of upwardly mobile or sterilely static middle classes or working classes, black or white, from which they had fled.

21. Robert Hass, Beach Lecture, University of Minnesota, Minneapolis, 13 Apr. 2000.

22. "Family Breadwinner," *The Pilot* 31 May 1946: 7. For more extensive treatments of Kaufman's biography, see Maria Damon, *The Dark End of the Street: Margins in American Vanguard Poetry* (Minneapolis: University of Minnesota Press, 1993) 32–76, and "Introduction," *Callaloo* 25:1 (Winter 2002): 105–11.

23. See Joseph Torra, ed., *Stephen Jonas: Selected Poems* (Hoboken, NJ: Talisman House, 1994) 1–12.

24. Preston Whaley, Jr., *Blows Like a Horn: Beat Writing, Jazz, Style, and Markets in the Transformation of U.S. Culture* (Cambridge, MA: Harvard University Press, 2004) 50–53.

25. For an anecdote about poet Jack Spicer's scribbling the word "Nigger" across a presentation copy of Kaufman's broadside *The Abomunist Manifesto*, where he knew Kaufman would see it, and Kaufman's response, see Kevin Killian and Lew Ellingham, *Poet Be Like God: Jack Spicer and the San Francisco Renaissance* (Middletown, CT: Wesleyan University Press) 138. Kaufman's clashes with the North Beach police are well documented. See, for example, David Henderson and Vic Bedoian, "Tribute to Bob Kaufman" (KPFA radio 26 Apr. 1991); Maria Damon, "'Unmeaning Jargon'/Uncanonized Beatitude: Bob Kaufman, Poet," *The Dark End of the Street: Margins in American Van-*

guard Poetry (Minneapolis: University of Minnesota Press, 1993) 33; and Jeffrey Falla, "Bob Kaufman and the (In)visible Double," *Callaloo* 25:1 (Winter 2000): 183–89. Falla discusses usefully Kaufman's double bind, as a person of color, of being both hypervisible and invisible.

26. For a discussion of "percussion: drumming, beating, striking" and the relationship of poetry/music, percussion, and social violence, see John Mowitt's book of the same name (Durham, NC: Duke University Press, 2002).

27. Albert 60.

28. Du Bois, *The Souls of Black Folk* (New York: Signet Classics, 1969) xii. For a fuller discussion of the doubling inherent in this and other work by Du Bois, see Shamoon Zamir, *Dark Voices: W.E.B. Du Bois and American Thought 1888–1903* (Chicago: University of Chicago Press, 1995); for an exploration of Du Bois's connection to anthropology, see *Critique of Anthropology* 12.3 (1992), special issue on Du Bois and Anthropology, and especially a treatment of his ambiguous valuation of double consciousness in Ernest Allen, Jr., "Ever Feeling One's Twoness: 'Double Ideals' and 'Double Consciousness' in *The Souls of Black Folk*" 261–75.

29. John Wieners, *707 Scott Street* (Los Angeles, CA: Sun and Moon Press, 2000) 53–54.

30. Johannes Fabian, *Time and the Other: How Anthropology Makes Its Object*. (New York: Colombia University Press, 1983).

31. Wieners, *707 Scott Street* 105.

32. Jeff Derksen, "I Need to Know If This Is Normal," *XCP Cross Cultural Poetics* 2.

33. John Wieners, "To Sleep Alone," in *Selected Poems*, ed. Raymond Foye (Santa Barbara, CA: Black Sparrow Press, 1986) 238.

34. Gilles Deleuze and Félix Guattari, *Kafka: Toward a Minor Literature* (Minneapolis: University of Minnesota Press, 1986) 24ff.

35. Fabian, "Ethnographic Objectivity" 31–32.

36. John Wieners, "Children of the Working Class," in *Selected Poems* 175.

10. Poetries, Micropoetries, Micropoetics

1. "Micropoetries," *XCP: Cross Cultural Poetics* 16, Word issue 235. Another inspiration for the term "micropoetries" was "micromovements," choreographer Emilie Conrad's coinage to describe the smallest perceptible movement that one can deliberately initiate and sustain in any part of the body. She has incorporated this concept into the system of movement awareness she calls Continuum, and into work with paralytics and other movement-challenged people. Thus the term refers to a minute but effectively expansive technique for restoring abilities; in the same way, "micropoetries" aims at de-alienating poetic language from everyday life.

2. James N. Osterberg, Jr. [Iggy Pop], "I Wanna Be Your Dog," *The Stooges*, Elektra, 1969. Italic added.

3. Peter Sacks, *The English Elegy: Studies in the Genre from Spenser to Yeats* (Baltimore: Johns Hopkins University Press, 1985) 3 ff.

4. Susan Lannen, telephone interview by the author, 31 May 2006.

5. "I was taking a class in therapeutic writing for my MA program [in expressive therapies]; I opened up one of the textbooks for the class [Gabriele Rico's *Writing the Natural Way*] to a page of writing by someone who had seen the Viet Nam Memorial. I couldn't stop working on it until it found its final form the next day; I used a technique we'd learned in class, 'clustering.' ... I couldn't think about anything else until it was done. It was my way of dealing with what I had read [the *Phoenix* article on virtual memorials]; it was hard to read and I had to deal with it through creative energy." Lannen, interview.

6. Annie Kessler, interview by the author, 30 May 2006.

7. Lannen, interview.

8. Kessler, interview.

9. See <http://arrielgurl.livejournal.com/>.

10. Camille Dodero, "They Have MySpace in Heaven, Right? Inevitably, the Social-Networking Site Has Become a Virtual Graveyard," *Boston Phoenix* 28 Mar. 2006 <www.thephoenix.com/Article.aspx?id=7187&page=1>.

11. See the Web site <http://www.bigbridge.org/issue10/elegymand.htm>; see also my own description of the memorial at <www.bigbridge.org/issue10/elegymdamon.htm/>.

12. See the Web site <http://www.spidertangle.net/liquidtext.com/lyxstitch.html/>.

13. See the Web site <http://joglars.org/EnterWriting/index.php?pagename=WritingDubuffetsTitles&PHPSESSID=c026e953d7c0cd364f96c9a76e33ee19/>.

14. See the Web Site <http://www.dreamtimevillage.org/>.

11. Electronic Poetics Assay

1. Thanks to the following people for suggestions and feedback: Loss Glazier, John Cayley, Rita Raley, Jani Scandura, Ed Cohen, Joanna O'Connell, and Anca Parvulescu, Sara Cohen, Barrett Watten, and Carrie Noland.

2. These pieces can be seen at <www.joglars.org/>.

3. Nathaniel Mackey, *Discrepant Engagement: Dissonance Cross-Culturality and Experimental Writing* (Cambridge, Eng.: Cambridge University Press, 1993).

4. Talan Memmott, conversation with the author and Rita Raley, 17 July 2002.

5. Walter Benjamin, "Theses on the Philosophy of History," *Illuminations*, trans. Harry Zohn (New York: Schocken, 1969), 254, 255, 257.

6. Walter Benjamin, "On Some Motifs in Baudelaire," *Illuminations* 176.

7. Carrie Noland, e-mail to author, 5 Aug. 2005.

8. See Brent Hayes Edwards, "Langston Hughes and the Futures of Diaspora," *American Literary History* 19.3 (2007): 689–711.

9. Noland, e-mail.

10. In, for example, *The Poetics of Imperialism: Translation and Colonization from "The Tempest" to "Tarzan"* (New York: Oxford University Press, 1991), otherwise not a text devoted to Jewish identity or literary matters, Eric Cheyfitz's introduction asserts his belief that "today in the United States, in stark contrast to Afro-Americans and Native Americans, Jews, except for the very orthodox, are comfortably integrated *for the moment*" (xiii). In an implicit rationale for why a nice Jewish boy can/should write about other more direly othered US Others (a self-reflective gesture of disclosure very common in the early 1990s), his italics indicate his own sense of contingency and preparedness for the other shoe to drop at any time.

11. "Re where I 'come from'—I didn't have anything to do with Fluxus or post-punk—if anything I come from the body-art/industrial music scene of the 70s and 80s—an important distinction for me, but perhaps not relevant. My closest friend was [Vito] Acconci; my closest musical ties were first the new thing music of Albert Ayler etc. and then later the work of SPK, Cabaret Voltaire, etc." (Alan Sondheim, personal communication, 26 Nov. 2002). The following several quotations from Sondheim are from this source.

12. "The description of the performance is great; of course it relates also to the laptop performance music going on now—I'm well aware of this—" (Sondheim, personal communication).

13. "'(think Lenny Bruce, Gertrude Stein, the Marx Brothers, Franz Kafka, Frankétienne, Nathaniel Mackey, or even James Brown's vocables)'—absolutely right on!" (Sondheim, personal communication).

14. "You say work is set adrift with often no clear origin or destination, and travels rather than in a fixed telos or predicable trajectory—absolutely—this parallels first, my identification with holocausts of all sorts (the apocalyptic politics and readings) and second, the notion I use of emission/spew/dispersal—building a broken semiotics out of the terms—" (Sondheim, personal communication).

15. Jerrold Shiroma, email to Poetics@listserv.buffalo.edu, July 19, 2002.

16. "Just saw also that you do provide an explanation of the rwx etc. . . ." (Sondheim, personal communication).

17. "I also don't see the 'sieve' or other texts as 'fragments'—which imply both an incompletion and a whole—I use the word 'texts' in fact, but dislike that because it conjures up Fr. Instead, I think (and fairly often) of Adorno's *Minima Moralia* Celan's taut work, Horkheimer's *Daybreak* etc.—it might not look it, but these are inspiration for me, and the work is far more polished than it might appear at first glance" [. . .] "Just realized 'fragments' also relates to German Romanticism of course in its full Capital glory!" (Sondheim, personal communication).

18. Daniel Boyarin and Jonathan Boyarin, *Powers of Diaspora: Two Essays on the Relevance of Jewish Culture* (Minneapolis: University of Minnesota Press, 2002).

19. See, for example, Jonathan Boyarin, *Storm from Paradise: The Politics of Jewish Memory* (Minneapolis: University of Minnesota Press, 1992).

20. Thanks to Barrett Watten for providing me with the appropriate formulations for exploring this obvious difference (e-mail to the author, August 2005).

21. Noland, e-mail.

22. Watten, e-mail.

23. Alan Sondheim, e-mail to the author, 23 Jan. 2005.

24. "You're right about silliness—I contrast it with 'humorous' myself, seeing silliness as in fact cutting, like the Diamond Sutra in a way or Zen koan; worlds can shatter. It's the other curled side of annihilation—Monty Python's killing joke, or the comment about the show that when they didn't know what to do, they blew things up" (Sondheim, 23 Jan. 2005).

25. "My own work relates to trauma, I think, as fundamental—" (Sondheim, 23 Jan. 2005).

26. "Can already tell that we are on very similar paths of pursuit in many ways with regard to issues of 'silliness,' 'filler,' etc. . . . I can also tell that I disagree with you about some particulars (at least regarding Flarf, esp. around the theme of competition), which is inevitable and more importantly stimulating." (K. Silem Mohammad/Sir Flarfalot, personal communication to the author, 31 Oct. 2002).

"3. How important is community (small) to flarfing." "Very important, I think. Not only does the list constitute what I consider to be my 'audience,' but it literally brings specific things to fruition. It also determines to great extent tone (largely ironic, but not always), and inspires inventiveness (via competitiveness)" (Gary Sullivan/Flarfy answering a questionnaire posted by Mike Magee/The Flarfologist, 4 Nov. 2002).

27. "I thought what you said about flarf and the list was completely dead on, except for maybe the gender stuff, because while on the one hand I do agree that it's usually thought of as 'guy' humor, both Nada and Katie have no problems writing it. Nada would have written much more to the list over the last year & a half, but she has to be careful because of her repetitive strain injury. And, have you ever read Sharon Mesmer's work? I can't believe she hasn't flarfed yet–her 'real' writing is very flarfy. But, that's a minor point" (Gary Sullivan/Flarfy, personal communication to the author, 9 Nov. 2002).

"I don't know if you can use this or not, but I think I might disagree somewhat with Gary–gender IS an issue. I know that there is a constant anxious friction in many posts surrounding the possible transgressions of acceptable gender interaction they enact. I'm probably more guilty of this than anyone else, actually. Referring to Katie as '16 years old,' getting comic mileage from misogynist rants and 'gurl talk' in blogs and chat rooms, etc. It seems to me to be part of the general exorcising of conscious and subconscious cultural no-no's that flarf performs, whether sexual, racial, political, or whatever. I don't really know what to do with this self-observation. I'm just saying" (K. Silem Mohammad/Sir Flarfalot, personal communication to the author, 30 Nov. 2002).

"I see Kasey's points below, and think he's right. I can't remember what I said, actually, but I think I was more saying that the kind of writing that this is—abrassive silliness? or something?–isn't *necessarily* in & of itself a gender-specific kind of writing. Or maybe that it needn't be—and that, Katie for instance, wrote some of the most abrassive (or transgressive) pieces—that 'WTC +cupcake' piece, for instance. But, yeah, specific things that get used and how they get used, definitely, there are issues of gender there" (Gary Sullivan/Flarfy, personal communication to the author and K. Silem Mohammad, 1 Dec. 2002).

28. Thomas Swiss, "Distance, Homelessness, Anonymity, and Insignificance: An Interview with Young Hae Chang Heavy Industries," *Iowa Web Review*, <www.uiowa.edu/~iareview/tirweb/feature/younghae/interview.html/>.

Bibliography

Abu-Lughod, Lila. *Veiled Sentiments: Honor and Poetry in a Bedouin Society*. Berkeley and Los Angeles: University of California Press, 1986.

Adorno, Theodor. "Lyric Poetry and Society." *Telos* 20 (1974): 56–71.

Agamben, Giorgio. *The Coming Community*. Minneapolis: University of Minnesota Press, 1994.

Albert, Bruce. "'Ethnographic Situation' and Ethnic Movements: Notes on Post-Malinowskian Fieldwork." *Critique of Anthropology* 17:1 (1997): 53–65.

Alcalay, Ammiel. *After Jews and Arabs: Remaking Levantine Culture*. Minneapolis: University of Minnesota Press, 1993.

Algarín, Miguel, and Bob Holman, eds. *Aloud! Voices from the Nuyorican Poets' Café*. New York: Holt, 1994.

Algarín, Miguel, and Miguel Piñero, eds. *Nuyorican Poetry: An Anthology of Puerto Rican Words and Feelings*. New York: Morrow, 1975.

Alighieri, Dante. *De Vulgari Eloquentia*. Ed. and trans. Steven Botterill. Cambridge: Cambridge University Press, 1996.

Allen, Ernest, Jr. "Ever Feeling One's Twoness: 'Double Ideals' and 'Double Consciousness' in *The Souls of Black Folk*." *Critique of Anthropology* 12:3 (1992): 261–75.

Allen, Woody. "The Scrolls." *Without Feathers*. New York: Warner Books, 1976.

Anderson, Benedict. *Imagined Communities*. 1983. New York: Verso, 1991.

Antin, David. "Dialogue." *tuning*. New York: New Directions, 1984. 219–68.

Armstrong, Louis. *Satchmo: My Life in New Orleans*. New York: Da Capo, 1954.

Aronowitz, Stanley. "Is a Democracy Possible? The Decline of the Public in the American Debate." *The Phantom Public Sphere*. Ed. Bruce Robbins. Minneapolis: University of Minnesota Press, 1993. 75–92.

Arteaga, Alfred. *Chicano Poetics: Heterotexts and Hybridities*. New York: Cambridge University Press, 1997.

Baker, Houston A. *Blues, Ideology, and Afro-American Literature*. Chicago: University of Chicago Press, 1984.

———. *Modernism and the Harlem Renaissance*. Chicago: University of Chicago Press, 1987.

Baraka, Amiri. *The Autobiography of Amiri Baraka/LeRoi Jones*. New York: Morrow, 1984.

———. "SOS." *Transbluesency*. New York: Marsilio, 1995.

Barfield, Owen. *Poetic Diction*. Middletown, CT: Wesleyan University Press, 1973.

Beatty, Paul. *Big Bank Take Little Bank*. New York: Nuyorican Poets' Café Press, 1990.

Becker, Howard. *Art Worlds*. Berkeley and Los Angeles: University of California Press, 1982.

Behar, Ruth. *The Vulnerable Observer: Anthropology That Breaks Your Heart*. Boston: Beacon Press, 1996.

Beller, Steven. "Otto Weininger as Liberal?" *Jews and Gender: Responses to Otto Weininger*. Ed. Nancy A. Harrowitz and Barbara Hyams, Philadelphia: Temple University Press, 1995. 91–101.

Bendich, Albert. Conversation with the author. 10 August 1989.

Benitez-Rojo, Antonio. *The Repeating Island: The Caribbean and the Postmodern Perspective*. Durham, NC: Duke University Press, 1996.

Benjamin, Walter. "A Berlin Chronicle." *Reflections*. Ed. Peter Demetz. Trans. Edmund Jephcott. New York: Harcourt Brace Jovanovich, 1978. 3–60.

———. *Gesammelte Schriften*, vol. 2. Frankfurt: Suhrkamp, 1977.

———. *Illuminations*. Trans. Harry Zohn. New York: Schocken, 1967.

———. "On Some Motifs in Baudelaire." *Illuminations*. Trans. Harry Zohn. New York: Schocken, 1967.

———. "Theses on the Philosophy of History." *Illuminations*. Trans. Harry Zohn. New York: Schocken, 1967. 155–200.

———. "The Work of Art in the Age of Mechanical Reproduction." *Illuminations*. Trans. Harry Zohn. New York: Schocken, 1967. 217–53.

Bernstein, Charles. *My Way*. Chicago: University of Chicago Press, 1999.

———. *A Poetics*. Cambridge, MA: Harvard University Press, 1992.

Beverley, John. *Against Literature*. Minneapolis: University of Minnesota Press, 1993.

Biale, David. *Eros and the Jews: From Biblical Israel to Contemporary America*. Berkeley and Los Angeles: University of California Press, 1982.

Blaser, Robin. "The Practice of Outside." *The Collected Books of Jack Spicer*. Santa Barbara: Black Sparrow Press, 1975. 271–329.

Boyarin, Daniel, and Jonathan Boyarin. *Powers of Diaspora: Two Essays on the Relevance of Jewish Culture*. Minneapolis: University of Minnesota Press, 2002.

Boyarin, Jonathan. *Storm from Paradise: The Politics of Jewish Memory*. Minneapolis: University of Minnesota Press, 1992.

Brennan, Tim. "Critical Response II, Rap Redoubt: The Beauty of the Mix." *Critical Inquiry* 22 (Autumn 1995): 159–61.

———. "Off the Gangsta Tip: A Rap Appreciation, or Forgetting About Los Angeles." *Critical Inquiry* 20.4 (Summer 1994): 663–93.

Brodersen, Momme. *Walter Benjamin: A Biography*, Trans. Malcolm R. Green and Ingrida Ligers. London: Verso, 1996.

Brossard, Chandler. *Who Walk in Darkness*. New York: Grove Press, 1952.

Brown, James (with Dave Marsh). *James Brown, the Godfather of Soul*. New York: Thunder's Mouth Press, 1990.

Bruce, Honey. *Honey: The Life and Loves of Lenny's Shady Lady*. Chicago: Playboy, 1974.

Bruce, Lenny. *The (Almost) Unpublished Lenny Bruce: From the Private Collection of Kitty Bruce*. Philadelphia: Running Press, 1984.

———. *The Essential Lenny Bruce*. New York: Ballantine, 1967.

———. *How to Talk Dirty and Influence People*. Chicago: Playboy Press, 1972.

———. Trial manuscript, 1962. Unpublished.

———. *What I Got Arrested For*. Fantasy Records, 1971. LP.

Buff, Rachel. *Immigration and the Political Economy of Home: West Indian Brooklyn and American Indian Minneapolis*. Berkeley and Los Angeles: University of California Press, 2001.

Burgess, Robert G., ed. *Field Research: A Sourcebook and Field Manual*. London: George Allen and Unwin, 1982.

Cándida Smith, Richard. *Utopia and Dissent: Art, Poetry, and Politics in California*. Berkeley and Los Angeles: University of California Press, 1995.

Caton, Steven C. *"Peaks of Yemen I Summon": Poetry as Social Practice in a Northern Yemeni Tribe*. Berkeley and Los Angeles: University of California Press, 1990.

Chauncey, George. "The Strange Career of the Closet." University of Minnesota, Minneapolis, 19 May 1998. Lecture.

Cheyfitz, Eric. *The Poetics of Imperialism: Translation and Colonization from "The Tempest" to "Tarzan."* New York: Oxford University Press, 1991.

Clifford, James. "Identity in Mashpee." In *The Predicament of Culture*. Cambridge, MA: Harvard University Press, 1988. 277–346.

———. *The Predicament of Culture*. Cambridge, MA: Harvard University Press, 1988.

———. "Traveling Culture." *Cultural Studies Now and in the Future*. Ed. Cary Nelson, Larry Grossberg, and Paula Treichler. New York: Routledge, 1991. 96–116.

Collier, John Lincoln. *Benny Goodman and the Swing Era*. New York: Oxford University Press, 1989.

Collins, Lisa Gail. "Anguished Pleasures: Black Female Sexual Politics and Poetics." *Colors: Opinion & the Arts in Communities of Color* 4.5 (September–October 1995): 26–30.

Creeley, Robert. *The Collected Poems of Robert Creeley, 1945–75.* Berkeley and Los Angeles: University of California Press, 1982.

Crenshaw, Kimberle. "Demarginalizing the Intersection of Race and Sex: A Black Feminist Critique of Antidiscrimination Doctrine, Feminist Theory and Antiracist Politics." *University of Chicago Legal Forum* (Summer 1989): 139–67.

Crow, Bill. *Jazz Anecdotes.* New York: Oxford University Press, 1990.

Damon, Maria. *The Dark End of the Street: Margins in American Vanguard Poetry.* Minneapolis: University of Minnesota Press, 1993.

———. "Gertrude Stein's Doggerel 'Yiddish': Women, Dogs, and Jews." *The Dark End of the Street: Margins in American Vanguard Poetry.* Minneapolis: University of Minnesota Press, 1993. 202–35.

———. "Inside/Outside: Jewish Cultural Signification." American Studies Association Conference. New Orleans, LA. 11 Nov. 1990. Panel: Inside/Outside: Jewish Cultural Signification.

———. "Introduction." *Callaloo* 25:1 (Winter 2002): 105–11.

———. "Jazz-Jews, Jive and Gender: Ethnic Anxiety and the Politics of Jazz Argot?" *Jews and Other Differences: The New Jewish Cultural Studies.* Ed. Daniel Boyarin and Jonathan Boyarin.

———. "Micropoetries." *XCP: Cross Cultural Practices* 15/16 (2006): 235 (Word Issue). Minneapolis: University of Minnesota Press, 1996.

———. "The Jewish Entertainer as Cultural Lightning Rod: The Case of Lenny Bruce." *Postmodern Culture* 7.2 (January 1997).

———. "'The Journal of John Wieners, /Is to Be Called/707 Scott Street': Callow But Not Shallow." *XCP: Cross Cultural Poetics* 3 (1998): 137–47.

———. "Other Beats." *Hambone* 13 (Spring 1997): 177–85.

———. Rev. of *707 Scott Street,* by John Wieners. *XCP: Cross Cultural Poetics* 3 (1997): 137–47.

———. "Talking Yiddish at the Boundaries." *Cultural Studies* 5.1 (1991): 14–29.

———. "Triangulated Desire and Tactical Silences in the Beat Hipscape: Bob Kaufman and Others." *College Literature* 27:1 (Winter 2000): 139–57.

———. "'Unmeaning Jargon'/Uncanonized Beatitude: Bob Kaufman, Poet." *The Dark End of the Street: Margins in American Vanguard Poetry.* Minneapolis: University of Minnesota Press, 1993. 32–76.

———. "Victors of Catastrophe: Beat Occlusions." *Beat Culture and the New America, 1950–1965.* Ed. Lisa Phillips. New York: Whitney Museum of American Art, 1995.

———. "When the Nuyoricans Came to Town: (Ex)changing Poetics." *XCP: Cross Cultural Poetics* 1 (1997): 16–40.

———, and Ira Livingston, eds. *Poetry and Cultural Studies: A Reader.* Champaign: University of Illinois Press, 2009.

Davies, Ioan. "Lenny Bruce: Hyperrealism and the Death of Jewish Tragic Humor." *Social Text* 22 (Spring 1989): 92–114.

Davis, Miles, and Quincy Troupe. *Miles: The Autobiography*. New York: Simon and Schuster, 1989.

De Grazia, Edward. *Girls Lean Back Everywhere. The Law of Obscenity and the Assault on Genius*. New York: Random House, 1992.

Deleuze, Gilles, and Félix Guattari. *Kafka: Toward a Minor Literature*. Trans. Dana Polan. Minneapolis: University of Minnesota Press, 1986.

D'Emilio, John. *Sexual Politics, Sexual Communities: The Making of a Homosexual Subculture, 1940–1980*. Chicago: University of Chicago Press, 1986.

Derksen, Jeff. "But I Could Make a Living from It." *Arras* 4 (November 2001): 53–65.

———. "I Need to Know If This Is Normal." *XCP: Cross Cultural Poetics* 2.

Dodero, Camille. "They Have MySpace in Heaven, Right? Inevitably, the Social-Networking Site Has Become a Virtual Graveyard." *Boston Phoenix*, 28 Mar. 2006. <www.thephoenix.com/Article.aspx?id=7187&page=1/>.

Du Bois, W.E.B. "Of the Sorrow Songs." *The Souls of Black Folk*. New York: Signet Classics, 1969. 264–76.

———. *The Souls of Black Folk*. New York: Signet Classics, 1969.

Duncan, Robert. "An African Elegy?" *The Years as Catches*. Berkeley, CA: Oyez, 1966.

———. "The Homosexual in Society." *Politics* (August, 1944): 290–11.

———. "The Song of the Borderguard." *Selected Poems*. Ed. Robert Bertholf. New York: New Directions, 1993. 22–23.

Dylan, Bob. "Highway 61 Revisited." *Highway 61 Revisited*. Columbia, 1965. LP.

———. "What's a Sweetheart Like You Doing in a Place Like This?" *Infidels*. Columbia, 1984. CD.

Edwards, Brent Hayes. "Langston Hughes and the Futures of Diaspora." *American Literary History* 19.3 (2007): 689–711.

Ellington, Duke [Edward Kennedy]. "Categories." *Music Is My Mistress*. New York: Da Capo, 1973. 38.

———. *Music Is My Mistress*. New York: Da Capo, 1973.

Ellison, Ralph. *Invisible Man*. New York: Vintage, 1980.

Fabian, Johannes. *Anthropology with an Attitude*. Stanford, CA: Stanford University Press, 2001.

———. *Time and the Other: How Anthropology Makes Its Object*. New York: Columbia University Press, 1983.

Falla, Jeffrey. "Bob Kaufman and the (In)visible Double." *Callaloo* 25.1 (Winter 2000): 183–89.

"Family Breadwinner." *The Pilot* 31 May 1946: 7.

Feather, Leonard, and Jack Tracy. *Laughter from the Hip*. 1963. New York: Da Capo, 1979.

Fineman, Joel. Lecture. Stanford University, Stanford, CA, 9 October 1987.

Fischer, Michael. "Ethnicity and the Post-Modern Arts of Memory." *Writing Culture*. Ed. George Marcus and Michael Fischer. Berkeley and Los Angeles: University of California Press, 1986.

Fishberg, Maurice. *The Jews: A Study in Race and Environment*. London: Walter Scott Publishing, 1911.

FitzGerald, Russell. *The Diary of Russell FitzGerald*. Unpublished manuscript. n.d.

Flores, Juan, and George Yudice. "Living Borders/Buscando America: Languages of Latino Self-formation." *Social Text* 24 (1990): 57–84.

Fraser, Nancy. "Rethinking the Public Sphere: A Contribution to the Critique of Actually Existing Democracy." *The Phantom Public Sphere*. Ed. Bruce Robbins. Minneapolis: University of Minnesota Press, 1993. 1–32.

Freud, Sigmund. *Jokes and Their Relation to the Unconscious*. Trans. James Strachey. New York: Norton, 1960.

Gale, Bob. Personal interview. October 1996.

Gans, Herbert. "The Participant Observer as Human Being: Observations on the Personal Aspects of Fieldwork." *Field Research: A Sourcebook and Field Manual*. Ed. Robert G. Burgess. London: Allen and Unwin, 1982. 53–61.

García Canclini, Néstor. *Hybrid Cultures: Strategies for Entering and Leaving Modernity*. Trans. Christopher L. Chiappari and Silvia L. López. Minneapolis: University of Minnesota Press, 1995.

Gates, Henry Louis, Jr. *The Signifying Monkey: A Theory of African-American Literary Criticism*. New York: Oxford University Press, 1988.

———. "Sudden Def." *New Yorker* 19 June 1995: 34–42.

———. "Writing 'Race' and the Difference It Makes." *"Race," Writing and Difference*, ed. Henry Louis Gates, Jr. New York: Oxford University Press, 1985.

Genet, Jean. *The Thief's Journal*. Trans. Bernard Frechtman. New York: Grove Press, 1964.

Gillespie, Dizzy [John Birks] (with Al Fraser). *To Be or Not to Bop: Memoirs of Dizzy Gillespie*. New York: Da Capo, 1979.

Gilman, Sander L. *Jewish Self-Hatred: Anti-Semitism and the Hidden Language of the Jews*. Baltimore: Johns Hopkins University Press, 1986.

———. *The Jew's Body*. New York: Routledge, 1991.

———. "Weininger and Freud: Race and Gender in the Shaping of Psychoanalysis." *Jews and Gender: Responses to Otto Weininger*. Ed. Nancy A. Harrowtiz and Barbara Hyams. Philadelphia: Temple University Press, 1995. 103–20.

Gilroy, Paul. *The Black Atlantic: Modernity and Double Consciousness*. Cambridge, MA: Harvard University Press, 1993.

Ginsberg, Allen. "Caw Caw." *Holy Soul Jelly Roll*. Prod. Hal Willner. Rhino Records 1994. Liner notes.

———. "Howl." *Howl and Other Poems*. San Francisco: City Lights, 1961.

———. *Kaddish and Other Poems*. San Francisco: City Lights, 1961.

Graham, Jorie. Interview. *A View from the Loft*. Minneapolis: The Loft, 1994.

Handler, Richard. "The Dainty Man and the Hungry Man: Literature and

Anthropology in the Work of Edward Sapir." *Observers Observed: Essays on Ethnographic Fieldwork.* Ed. George W. Stocking, Jr. Madison: University of Wisconsin Press, 1983. 208–31.

Harrington, Joseph. *Poetry and the People.* Middletown, CT: Wesleyan University Press, 2001.

Harrowitz, Nancy A., and Barbara Hyams, eds. *Jews and Gender: Responses to Otto Weininger.* Philadelphia: Temple University Press, 1995.

Harshav, Benjamin. *The Meaning of Yiddish.* Berkeley and Los Angeles: University of California Press, 1990.

Hass, Robert. Beach Lecture. University of Minnesota, Minneapolis. 13 Apr. 2000.

Hentoff, Nat. *Boston Boy.* New York: Knopf, 1986.

Herskovits, Melville. *Franz Boas: The Science of Man in the Making.* New York: Charles Scribner's Sons, 1953.

———. *The Myth of the Negro Past.* 1941. Boston: Beacon Press, 1958.

Holbrook, Carolyn. Personal interview. 15 Aug. 1996.

Holiday, Billie (with William Dufty). *Lady Sings the Blues.* London: Barrie and Jenkins, 1973.

Jonas, Stephen. "Boston, Mar. 2, 1961" (letter to Cid Corman). *That: short sets of writing,* 23 (July 1993) 1.

———. *Selected Poems.* Ed. Joseph Torra. Hoboken, NJ: Talisman House, 1994.

Jones, Hettie. *How I Became Hettie Jones.* New York: Penguin, 1991.

Karasick, Adeena. *Dyssemia Sleaze.* Vancouver, BC: Talonbooks, 2000.

———. *The House That Hijack Built.* Vancouver, BC: Talonbooks, 2004.

Kaufman, Bob. *Abomunist Manifesto. Solitudes Crowded with Loneliness.* New York: New Directions, 1965.

———. *The Ancient Rain: Poems 1956–1978.* New York: New Directions, 1981.

———. "Bagel Shop Jazz." *Solitudes Crowded with Loneliness.* New York: New Directions, 1965. 14–15.

———. *Golden Sardine.* San Francisco: City Lights Books, 1968.

———. "Perhaps." *Solitudes Crowded with Loneliness.* New York: New Directions, 1965. 54.

Kessler, Annie. Personal interview. May 2006.

———. *Solitudes Crowded with Loneliness.* New York: New Directions, 1965.

Killian, Kevin, and Lew Ellingham. *Poet, Be Like God: Jack Spicer and the San Francisco Renaissance.* Middletown, CT: Wesleyan University Press, 1998.

Knobloch, Frieda. *The Culture of Wilderness: Agriculture as Colonization in the American West.* Chapel Hill: University of North Carolina Press, 1996.

Kofsky, Frank. *Lenny Bruce: The Comedian as Social Critic and Secular Moralist.* New York: Monad Press, 1974.

Kugelmass, Jack. *The Miracle of Intervale Avenue.* New York: Schocken, 1986.

Lannen, Susan. Telephone interview. May 2006.

Lavie, Smadar. *The Poetics of Military Occupation: Mzeina Allegories of Bedouin*

Identity under Israeli and Egyptian Rule. Berkeley and Los Angeles: University of California Press, 1990.

Lavie, Smadar, Kirin Narayan, and Renato Rosaldo. *Creativity/Anthropology*. Ithaca, NY: Cornell University Press, 1993.

Lerner, Michael. "Jews Are Not White." *Village Voice* 18 May 1993. Special section: "White Like Who?" 33–34.

Lipsitz, George. "Listening to Learn and Learning to Listen: Popular Culture, Cultural Theory, and American Studies." *American Quarterly* 42.4 (December 1990): 615–36.

———. "Popular Culture: This Ain't No Sideshow." *Time Passages: Collective Memory and American Popular Culture*. Minneapolis: University of Minnesota Press, 1992. 3–20.

———. Unpublished panel proposal. Manuscript. 1997.

"Literary Model: The Loft Grows Up, Reaches Out." *Minneapolis Star Tribune* 10 Oct. 1996: A26.

Louis, Adrian. Letter to the Editor. *A View from the Loft: A Magazine about Writing* 16:6 (January 1994): 17.

Lubiano, Wahneema. "'Elbow Room' and Shuckin' Off the 'Native Other.'" Modern Language Association Annual Convention. New York. 27–30 Dec. 1987.

Mackey, Nathaniel. *Bedouin Hornbook*. 1986. Los Angeles: Sun and Moon, 1997.

———. *Discrepant Engagement: Dissonance, Cross-Culturality, and Experimental Writing*. Cambridge: Cambridge University Press, 1993.

Mailer, Norman. "The White Negro." *Advertisements for Myself*. 1959. Cambridge, MA: Harvard University Press, 1992.

Malinowski, Bronislaw. *Argonauts of the Western Pacific*. New York: Dutton, 1961.

———. *A Diary in the Strict Sense of the Term*. Trans. Norbert Guterman. Stanford, CA: Stanford University Press, 1989.

———. "W katedrze na Wawelu" ("In Wawel Cathedral"). Trans. Frank L. Vigoda. Unpublished. Yale University Library Special Collections, New Haven.

Marcus, Greil. *Lipstick Traces: A Secret History of the Twentieth Century*. Cambridge, MA: Harvard University Press, 1989.

Mauss, Marcel. *The Gift: Forms and Functions of Exchange in Archaic Societies*. Trans. W. D. Halls. New York: Norton, 1967.

Memmott, Talan. Conversation with the author and Rita Raley. 17 July 2002.

Mesmer, Sharon. *Annoying Diabetic Bitch*. New York: Combo Books, 2007.

Mezzrow, Mezz, and Bernard Wolfe. *Really the Blues*. 1946. New York: Citadel, 1990.

Monroe, Jonathan. "Poetry, the University, and the Culture of Distraction." *Diacritics* 26.3–4 (1996): 3–30.

———. *A Poverty of Objects: The Prose Poem and the Politics of Genre*. Ithaca, NY: Cornell University Press, 1987.

Morales, Ed. "The Last Hispanic." *Aloud: Voices from the Nuyorican Poets Café*. Ed. Miguel Algarín and Bob Holman. New York: Henry Holt, 1992. 99.

Morris, Tracie. *Chap-t-her Won: Some Poems by Tracie Morris*. Brooklyn, NY: TM Ink, 1992.

Morrison, Toni. *Playing in the Dark: Whiteness and the Literary Imagination*. Cambridge, MA: Harvard University Press, 1991.

Mowitt, John. *Percussion: Drumming, Beating, Striking*. Durham, NC: Duke University Press, 2002.

Nelson, Cary, Larry Grossberg, and Paula Treichler, eds. *Cultural Studies Now and in the Future*. New York: Routledge, 1991.

Nielsen, Aldon Lynn. *Black Chant: Languages of African American Postmodernism*. New York: Cambridge University Press, 1996.

Nowak, Mark. "Open Book, Case Closed: The Democratic Paradox of Minnesota's New Literary Center." *Workers of the Word, Unite and Fight!* Los Angeles: Palm Press, 2005.

———. *Revenants*. Minneapolis: Coffee House Press, 2000.

Nuyorican Symphony. Imago/Nuyo Records, 1994. CD.

Osterberg, James N., Jr. [Iggy Pop]. "I Wanna Be Your Dog." *The Stooges*. Prod. John Cale. Electra Records, 1969.

Ozick, Cynthia. "A Critic at Large: Sholem Aleichem's Revolution." *New Yorker* 28 Mar. 1988: 99.

Perelman, Bob. "Write the Power." *American Literary History* 6.2 (1994): 306–24.

Piña, Javier. "Bilingual in a Cardboard Box." *The United States of Poetry*. Ed. Joshua Blum et al. New York: Abrams, 1996. 92–93.

Plato. *The Republic*. Trans. Desmond Lee. London and New York: Penguin Books, 1995.

Pratt, Mary Louise. *Imperial Eyes: Travel Writing and Transculturation*. New York: Routledge, 1992.

Prell, Riv-Ellen. *Fighting to Become Americans: Assimilation and the Trouble between Jewish Women and Jewish Men*. Boston: Beacon Press, 2000.

———. "Why Jewish Princesses Don't Sweat: Desire and Consumption in Post-war American Jewish Life." *People of the Body*. Ed. Howard Eilberg-Schwartz. New York: SUNY Press, 1992. 329–60.

Richards, Mary Caroline. *Centering in Pottery, Poetry, and the Person*. Middletown, CT: Wesleyan University Press, 1989.

Rimbaud, Arthur. *Poésies*. Paris: Librairies Générales Françaises, 1972.

Robbins, Bruce, ed. *The Phantom Public Sphere*. Minneapolis: University of Minnesota Press, 1993.

Roediger, David. *The Wages of Whiteness*. New York: Routledge, 1993.

Rogin, Michael. "Blackface, White Noise: The Jewish Jazz Singer Finds His Voice." *Critical Inquiry* 18.3 (Spring 1992): 417–53.

Rosaldo, Renato. *Culture and Truth: The Remaking of Social Analysis*. Boston: Beacon Press, 1989.

Rose, Tricia. *Black Noise: Rap Music and Black Culture in Contemporary America.* Middletown, CT: Wesleyan University Press, 1994.

Ross, Andrew: *No Respect: Intellectuals and Popular Culture.* New York: Routledge, 1989.

Sacks, Peter. *The English Elegy: Studies in the Genre from Spenser to Yeats.* Baltimore: Johns Hopkins University Press, 1985.

Said, Edward. "Representing the Colonized: Anthropology's Interlocutors." *Critical Inquiry* 15.2 (Winter 1989): 205–25.

Saldívar, José. *Border Matters: Remapping American Cultural Studies.* Berkeley and Los Angeles: University of California Press, 1997.

San Juan, E. "The Culture of Ethnicity and the Fetish of Pluralism." *Cultural Critique* 18 (Spring 1991): 215–29.

Sarris, Greg. *Mabel McKay: Weaving the Dream.* Berkeley and Los Angeles: University of California Press, 1997.

———, ed. *The Sound of Rattles and Clappers: An Anthology of California Native American Writing.* Tucson: University of Arizona Press, 1994.

Schechner, Mark. "Dear Mr. Einstein: Jewish Comedy and the Contradictions of Culture." *Jewish Wry.* Ed. Sarah Blacher Cohen. Bloomington: Indiana University Press, 1983.

———. "Woody Allen and the Failure of the Therapeutic." *From Hester Street to Hollywood: The Jewish American Stage and Screen.* Ed. Sarah Blacher Cohen. Bloomington: Indiana University Press, 1983.

Schultz, Bruno. *Letters and Drawings of Bruno Schultz.* Ed. Jerzy Ficowski. Trans. Walter Arndt with Victoria Nelson. New York: Harper and Row, 1988.

Schusterman, Richard. "Critical Response I, Rap Remix: Pragmatism, Postmodernism, and Other Issues in the House." *Critical Inquiry* 22 (Autumn 1995): 150–58.

Shapiro, Karl. "The Interlude." *Collected Poems 1940–78.* New York: Random House, 1978. 83–84.

Shapiro, Nat, and Nat Hentoff. *Hear Me Talkin' to Ya.* New York: Dover, 1955.

Shohat, Ella. *Israeli Cinema: East/West and the Politics of Representation.* Austin: University of Texas Press, 1989.

Sidran, Ben. *Black Talk.* 1971. New York: Da Capo, 1981.

Slobin, Mark. *Subcultural Sounds: Micromusics of the West.* Middletown, CT: Wesleyan University Press, 1993.

———. *Tenement Music.* Urbana: University of Illinois Press, 1982.

Spector, Ronnie (with Vince Waldron). *Be My Baby.* New York: HarperCollins, 1990.

Spicer, Jack. *The Collected Books of Jack Spicer.* Ed. Robin Blaser. Santa Rosa, CA: Black Sparrow Press, 1975.

Stein, Gertrude. *Bee Time Vine and Other Pieces (1913–1927).* New Haven: Yale University Press, 1953.

———. *How to Write.* 1931. New York: Dover, 1975.

————. "Identity a Poem." *What Are Master-pieces*. New York: Pitman, 1940.

————. "Lecture 2: Narration." *The Poetics of the New American Poetry*. Ed. Donald Allen. New York: Grove, 1973.

————. *The Making of Americans*. 1925. New York: Harcourt Brace, 1966.

————. *Painted Lace and Other Pieces (1914–1937)*. New Haven: Yale University Press, 1955.

————. *Paris France*. 1940. New York: Liveright, 1970.

————. *Q.E.D. Fernhurst, Q.E.D. and Other Early Writings*. New York: Liveright, 1971.

————. *Tender Buttons: Selected Writings of Gertrude Stein*. 1914. Ed. Carl Van Vechten. New York: Random House, 1962.

————. *Three Lives*. 1909. New York: Vintage, 1983.

————. "Yet Dish." *The Yale Gertrude Stein*. Ed. Richard Kostelanetz. New Haven, CT: Yale University Press, 1981.

Stierle, Karlheinz. "Identité du discours et transgression lyrique." Trans. Jean-Paul Cohn. *Poétique* 32 (November 1977): 422–41.

Stocking, George W., Jr. "The Ethnographer's Magic: Fieldwork in British Anthropology from Tylor to Malinowski." *Observers Observed: Essays on Ethnographic Fieldwork*. Ed. George W. Stocking, Jr. Madison: University of Wisconsin Press, 1983. 70–120.

————, ed. *Observers Observed: Essays on Ethnographic Fieldwork*. Madison: University of Wisconsin Press, 1983.

Swiss, Thomas. "Distance, Homelessness, Anonymity, and Insignificance: An Interview with Young Hae Chang Heavy Industries." *Iowa Web Review*. <http://www.uiowa.edu/~iareview/tirweb/feature/younghae/interview.html/>.

Taussig, Michael. *The Magic of the State*. New York: Routledge, 1996.

Thomas, Nicholas. "Against Ethnography." *Cultural Anthropology* 6.3 (August 1991): 306–22.

Torra, Joseph, ed. *Stephen Jonas: Selected Poems*. Hoboken, NJ: Talisman House, 1994.

Torres, Edwin. *I Hear Things People Haven't Really Said: A Collection of Poetry by Edwin Torres*. New York: Edwin Torres, 1991.

————. "Indian Hand Poem." *I Hear Things People Haven't Really Said: A Collection of Poetry by Edwin Torres*. New York: Edwin Torres, 1991. n. pag.

————. *SandHomméNomadNo*. New York: Edwin Torres, 1997.

————. "Seeds Sown Long Ago: Are You the Layer?" *XCP: Cross Cultural Poetics* 1.1 (1997): 89–91.

————. "Ugilante." *I Hear Things People Haven't Really Said: A Collection of Poetry by Edwin Torres*. New York: Edwin Torres, 1991. n. pag.

Vasquez, Diego. Interview. *SHOUT! A Community Newspaper for Poets Storytellers and Performance Artists*. November 1996.

Vereen, Ben. "I'll Make Me a World: A Twentieth-Century History of African Americans in the Arts." Interview. PBS. 1 Feb. 1999.

Vincent, Stephen. "Re: Outsider Art." Posted 10 Mar. 2007. <poetics@poetics@ listserv.buffalo.edu>.

Watten, Barrett. *The Constructivist Moment: From Material Text to Cultural Poetics.* Middletown, CT: Wesleyan University Press, 2003.

———. *The Grand Piano, Part 3: San Francisco, 1975–1980: An Experiment in Collective Autobiography.* Ed. Steve Benson et al. Detroit, MI: Mode A, 2007. 85.

Weininger, Otto. *Sex and Character.* Trans. from 6th German ed. London: Heinemann, 1906.

Weinreich, Max. *The History of the Yiddish Language.* Chicago: University of Chicago Press, 1980.

Whaley, Preston, Jr. *Blows Like a Horn: Beat Writing, Jazz, Style, and Markets in the Transformation of U.S. Culture.* Cambridge, MA: Harvard University Press, 2004.

Whitman, Walt. "Democratic Vistas." *Whitman: Poetry and Prose.* Ed. Justin Kaplan. New York: Library of America, 1982. 929–94.

Wieners, John. *Selected Poems, 1958–1984.* Ed. Raymond Foye. Santa Barbara, CA: Black Sparrow Press, 1986.

———. *707 Scott Street.* Los Angeles: Sun and Moon, 1997.

Wikan, Unni. "Toward an Experience-Near Anthropology." *Cultural Anthropology* 6.3 (August 1991): 285–305.

Zamir, Shamoon. *Dark Voices: W.E.B. Du Bois and American Thought, 1888–1903.* Chicago: University of Chicago Press, 1995.

Zamora, Bernice. *Restless Serpents.* Menlo Park, CA: Diseños Literarios, 1994.

Zipes, Jack. *The Operated Jew.* New York: Routledge, 1991.

Index

Note: Page numbers in *italics* refer to illustrations.

CONTEMPORARY NORTH AMERICAN POETRY SERIES

Industrial Poetics: Demo Tracks for a Mobile Culture
By Joe Amato

Postliterary America: From Bagel Shop Jazz to Micropoetries
By Maria Damon

On Mount Vision: Forms of the Sacred in Contemporary American Poetry
By Norman Finkelstein

Jorie Graham: Essays on the Poetry
Edited by Thomas Gardner
University of Wisconsin Press, 2005

Gary Snyder and the Pacific Rim: Creating Countercultural Community
By Timothy Gray

Urban Pastoral: Natural Currents in the New York School
By Timothy Gray

We Saw the Light: Conversations between the New American Cinema and Poetry
By Daniel Kane

History, Memory, and the Literary Left: Modern American Poetry, 1935–1968
By John Lowney

Paracritical Hinge: Essays, Talks, Notes, Interviews
By Nathaniel Mackey
University of Wisconsin Press, 2004

Frank O'Hara: The Poetics of Coterie
By Lytle Shaw

Radical Vernacular: Lorine Niedecker and the Poetics of Place
Edited by Elizabeth Willis